"While popular portrayals of women and sex are glossy, voyeuristic, simplified, unemotional, or trite, *Hard to Get* offers rarely heard detailed stories told with emotional resonance and connection to women's full lives and selves. Bell has made a superb contribution to our understanding about how women navigate sexuality in young adulthood in an era when they no longer must be married, and thus she has enlightened our understanding of women's social, sexual, and psychological lives."

—Karin A. Martin, author of *Puberty, Sexuality, and the Self: Boys and Girls at Adolescence*

"Can today's young women be independent and sexual agents while also satisfying their relational needs for intimacy? Bell believes that they can, and insightfully uses women's stories to reveal the inner and outer barriers to having it all."

—Paula England, New York University

"Bell offers a profoundly original and important argument about why—despite gains in education and employment—young women in America continue to be shortchanged in sex and intimacy. And she gives us a new, compelling vision of what it would mean for them to attain true sexual liberation."

—Amy Schalet, author of *Not under My Roof: Parents, Teens, and the Culture of Sex*

"*Hard to Get* is a brilliant intervention into recent debates about women's sexuality. While theoretically sophisticated, the book is so beautifully written that it is hard to put down. Therapists, sexuality scholars, and young women will find this book a powerful tool in making sense of the pleasures and dissatisfactions of young adulthood today."

—Elizabeth A. Armstrong, University of Michigan

"Female sexuality provides endless fascination; but how do *actual* young women find happiness in sex and love? Leslie Bell gives us an up-close look at twenty-something women at a cultural moment when they have more freedom than ever before, but their desires—sexual and relational—continue to confound. Bell navigates this complex terrain with compassion, keen insight, and an eye to social change."

—Daphne de Marneffe, author of *Maternal Desire: On Children, Love, and the Inner Life*

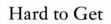

Hard to Get

Hard to Get

Twenty-Something Women and the Paradox of Sexual Freedom

Leslie C. Bell

UNIVERSITY OF CALIFORNIA PRESS

Berkeley   Los Angeles   London

University of California Press, one of the most distinguished university presses in the United States, enriches lives around the world by advancing scholarship in the humanities, social sciences, and natural sciences. Its activities are supported by the UC Press Foundation and by philanthropic contributions from individuals and institutions. For more information, visit www.ucpress.edu.

University of California Press
Berkeley and Los Angeles, California

University of California Press, Ltd.
London, England

Library of Congress Cataloging-in-Publication Data

Bell, Leslie C., 1970–
    Hard to get : twenty-something women and the paradox of sexual freedom / Leslie C. Bell.
        p. cm.
    Includes bibliographical references and index.
    ISBN 978-0-520-26149-5 (cloth : alk. paper)
    1. Young women--Sexual behavior.   2. Sexual freedom.   3. Man-woman relationships.   4. Sexual ethics.   5. Women--Identity.   I. Title.
    HQ29.B42 2013
    176'.4--dc23

                                                                    2012028369

Manufactured in the United States of America

22   21   20   19   18   17   16   15   14   13
10   9   8   7   6   5   4   3   2   1

In keeping with a commitment to support environmentally responsible and sustainable printing practices, UC Press has printed this book on Natures Natural, a fiber that contains 30% post-consumer waste and meets the minimum requirements of ANSI/NISO z39.48–1992 (R 1997) (*Permanence of Paper*).

For Alex

CONTENTS

ACKNOWLEDGMENTS

Acknowledgments first must go to the women I interviewed, who generously gave of their time and, most important, themselves to participate in this project. Their commitment to and interest in their own developmental processes made conducting the interviews a genuine pleasure. I also thank everyone who helped me to locate respondents, and whose interest and confidence in my work convinced young women to participate.

This book has benefited greatly from discussions with or comments by Natalie Boero, Nancy Chodorow, Marianne Cooper, Margaret Fitzsimmons, Laura Frame, Mark Harris, Meg Jay, Miranda Hoffman Jung, Maureen Katz, Ann Kring, Betsy Lerner, Daphne de Marneffe, Katharine Marshall, Dawne Moon, Elena Moser, Malkah Notman, Catherine Nye, C.J. Pascoe, Raka Ray, Toby Rogers, Cornelia St. John, and Pilar Strutin-Belinoff—gifted thinkers and clinicians who have seen the relevance of this project to a broader audience. Thanks to Lissa Caldwell, Paula England, and four anonymous reviewers whose careful reading and critiques of the manuscript in earlier drafts improved the book's theoretical rigor and historical grounding. I feel tremendously grateful to Nancy Chodorow, whose mentorship, training, advice, intellect, and criticism are unparalleled. She has insisted that I can have it all. Deep gratitude to my editor, Naomi Schneider, whose confidence and interest in this project have been as important as her keen editorial eye.

For their friendship and faith in me, I thank Mary Curtin, Margaret Fitzsimmons, Kaethe Morris Hoffer, Kirsten Miley Howell, Meg Jay, Maureen Kelly, Nancy Latham, Lea Queen, Marcy Reda, Julie Rice, Toby Rogers, Julie Shapiro, Juliana Van Cleve, Patti Wiley, and Cara Zeisloft. Special thanks to Rachel Sherman, my fellow traveler through the sociology department, whose discussions with me about sexuality, gender, and psychological processes generally greatly benefited this work, and whose support and love as a friend have been invaluable, and to Miranda Hoffman Jung, whose emotional and intellectual engagement in all things personal and professional has enriched my life immensely.

Thanks to my parents, Kathleen Bell and Wayne Bell, who have unfailingly supported me and had confidence in me, encouraging me always to pursue work that feeds and engages me. I am grateful for such a gift of freedom. I deeply appreciate my sister, Alison Bell, whose interest in and conversations with me about twenty-something women's sexuality have greatly benefited this work. Thanks to Kathryn Gronke and Bob Gronke, who have enthusiastically embraced my triumphs both personal and professional.

Profound thanks to Alex for taking so many risks with me.

Thanks to Vivian and Gloria for simply being themselves.

This research was made possible by fellowships from the Sexuality Research Fellowship Program of the Social Science Research Council, funded by the Ford Foundation; the U.C. Berkeley sociology department; the American Psychoanalytic Association; the Stoller Foundation; and the Woodrow Wilson Women's Studies National Fellowship Foundation. I am grateful to all of these funding sources.

CHAPTER ONE

The Paradox of Sexual Freedom

Excited yet embarrassed, Claudia, a twenty-eight-year-old postdoctoral researcher, told me about a one-night stand she'd had the night before our interview. I listened as she described the encounter: the fun of flirting with the man at a concert, the excitement and nervousness when it was still unclear what would happen, and the pleasure of being touched by someone she found so attractive. But I noticed that her pleasure gave way to worry that her strong sexual desires might get her into trouble. "I wish I weren't so horny, so I didn't need to go out and get it so much. I wish I could take a pill to kill my desire," she confided. Claudia felt some shame about her sexual desires and feared others might label her a "ho" for acting on them. She imagined that her Mexican Catholic family would be horrified if they knew about the number of sexual partners she'd had, that they would be devastated and disappointed that their daughter had not become the woman they raised her to be: a good girl who would marry her first boyfriend.[1] At the same time, the strength of her sexual desires sometimes frightened her, and she feared that men might find them overwhelming. Claudia also worried that being in a relationship would mean a loss of her identity, as she had witnessed her mother sacrifice her own dreams and adventurous spirit to be a wife and parent. Consequently, Claudia had not settled down, and she felt baffled at how difficult it had been to develop successful relationships with men. She had doggedly pursued her career goals as an academic and felt accomplished in that arena, but wondered why she hadn't had as much success in relationships.

At every turn and from every angle, Claudia was uncomfortable with the dimensions of her sexuality. Claudia, like many twenty-something women, was not playing hard to get. But good sex and relationships were proving elusive.

This is not the outcome Claudia's feminist foremothers dreamed of for her. Today's young women are supposed to be liberated from old edicts about sex and love. Their twenties ought to be a decade of freedom and exploration. But in interviews and in my psychotherapy practice with young women, I have found them to be more confused than ever about not only *how* to get what they want, but *what* they want.

Did Claudia want a relationship? Maybe, but not too serious a relationship; she didn't want to be held back from pursuing her goals. Did she want casual sex? Maybe, but only if she could feel safe enough. Did she want to have regular orgasms? Yes, but she was afraid of losing too much control.

In this book, I explore what is going on with highly educated twenty-something women when they're not busy advancing their careers and professional lives in the twenty-first century. Freed from economic, social, and biological pressure to marry and reproduce in their twenties, I explore what's happening in their love and sex lives. A glance at young women in the media—

see, for example, Natalie Portman's portrayal of the emotionally detached and high-achieving Emma in the 2011 film *No Strings Attached,* stories of twenty-something women outearning men, and reports of women outnumbering men on college campuses—might lead one to think that they're happily playing the field, sowing their wild oats, loving their independence and freedom, and building their careers before they settle down in their thirties.[2] But this new developmental period is more complicated than simplified media representations would have us believe.[3] Marriage and motherhood used to mark the transition to adulthood for women—highly educated or not. No longer is this the case. The black box of the twenties for contemporary women, the beneficiaries of so many gains for women in education, work, and sex, needs to be opened.

Young women who are college-educated and childless are part of a new generation that has a longer time for self-exploration than did earlier generations of women. For many women, the twenties are no longer a time principally devoted to either partnership or children. They have more freedom than women a few generations ago would have imagined possible. This period would seem to be ripe with possibilities for sexual and relationship satisfaction.[4]

I take a look at this new in-between period of early adulthood for twenty-somethings and how it offers women a mixed bag: opportunities, to be sure, but also retrograde messages about their identities as sexual beings, partners, and future mothers. And while they have plenty of training in how to be successful and in control of their careers, young women have little help or training, apart from the self-help aisle in their local bookstore, in how to manage these freedoms, mixed messages, and their own desires to get what they want from sex and love.

The absence of such useful training, combined with the new freedoms and mixed messages that characterize their twenties, contribute to a paradox of sexual freedom.[5] Young women may appear to have more choices than ever before, but the opening up of cultural notions of what is acceptable for women generates great confusion, uncertainty, and anxiety. Some women then find shelter in the process of splitting—a defense that involves seeing the world in black-and-white terms—to resolve the internal conflicts they feel about their desires. Through the series of case studies in the chapters that follow, I tease out various strands of the internal conflicts that some women feel as they attempt to navigate early adulthood without, in many cases, being conscious of their panoply of mixed desires and motivations.

THE PARADOX OF SEXUAL FREEDOM

This in-between period of early adulthood provides a window into the social, cultural, and economic changes that have been afoot for the past five decades.[6] And twenty-something women bear the imprint of those changes. For these resourceful women, sex and relationships really can occur independent of marriage and reproduction in their twenties. The current average age of first sexual intercourse for girls is seventeen, leaving ten years of sexual and relationship activity before the current average age of marriage at twenty-seven. These women don't think twice about cohabiting with a partner, or about delaying marriage until their own careers are on track.

In formulating this study, I thought that these women would describe this time in their lives as one in which they were relatively free from social restrictions and proscriptions on sexuality and relationships, but through my research and my psychotherapy practice, I discovered a different story. Instead of feeling free, twenty-something women are weighed down by vying cultural notions about the kind of sex and relationships they should be having in their twenties. Be assertive, but not aggressive. Be feminine, but not too passive. Be sexually adventurous, but don't alienate men with your sexual prowess. Be honest and open, but don't overwhelm someone with too much personal information. They are taught to seek out a companionate relationship of equals. But at the same time they are instructed by increasingly popular arguments from the burgeoning field of evolutionary psychology about irreconcilable differences between men and women. Meanwhile, they spend their twenties hearing gloomy forecasts about their chances of marriage if they don't marry before thirty, and their chances of conceiving a baby if they don't get pregnant before thirty-five. Given the discordant nature of these prescriptions, it's no wonder that the women I interviewed and counsel struggle to square these contradictory messages with their own individual experiences.

With relationships, women hear that they ought to use their twenties to "live it up" and not necessarily to be serious about relationships. Indeed, they ought not care very much about relationships, and shouldn't be devastated when relationships don't work out. Hearing advice across the self-help spectrum— from *The Rules,* which admonishes them to pretend to be independent to get into a relationship, to *He's Just Not That into You,* which entreats them to stop being so needy and get on with their lives after a breakup—young women often struggle to admit that they need anyone, but it's particularly difficult to say that they need a man. At the same time, they are enjoined to remember that partnership and marriage are just around the corner, when they turn thirty, so the dating and experimentation of their twenties must result in a relationship, and must come to an end. At that point, books such as *Marry Him* advise that they find someone who is "good enough" and hold on to him for dear life.[7]

This is a confusing set of messages with high stakes. If the goal is still marriage, what should young women do with all of their training in not needing anyone? What kind of a marriage should they hope for? It's difficult to square their experiences in their twenties with marriage, which inevitably involves need, compromise, dependence, and vulnerability.

When it comes to sex, women hear that they ought to spend their twenties being sexually experimental, but only to a point. There is a fine line between being experimental and being a slut. Their peers, television shows such as *Sex and the City*, and movies seem to encourage sexual experimentation. And they may find advice about sexual positions to try in *Glamour* or *Cosmopolitan* magazines. But at the same time, books, such as *Unhooked* and *A Return to Modesty*, advise them to return to courtship practices from the early 1900s.[8] And real women, not those in magazines, books, and movies, often contend with messages from their families, religions, and partners that they ought not to be sexually assertive, or sexually active at all.

These contradictory directives leave young women in a bind, and without much help in figuring out what they actually want. Every piece of "modern" advice about maintaining independence and using their twenties to explore and experiment sexually is layered over a piece of "old-fashioned" advice about getting married before it's "too late," not being too assertive or passionate in sex, and not being too sexually experienced.

These confusing messages are in contrast to the clear and helpful direction young women in the twenty-first century receive about how to succeed academically and professionally. Parents, educational institutions, workplaces, companies, and countless nonprofit organizations have focused on empowering girls and women to get ahead in fields and endeavors where they had lagged behind for generations. This training has often focused on developing a sense of control and mastery, and these efforts have largely succeeded. Today more women attend college than do men, and women make up close to half of all law and medical school graduates, although their entry into the highest echelons of these professions is still limited.[9] But the skills twenty-something women have developed in getting ahead educationally and professionally have not translated well into getting what they want and need in sex and relationships.

When I began this project, I was a feminist sociologist starting my training as a psychotherapist. In my practice, I found that I was seeing a number of high-achieving twenty-something women who had trouble letting down their guard, who had difficulty being vulnerable and expressing needs, and who, despite their professed desire for satisfying sex and relationships, put a great deal of energy into protecting themselves from getting hurt. I wanted to understand what was going on with my patients and, more importantly, how I could use that understanding to help them get more of what they wanted. For reasons of confidentiality, I do not discuss patients in this book, but their experiences certainly inform my thinking about twenty-something women. The women described in detail in this book are those whom I interviewed. As a sociologist, feminist, and psychotherapist, I bring multiple perspectives to my analysis.

FREEDOM IN CONTEXT

It is not coincidental that women born after 1972, a turning point in U.S. history for women in gaining formal equality with men, are the subject of this book. Title IX, which protects people from discrimination based on sex in educational programs that receive federal funding, passed in 1972 and has had a tremendous impact on girls' access to academics and athletics. By 1971, President Johnson's Executive Order 11375, which prohibits federal contractors from discrimination in employment on the basis of sex and mandates "affirmative" measures to eliminate job segregation by gender, had been fully implemented by the Equal Employment Opportunity Commission. And in 1973, *Roe v. Wade* made restrictions on abortion illegal throughout the country. The early 1970s also saw a dramatic decline in the proportion of families that lived with a father who earned a "family wage," one able to support his entire family without income generated by another parent; the proportion had held steady for the previous two decades. Women born after 1972 were among the first in the late twentieth century to have been born into a country without formal discrimination in the workforce and educational institutions and with affirmative action and the legal right to abortion. With these formal rights came great changes in their family experiences in childhood, and in their opportunities in the workforce in adulthood.

These women's experiences anticipate the social changes and trends that will characterize the lives of young women to come. Their entire lives have been marked by unprecedented sexual, educational, and professional freedoms. At the same time, some of these freedoms have had contradictory and paradoxical consequences. Not everything turned out exactly as hoped and planned by the feminist movement of the 1960s and 1970s. As a feminist who advocates for greater social, educational, economic, and sexual freedom for women, I feel a sense of urgency to understand which versions of freedom are truly liberating for women and which versions come with their own, new limitations.

For readers versed in the progress of the feminist movement and its central and guiding ideals, the next few pages include material that may be well known. But for readers unfamiliar with this history, they provide a historical context for understanding twenty-something women today. In earlier days of the feminist movement, freedom was a clear and important goal, one whose accomplishment seemed unambiguously positive. With the 1963 publication of *The Feminine Mystique,* Betty Friedan helped to spark a movement that challenged women's confinement to roles as passive wives, mothers who derived their sense of meaning and self solely from domestic work, or sex objects.[10] Feminists at the time critiqued these domestic ideals and fought for women's equality in educational institutions and the workplace, and for the control of their reproductive and personal lives. Important achievements included legal protection from employment discrimination, inclusion in affirmative action, and increased representation in the media.[11] Other feminist activists fought for and won reforms of the law's traditionally ·punitive stance toward victims of rape and domestic violence.[12] Feminist scholars in the social sciences targeted the traditional nuclear family and its division of labor between the public sector of work and the private sector of home as the cause of much of women's oppression; since the 1960s, what constitutes a family and how it operates have changed dramatically.[13]

As a consequence of these achievements, many women born after 1972 had childhoods characterized by fathers (and sometimes mothers) coaching their soccer teams and encouraging them in sports and school. They grew up prior to the rise of the princess culture for young girls, which began in 2000 when Disney created and marketed a wildly successful line of princess products that promotes regressive versions of femininity.[14] Girls in the 1970s and 1980s could do anything boys could do in the classroom and on the field, and, many argued at the time, they could even do it better than boys. "Girl power," with its emphasis on self-reliance, ambition, and assertiveness, had its ascendance in the 1990s, when these women were in high school. With girlhood characterized by an "anything you can do, I can do better" attitude, and adolescence replete with a girl-power stance, women born after 1972 would seem to be poised for agency and independence in adulthood.

Yet at the same time that schools proclaimed that girls could do and be anything, they still encouraged particular versions of femininity for girls and masculinity for boys, and dissuaded girls from being as competitive or aggressive as boys. Sociologists of education have documented the ways that schools in the 1970s and 1980s subtly, and not so subtly, reinforced differences between boys and girls.[15] Even after the passage of Title IX, researchers in the field of education found that girls were instructed with less focus and precision than boys— regardless of their behavior, boys got more time and attention from teachers.[16] At the same time that birth control became more accessible to adolescent girls than it had been to earlier generations, abstinence-only sex education curricula in schools made using birth control increasingly confusing for girls whose parents didn't speak openly and frankly with them about sex.[17] And even as services increased for survivors of sexual assault, and some legislation was passed to protect survivors' rights and safety, sexual violence against women remained persistent, widespread, and, at least tacitly, socially acceptable. Women born after 1972, then, had formal freedom to be and do as they wished, but constraints regarding sex and gender persisted.

In their family lives, women born after 1972 grew up very differently than had previous generations of women, as a consequence of the freedoms their mothers enjoyed. Their mothers were more likely to work outside the home than were mothers of earlier generations, and their fathers were more likely to be involved in their care than were fathers of earlier generations.[18] At the same time, they were among the first generation of children widely affected by divorce, and were less likely to grow up in a "traditional" nuclear family, composed of a married biological father and mother and biological children living together, than were girls of earlier generations.[19] During the 1970s and 1980s, "nontraditional" families including stepparents, stepsiblings, gay and lesbian parents, grandparents, and extended family members became increasingly common.[20]

These changes in family life have had both positive and negative effects. Possibilities for community and connection increase as family forms change dramatically to include stepfamilies, gay and lesbian families, and families that include multiple members not related by blood.[21] At the same time, as two wages have become essential for many families' economic survival, men have been hesitant to share the labor at home, and employers have been slow to respond to the needs of families in which both parents work.[22] These changes in family formation and roles within families have been important in establishing young women's new expectations for relationships and family life.[23]

Alongside the feminist movement, movements for gay and lesbian liberation in the same period challenged and expanded social understandings of "normal" sexuality to include gay and lesbian sexual orientations and relationships. The Stonewall riots of 1969, in which a group of gay male, lesbian, and transvestite patrons of a bar in New York City resisted a police raid, provided a rallying point for the movement. The movement succeeded in helping lesbians and gay men to begin to counter shame over their sexual orientation with gay pride. An important achievement was the removal, in 1973, of homosexuality as a psychiatric diagnosis from the American Psychiatric Association's *Diagnostic and Statistical Manual*. Later iterations of social movements for gay and lesbian rights have fought for legal same-sex sexual activity (effective nationally as of 2003 due to the Supreme Court decision in *Lawrence v. Texas*), protections against discrimination based on sexual orientation in the workplace (in place in twenty states but not at the federal level as of this writing in 2012), same-sex civil unions (legal in thirteen states) and marriage (legal in six states and the District of Columbia), and the right to serve as openly gay or lesbian in the military (in effect since 2011). These expanded rights and acceptance of gay and lesbian people have dramatically affected young women's hopes for and expectations of diverse sexual lives.

As schools, families, and workplaces have absorbed and responded to these profound social and economic changes, the goals of the feminist movement have become less unifying, and the notion of freedom less clear.[24] In the 1990s and 2000s, various feminists bristled at the notion that there was only one way to be a feminist, a modern woman, or a liberated woman. Many argued that the early feminist movement confined women to being androgynous, rather than diversely gendered. During this same period, queer theorists emerged and critiqued the feminist movement for depicting women in an essentialist way, equating female bodies with only particular versions of femininity and not seeing possibilities for more fluid versions of gender.[25] Arguing that the movement had neglected poor women and women of color, whose experiences of gender have been complicated by their particular class and race oppression throughout history, writers of color critiqued the movement's goals for assuming the privileges of white middle-class women: not having to work or face racial discrimination.[26] Sex-positive writers argued that earlier theorists' focus on the oppressive nature of sex for women deprived women (including sex workers and women involved in pornography) of an important arena of potential empowerment and pleasure.[27]

In recent years, then, it has become unclear what it means to be a woman, especially a liberated woman. Freedom and liberation have been marked by gaps and contradictions. Is work a liberating experience? Or does it constitute participation in patriarchal institutions? Is sex an empowering experience? If so, under which conditions? With whom? Is it restrictive to dress and act in traditionally feminine ways? Or are such women merely playing with one of many versions of gender? Is a relationship an important part of a woman's life? Or should relationships take a backseat to work? This confusion about both freedom and what it is to be a woman lays the feminist groundwork for the in-between period I discuss in this book.

In addition to uncertainty about the meaning and consequences of freedom, new economic pressures have come to play a role in women's decision making about the timing of marriage and childbearing. Young families today often require greater income than did previous generations in order to afford to buy a home and pay for child care. From 1970 to 2008, housing costs rose disproportionately to income growth.[28] Child care costs in major metropolitan areas can approach twenty-five hundred dollars per month for full-time care for one child. The return on a college degree continues to be significant, but a graduate degree is often considered necessary to earn a sustainable salary in an urban area. High-powered and high-paying jobs often require well over forty-hour work weeks.[29] And with very few social supports for working women, the ideal of being a working parent often clashes with the overwhelming financial and logistical realities of doing so.

As a result of these freedoms and economic realities, women are developing relationships and families more slowly than did previous generations of women. College-educated women now marry, on average, at twenty-seven, and women in general have their first child at age twenty-five, in contrast to 1970, when they did both, on average, at twenty-one.[30] Particularly striking are the findings that, from 1970 to 2009, the proportion of women ages twenty-five to twenty-nine who had never married quadrupled, from 11 percent to 47 percent,[31] and between 2000 and 2006, 69 percent of college-educated women ages twenty-five to twenty-nine had never borne a child. These trends have only accelerated over the past few years. In 2009, an astounding 23 percent of adult women had never been married, the largest percentage in the past sixty years.[32] These demographic shifts, the result of the many social and economic forces outlined above, have profound implications for women's lives.

SPLITTING

In seeking to understand how women respond to the freedoms, opportunities, and accompanying confusion, uncertainty, and anxiety of their twenties, I turned to psychoanalytic theory. From my viewpoint as a psychotherapist, I found that psychoanalytic insights could help us to understand how people respond to anxiety, and how and why people may report wanting something and yet seem to thwart themselves in their efforts to get that thing. Freud and other early psychoanalytic theorists have been rightly critiqued for focusing on men, assuming heterosexuality, depriving mothers of subjectivity, and having a biological determinist bent. At the same time, I (and many other feminists) have found psychoanalytic theory to be one of the most effective tools we possess to account for how women and men, sometimes unwittingly, perpetuate gender inequality. Psychoanalytic theories help us to understand why women, with the best and clearest of intentions, may unconsciously undermine their ability to reach their goals.[33]

The contradictions and uncertainties that characterize today's young women's lives lead many of them to systematically employ certain unconscious defenses to resolve their internal conflicts and anxiety, often to their detriment. I contend that splitting—a tendency to think in either/or patterns and to insist that one cannot feel two seemingly contradictory desires at once—has become a widespread sociological phenomenon among young women. This process has become a means for women to reconcile the disconcertingly uneven progress of their psychological, economic, and emotional lives in the twenty-first century.

Psychoanalytically oriented psychotherapists employ the notion of splitting, sometimes referred to as dualistic or binary thinking, widely in their work with patients, although it's fallen out of favor in the field of cultural anthropology, where it is associated with the structuralism of Claude Lévi-Strauss. Splitting continues to be a helpful concept in clinical work because it describes the defensive processes of so many patients, including many of the women with whom I spoke. These are neither total nor absolute splits in the grand narrative sense of the term—splits between black and white or masculine and feminine that undergird the foundations of society—but multiple splits that people invoke at different times and in various situations to manage anxiety and to defend against uncertainty. I therefore discuss multiple and shifting psychological and social splits as a way to make sense of the lived experiences of twenty-something women as they navigate sex and relationships. For an expanded discussion of the concept of splitting and its use by psychoanalytic, queer, and poststructuralist theorists, please see appendix I.

I argue that splitting came to predominate among many of the women with whom I spoke, not because they were in any way pathological, but because of the unsettled nature of this new in-between period of early adulthood for women, and the uncertainty and anxiety that accompany it.[34] Confused about freedom and what it is to be a woman today, young women often split their social and psychological options—into independence, strength, safety, and control versus relatedness, vulnerability, need, and desire—as though they're mutually exclusive and not equally important to human development.[35] Despite all the advances of women over the past fifty years, these experiences are frequently split into masculine and feminine ones, with the masculine being overvalued socially and psychologically. In modern western culture, autonomy and all that accompany it are much more highly valued than are interdependence and all that accompany it. Splitting leads some women to assume that they cannot be strong and autonomous when they are interdependent with others, vulnerable, and intimate. Vulnerability, needs, desires, and intimacy, then, often become new taboos for young women—experiences to be avoided rather than embraced.

It's no wonder that splitting is often young women's preferred method to make sense of the dizzying array of freedoms before them. A group of people trying to be autonomous and successful at work, and to have love and sex lives in which they express their vulnerability, need, and desire, is groundbreaking and historically unprecedented. This new in-between developmental period brings these two life spheres together at a time when neither is yet firmly established. But splitting makes young women feel that their options are limited as opposed to expansive.

STRATEGIES OF DESIRE

I argue that the women I spoke with employed *strategies of desire* to solve the problems at hand—problems of desire, autonomy, agency, intimacy, and safety—in a new in-between developmental period in which the rules aren't clear. These strategies of desire were sometimes conscious, sometimes unconscious, and women developed varying ones based on the cultural tools available to them, their psychological tendencies, their family backgrounds, and their relationship experiences. They were after—albeit with different degrees of internal conflict—sexual experiences, relationship experiences, safety, and control. This notion of a strategy helps describe the ways in which these women both had agency and were limited by the cultural notions available to them.[36]

In my research and clinical practice, I've found that the women to whom I've spoken have tended to employ strategies of desire clustered in three types. These strategies are based on the degree of conflict over sexual and relational desires that women are able to tolerate. My three archetypes—those of the Sexual Woman, the Relational Woman, and the Desiring Woman—are ways to interpret broad sets of behavior. Of course, they flatten out individual experiences to a degree, but they provide a broad paradigm for understanding how contemporary women cope with a confusing and sometimes conflicting set of beliefs and behaviors.

Women mobilized defensive strategies of the Sexual Woman and the Relational Woman when they were unable to tolerate the degree of internal conflict and anxiety that they felt over sexual and relational desires.[37] Both archetypes defensively split their desires, leaving them frustrated in their ability to get what they want.

Women who had little conflict over sexual desire and a high degree of conflict over relational desire used the strategies of desire of the Sexual Woman.[38] These women had benefited from the increased sexual freedom that characterized their childhood, adolescence, and twenties, and they succeeded in developing comfort with their sexual desires. Revealing sexual desire did not fill them with fear and dread and did not threaten their identity or sense of self. However, they feared losing their identities and independence through being in an intimate relationship. So they felt conflicted about having and letting somebody in on their relational desire.[39] For many women, these strategies reflected a split between a strong and independent identity and a relationship. They used strategies that allowed the expression of sexual desire but preserved their identities and independence from the perceived threat of relationships.

For example, one of my informants, twenty-nine-year-old Jayanthi, delighted in defying her Indian parents' expectations by sleeping with as many men as she could in her early twenties. She enjoyed sex a great deal, and over the course of her twenties learned how to regularly have an orgasm. But Jayanthi also derived pleasure from being able to attract men and turn them on, and from the control that she felt in not getting emotionally attached to men even when they may have felt attached to her. As she moved into her late twenties, though, she was left with a nagging desire for something more intimate and lasting than a mere sexual encounter. But she worried about losing control, and losing herself, in intimate relationships with men. Women such as Jayanthi represent a new take on the dilemma of female desire: at ease with sexual desire, but ill at ease with desire for a relationship.

Women who had little conflict over relational desire but a high degree of conflict over sexual desire gravitated toward the strategies of desire of the Relational Woman.[40] These women were comfortable feeling and expressing their desire for relationships but feared that either a man or a relationship couldn't withstand their strong sexual desire. They felt conflicted about having and expressing sexual desire and so gave it up. Unlike good girls of yesteryear, women who employed strategies of the Relational Woman had felt and understood the power of sexual desire. It was for this reason that they avoided it. They worried that asserting their sexual desires might overwhelm the men (or women, although this was more rare) with whom they wanted to be in relationships. Or they worried that their strong sexual desire might be incompatible with a stable relationship. These women then developed strategies of desire that inhibited their desires for sex. They illustrate the problem of splitting sexual desire from safety and stability in relationships.

For example, twenty-eight-year-old Alicia might, at first glance, have looked like a good girl of old. She delayed sex until after college, acted demurely, and was only subtly flirtatious with men, and she wanted more than anything to be part of a traditional family. Alicia also felt inhibited from expressing her sexual desires to men and was more comfortable with being passive in sex than she was with initiating sex. But Alicia, unlike a prototypical good girl, knew what she wanted from sex and actively fantasized about it. She didn't, however, share those desires with the men with whom she was in relationships. She worried that her sexual desires would be incompatible with the kind of committed relationship that she wanted, so she held herself back from expressing them.

Women who could tolerate the conflicts they felt over sexual and relational desire made use of the productive strategies of desire of the Desiring Woman. These women used their conflicts to inform how they could pursue their desires; they were comfortable with and expressed their desires for sex and a relationship.[41]

For example, twenty-eight-year-old Maria managed to tolerate a reasonable amount of internal conflict between her desires and could acknowledge desires for both sex and relationships without defensively splitting. She then sought out intimate relationships with men who were interested in satisfying sex and who worked to sustain a good sex life, and she received such interest and efforts nondefensively.

THE STUDY

For all the talk of sex and relationships in American culture, it turns out we know very little about the sex and love lives of "ordinary" women. Much of what we know about these topics comes from cultural products, memoirs by writers with a particular agenda, writings by therapists about their patients, and anecdotal knowledge from friends and acquaintances, who are not always completely frank about the conflicts and inhibitions they feel. Because in-depth knowledge about the lives of everyday women is difficult to come by, I recruited and interviewed ordinary women, many of whom commented on how surprised they were at how much they told me.

At the time of the interviews, my respondents were between twenty-four and twenty-nine years old and lived in Northern California. They had all graduated from college, and none had children. Some were in relationships, some were not, and a few were married. Half of them were women of color and half were white. Half were lesbian, bisexual, or queer, and half were straight.[42]

In some ways, they were not representative of the population. College-educated women currently compose 35 percent of the population of women ages twenty-five to twenty-nine in the United States. And Northern California, particularly the San Francisco Bay Area, is known for its progressive sexual values and culture, in contrast to some other regions of the country. When it comes to religion and degree of religiosity, the women I spoke with were less religious (35 percent came from non-religious families, in contrast with 21 percent in California and 15 percent in the United States as a whole) and less Protestant (15 percent came from Protestant families, compared with 36 percent in California and 51 percent in the United States as a whole), on average, than the general population. They represent a range of class backgrounds, but, like most college graduates, they come disproportionately from upper-middle-class families: 55 percent from upper-middle-class families, which compose only 20 percent of the U.S. population as a whole.[43] Current numbers on the proportion of women in the United States who identify as lesbian, bisexual, or queer hover between 3.5 and 7 percent.[44] However, I chose to oversample lesbian/bisexual/queer women and women of color because of my frustration with studies of female sexuality that included predominantly straight white women and drew conclusions about all women based on the experiences of women belonging only to socially dominant groups. While the women I spoke with might not have been representative of all twenty-something women in the United States, they were representative of those most likely to benefit from the increased freedoms discussed above, and so give us a window into what many women will experience if national social trends toward more progressive sexual values continue.

In other respects, however, the women I spoke with represented the diversity of women their age. Although they lived in California at the time of the interviews, only half of them had grown up there. Half came from families in which their parents were still married, half from families in which their parents were divorced. Of those families of divorce, family formations ranged from blended families, to extended families involving grandparents, aunts, and uncles, to gay and lesbian families. And, in fact, in California in 2010, the population included only 40 percent non-Hispanic whites. More detailed information about the women I interviewed and the interview process can be found in appendix II.

I conducted a total of sixty interviews, interviewing twenty women three times in a process called clinical interviewing.[45] This technique, which involved conducting multiple interviews over the course of one to two months, was particularly appropriate in this study due to the feelings of shame, inadequacy, fear, competition, and exposure frequently associated with sex and love. Furthermore, because women's experiences of sexuality are often complicated by violence and coercion, building trust and safety over the course of a series of interviews was important to gain a full picture of young women's lives. And the women with whom I spoke were able to develop increasing levels of comfort with me and with the topic over the course of the three interviews, discussing increasingly vulnerable and revelatory material as the interviews went on. They and I could also notice ways in which they sometimes contradicted themselves, concluding one thing about a specific experience in one interview, and another thing about the same experience in a different interview.

People have asked how I managed to get my participants to speak with me about the very private matters of sex and love. The truth is that while many of the women I spoke with found it anxiety provoking to discuss their feelings about sex and love, they also found it to be a great relief to explore a topic on which there are so many internal and external prohibitions and proscriptions. They were relieved to feel understood, to hear their experiences reflected in those of other twenty-something women, and to feel that someone was attending to the particulars of their experiences as women in their twenties in the early twenty-first century. I heard women ask over and over again whether their experiences and feelings were normal, whether the contradictory feelings they had about sex and love were true for other women, whether their ambivalence about sexual and relational desire and pleasure was shared by other women, and whether there was hope for them to feel more comfortable with their desires for sex and relationships.

In my interviews and in my experiences with patients, I heard a lot of questioning, a lot of discontent, and a lot of angst. While some women with whom I spoke were getting exactly what they wanted and felt comfortable with their desires for both sex and relationships, a little over half of the women were not getting what they wanted from sex and love, and they felt very confused about what was getting in the way, and what to do about it. These young women didn't feel empowered or like they lived on top of the world. Instead, they felt lost.

THE STRUCTURE OF THE BOOK

The book unfolds in three parts, in which I examine how nine women grappled with sexual liaisons and relationships with varying degrees of internal conflict, anxiety, and uncertainty. The chapters progress from a focus on splits reflecting an inhibition of relational desire (between relationships and career, relationships and identity, and relationships and sexual desire) to a focus on splits reflecting an inhibition of sexual desire (between sexual desire and safety and between sexual passion and stability), and finally to the experiences and strategies that made it possible for some women not to split.

Part I: The Sexual Woman

In part I, I tease out the experiences of three women struggling with their desires for relationships, successful careers, strong identities, and independence. Katie, Jayanthi, and Claudia split relationships from various aspects of independence, leading them to develop strategies of desire of the Sexual Woman. In chapter 2, I profile Katie and introduce one of the fundamental splits that I saw in the women I interviewed: between relationships and career. Katie's sexual desires felt straightforward to her, but she felt a taboo on desiring a relationship as a successful scientist. Chapter 3 highlights Jayanthi and another important split: between relationships and a strong identity. Jayanthi enjoyed being a bad girl who "played" men and could control them sexually, but she worried that being in a relationship would mean the loss of her identity. Chapter 4 concerns Claudia and the split between relationships and strong sexual desire. Claudia was surprised at how difficult it had been to develop a relationship in her twenties, and her sexual desires sometimes felt so strong that she wishes she could "take a pill to kill" them.

Part II: The Relational Woman

In part II, I investigate the experiences of two women who grappled with their desires for sex, passion, safety, and stability. Alicia and Phoebe split sexual desire and passion from various aspects of security in relationships, leading them to develop strategies of desire of the Relational Woman. In chapter 5, I explore Alicia's experiences and introduce the split between sexual desire and safety. Alicia was a good girl who tried to create safety and security in her relationships, but kept getting hurt by her partners. Chapter 6 focuses on Phoebe and the split between sexual passion and stability. Phoebe was on the cusp of getting engaged to someone stable with whom she didn't have passionate and intimate sex, despite her history of good relationships with good sex.

Part III: The Desiring Woman

In part III, I explore the experiences of four women who developed productive strategies of desire that allowed them to have satisfying sex and relationships. In chapters 7 and 8, Maria, Susan, Sophia, and Jeanette demonstrate various ways of getting what they want and need. They did so by resisting the temptation to split either a strong identity and independence from relationships, or strong sexual desire from stability and safety in relationships. I uncover how they managed to develop comfort with their sexual desires and desires for a relationship, becoming the Desiring Woman. In chapter 7, Maria and Susan illustrate different paths to developing comfort with complicated desires for sex and relationships. These paths followed periods of struggle in their teens and early twenties during which they succumbed to splitting—relational desire from independence in Maria's case, and sexual desire from safety in Susan's case. Sophia's and Jeanette's experiences, in chapter 8, show how strong identities and a capacity for independence and vulnerability, crucial qualities in obtaining what they wanted from sex and relationships, can be facilitated in childhood. Because of their comfort with all of their desires, neither Jeanette nor Sophia resorted to splitting.

The women I interviewed who did get what they wanted and needed did so through sexual and relationship experiences in which they acknowledged their contradictory feelings, desires, and fears, but took risks anyway. They didn't work to ensure their safety above all else and sometimes they got hurt. But they survived the hurt and learned from it that they could continue to take risks, rather than learning that they needed to protect themselves from all future vulnerability.

In chapter 9, I argue for the kind of useful training that young women need to help them stop splitting, start resolving their internal conflicts about their desires for sex and relationships, and begin to have satisfying sex and relationships. The training that I advocate includes the acknowledgment that the desire for seemingly contradictory things—independence and dependence, passionate sex and stability, a strong identity and intimacy—is normal. Internal conflict about the things that matter most in life—love and work and sex—is natural and can be acknowledged as such. Of course, we have mixed feelings about the things that are important to us. Our internal conflict is, in part, what lets us know what really matters to us. Instead of being encouraged to split and disavow their desires, women who can acknowledge their desires and the conflicts that they feel about them can use such knowledge to pursue their desires in all of their complexity. This training can take place in relationships of various kinds: mentorships, romantic relationships, therapeutic relationships, and friendships. Of course, societal changes would help, too, such as changes in social representations of women, changes in the family, changes in the ways we learn about sex in schools, and changes in the ways work is structured.

In this historical moment of freer sexual mores for women, when traditional institutions no longer hold as much sway and no longer provide as much coherence as in the past, young women are left alone to do the cultural and psychological work necessary to navigate the murky waters of sex and love. Old ideals of sexual submissiveness and inhibition don't cohere with the new black box of the twenties for women. But neither do ideals of radical independence, safety, and control help women to develop satisfying relationships and sex lives characterized by mutuality.

I argue that it is possible to want and to get love and good sex, a career and a relationship, sex and relatedness—to integrate previously split desires. Young women can have it all, not in a glib sense or according to some checklist from a magazine, but in a real sense: by not cutting themselves off from their desires. But this involves giving up some control and entails some expression of vulnerability. Because of this paradox, for women such as Katie, whom we will meet in the next chapter, love and sex and work have never felt so hard to get.

PART I

The Sexual Woman

CHAPTER TWO

The New Taboo

Katie

An increasing number of twenty-something women face a new taboo, and it's not about sex or money or power. Instead, it's a taboo about that traditional province of women: relationships.[1] No longer is a romantic relationship the holy grail for college-educated women. Their mothers may have concerned themselves with such old-fashioned matters, but times have changed. Instead, relationships are often perceived as threatening educational attainment, career development, and personal growth. These women feel comfortable having and expressing sexual desire—that's not the problem. The problem is relationships that threaten to impinge upon personal and professional development.

Katie, a twenty-five-year-old graduate student born in 1978, with dark brown hair and bright green eyes, had a physical presence that made her seem taller than she was, and an intense gaze that she frequently turned on me when looking for help with her dilemmas.[2] She had known since high school that she wanted to be a chemist, but spent a few years after college working in labs and traveling, making sure she chose the right graduate school. Smart and accomplished, Katie landed a spot in a top graduate program. She seemed to have made all the right choices to position herself for a great career.

And the freedom that Katie felt and exhibited in her sexual development would appear to have set her up for a satisfying sex life. From a young age, Katie had felt free to explore her body—masturbating comfortably as a child and then letting her sexual curiosity and desires lead her to experimenting with various sexual practices and partners in her teens and college years. Old taboos and shame about female sexual desire seemed to have no place in Katie's experience.

But shortly into our conversations, Katie confided that she worried that her single-minded pursuit of a PhD might limit her ability to meet a man with whom she could build a life. Being stuck in a small college town for five to six years while earning a degree felt severely restrictive to Katie. This realization—that she might want to prioritize a relationship over her career—felt shocking to Katie, and she did not admit to it easily. In fact, she felt deeply ashamed by such thoughts, worried that they signaled weakness and dependence, qualities she did not admire. To put such a high premium on relationships was frightening to Katie. She worried that it meant she wasn't liberated and was still constrained by traditional expectations of women. Why should she, a young and highly educated woman in the twenty-first century, value relationships with men so highly?

I have heard Katie's dilemma echoed by countless women in their twenties. They, like Katie, feel a taboo on being too relationship-oriented in their twenties. Parents warn, "Do you really want to settle down so early? We just don't want to see you miss out on any opportunities." Friends intone, "How will you know what you like and want if you don't play the field? You're only young once. Now's the time to explore."

This taboo is a new kind of cultural pressure, unfamiliar to women of earlier generations. Katie's mother faced very different demands: to marry and have children early, to be sure to find a man who would support her financially. But Katie's mom, like many women of her generation, lost out in the marriage bargain. She divorced Katie's father soon after Katie was born because of his extramarital affairs, and thus she was cheated out of the assurances of protection that marriage had offered.

According to her mom, Katie had it made—she had a promising career ahead of her, she hadn't abandoned her own ambitions for a partner or children, and a relationship would come easily once she was ready for it. But Katie lacked confidence about her own life decisions. She felt much more uncertain about both her career and relationships than she liked to admit. And, like other women of her generation, she deeply feared that she wouldn't be able to have both a career and a relationship.

Katie, like many of the young women with whom I spoke, still struggled with having a relationship and a professional identity at the same time. Despite all the cultural advances we've made over the last century, it is still difficult to reconcile these two paths. In fact, the notion of "having it all" propagated by second-wave feminists seems like a pipe dream of yesteryear to young women such as Katie. This chapter explores why Katie feared that she couldn't have both professional success and a relationship. Why would a professionally accomplished and ambitious woman feel so threatened by the idea of wanting a relationship?

FREEDOM AND NEW TABOOS

While Katie had unprecedented freedoms in her educational opportunities, career options, sexual experiences, and relationship patterns, she did not feel quite as free as we might imagine. Katie could, ostensibly, have had whatever kind of relationship she wanted, and whenever she wanted it. But as with many experiences of increased choices, new social and psychological constraints have arisen in response to them: don't focus too much on relationships, don't settle down too soon, put your energy into developing yourself, commitment comes at the expense of your own development, and so forth.[3] These edicts didn't feel like freedom to Katie once she became interested in pursuing a relationship.

Earlier, when she had been focused on sexual and personal exploration during college and for a few years afterward, these injunctions did not feel so much like taboos, and in fact facilitated Katie's pursuit of what she wanted. She could enjoy her sexual freedom and explore sexual experiences with men and women. And she could do this all without feeling as though she were compromising either her academic and professional development or her chances of developing a relationship in the future. She could pursue her academic ambitions unfettered by the emotional and time commitments of a relationship.[4] And she didn't fear any derogatory sexual labels that would mark her as "nonrelationship material" in the future.

But in her midtwenties, Katie found herself in a bind. She professed to want a relationship in which she could develop emotional intimacy and so explore herself and her sexuality more deeply. But she felt the influence of the social and psychological taboo of being relationship focused, and she worried about the potential loss of independence and her focus on her career. As she grew older and wanted more emotional contact with a sexual partner, but also wanted to advance her career, Katie was in a terrible dilemma.

We see this age-old conflict between relationships and careers played out on television shows such as *Mad Men,* in which one of the ambitious female characters, Midge Daniels, the bohemian art illustrator who had an affair with Don Draper in season 1, insists on having only affairs and not relationships so that she can stay free. For Midge, this seems the only solution open to her, given the restrictions of marriage in the 1960s. She's reconciled herself to not having it all. It is striking, then, that in the new millennium Katie resolved the dilemma similarly: by having long-term affairs with men who already had girlfriends. This way, she enjoyed some emotional involvement in an ongoing sexual relationship, but there was no threat to her ambition and career because the relationship couldn't go anywhere. At the time that I spoke with her, however, this did not feel like a solution to Katie, and instead was the problem she most desperately wanted to solve.

Katie's solution to the dilemma of wanting an emotionally intimate sexual relationship at the same time that she wanted a career, although a particular manifestation of Katie's individual psychology and history, also came precisely from the freedoms that Katie's mother so envied.

SEXUAL FREEDOM

If having it all seemed elusive to Katie, then her sexual freedom would leave her feminist foremothers profoundly pleased. Rather than being consigned to "lie back and think of England,"

Katie felt free to explore her body and its pleasures without shame and to be sexually experimental with men and women. And unlike the limited freedoms advocated by the sexual revolution, which often privileged men's desires for unfettered access to women over women's prerogative to follow their own desires, Katie felt free to let her own sexual desires be her guide.

Unlike many young girls, Katie seemed to feel that her body really belonged to her and to no one else. She began masturbating when she was eleven, and figured out how to climax from masturbation a few years later. An early vivid memory involved sitting on the floor of her bedroom, leaning against her bed with no clothes on and looking at her reflection in her pet snake's aquarium. She felt curious about her body and sex and puzzled by how it all worked.

Although Katie felt her own desires strongly and clearly and was curious about sex, she felt generally unrecognized as a sexual being in high school. As an average-size white girl who judged herself to be "overweight and with small breasts," she felt desexualized by most boys around her, not someone anyone would pay attention to or whose body would interest boys. These experiences and insecurities left Katie in the curious position of knowing her sexual desires but being unconvinced that her body could arouse the same level of desire in others.

These insecurities make it all the more remarkable that in high school, Katie developed an impressive capacity, rare in teenage girls—as documented in scholarly research such as Deborah Tolman's *Dilemmas of Desire*—to know what she did and didn't want.[5] Katie felt curious and interested and was happy to make out with the first two boys she kissed. But with the boy she took to her prom, she felt turned off because he was so forceful. She recalled: "He was just awful. He was pushing my head down into his lap in the back of his car on the way there, and on the way to afterprom. Wanting to make me give him head. . . . I was curious and wanted to do things, but was feeling bad about how it was happening." She pushed him away and spent the rest of the night and weekend avoiding him. Rather than acceding to his demands, Katie pushed back. She wasn't confused about whether she was entitled to say no, or whether her reaction was reasonable. It was clear to her that his behavior was unacceptable and unappealing, but she also remained aware of her own desires. She recalled: "I was attracted to him and had a crush on him, and had he not been so aggressive, I probably would have been more sexually open with him and had some more experiences with him. But as soon as he sort of was forceful and I felt like meat instead of like he was actually interested or thought I was attractive or anything, I was just turned off." While Katie felt turned off by the boy's behavior, she still acknowledged the presence of her own desire. She didn't polarize sexual desire into something that only men possess, and that women must remain wary of.[6]

In college, Katie finally was able to do more sexual exploration with both men and women. She reveled in her ability to go to parties and, as she put it, "randomly make out" with people. Katie limited most of these encounters to sexual contact that didn't include intercourse. Because Katie had such clear knowledge of what she did and didn't want and was so comfortable expressing her desires, she never feared that things would go too far or get out of control, and they didn't.

Katie applied the same qualities that made her a good scientist—curiosity, perseverance, and objectivity—to sex while she was in college. She actively tried to learn about both women's and men's bodies, seeking to figure them out. She wanted to understand the mechanics of men's bodies, since she felt that she didn't really have a handle on how they worked. As a junior, she and a guy and a girlfriend were "talking about sex down on the porch, and our confusion, our mutual confusion, about the opposite sex's bodies." They then

> sat around in his apartment, naked, talking about our bodies and sexuality. And he was explaining to us, like, how a hand job is supposed to be done and how a good blowjob works. . . . We both wanted to know how to please. And so that was kind of a helpful lesson, but really asexual . . . it was very clinical . . . we were kind of showing him what feels good and, and it was very—it was not graphic. It was kind of like we were sitting there and pointing, kind of like, "This is the area that you should touch; this doesn't matter." And he was kind of like, he had his penis is his hands and was kind of lifting it up, and it was really, um, kind of the first time that I had been in daylight with a naked man and really gotten to see what it was all about. And I was, I remember being kind of struck by how testicles, how a scrotum, look like labia.

As Katie described this exchange, I pictured "circle time" in my mind—it sounded as straightforward as sharing in kindergarten. Only the content being shared was "This feels good when you stroke me here" and "This is what you touch and do to get me aroused" instead of stories of trips to the zoo. At this stage of her life, Katie was determined to gather sexual data as she would for an experiment run in the lab—methodically, purposefully, and without the intrusion of messy feelings.

Katie had sex for the first time with a good friend who lived in her dorm, but here things started to get complicated. She described her first time, as do many women, as somewhat underwhelming, more as something to be gotten out of the way than as something memorable. Katie was hoping they could work up to "good" sex. Before this time, she really had had no emotional expectations from sexual partners. But now she was interested in developing, maybe not a full-fledged relationship, but at least an ongoing sexual exploration in which she could learn how things worked with someone with whom she felt comfortable and close. The good friend, however, became awkward and distant after they'd had sex, and they didn't have sex again until they'd both returned from stints abroad. In the aftermath, he seemed to want less to do with her than she did with him. This left Katie feeling confused and hurt, and unsure of what she could or should expect from a boy with whom she wasn't in a relationship.

Unlike many other women, who say they felt pressured to have sex, Katie's own desires dictated her first sexual experiences. In short, her sexual history in college would have done the authors of *Our Bodies, Ourselves* proud.[7] She felt no shame or even much inhibition about her early sexual experimentation. Instead, Katie felt her early sexual encounters to be straightforward, exploratory, and consensual.

Not so clear and straightforward was what Katie should do with the emotional desires that kept showing up once she had had sex. On the face of it, Katie was not yet really interested in relationships. She was focused on gaining sexual experience and succeeding academically. And she had the freedom (and sometimes pressure) to experiment sexually and remain rather uninterested in relationships in college and her early twenties. But the desire for something more than sex cropped up despite Katie's best efforts to be scientific about it all.

Katie longed to be with someone she could get to know sexually, whom she could come to trust and feel comfortable with, and with whom she could be vulnerable enough to have an orgasm. These longings did not match up with her dismissal of relationships. As long as Katie didn't pursue relationships involving emotional connection, she was unlikely to develop the trust and comfort that she craved. So Katie's systematic acquisition of sexual knowledge, and her ability to orgasm while masturbating, did not guarantee orgasmic sex with casual partners.

This quandary left Katie with little practice at relationships. She had a decent number of one-time sexual encounters but not a lot of ongoing sexual experience; she feared depending upon a man; and she felt profound doubts about whether she could ever have both a successful career and a relationship—not a recipe for satisfaction from sex or relationships with men.

UNAVAILABLE MEN

The strategy of desire that Katie unconsciously developed as a solution, although it didn't feel like much of a solution to her, was to pursue relationships with men who were already involved with other women. She got many of the perks of a relationship: closeness, passion, sex with someone she felt close to, and companionship. What she didn't get were commitment, security, or any hope of a future. While disappointed by missing these emotional elements, Katie faced no risk that anything or anyone might compromise her ambition.

After disappointing sex in college, Katie continued to seek out ongoing sexual relationships that would help her to figure out "how sex worked." She felt sexually inexperienced relative to her peers, and was eager to catch up to them in terms of number of partners and amount of sex. Katie was not, however, interested in developing committed relationships with men. She assumed those would come later, when she was ready.

In her first year after college, Katie traveled several hours away for "weekends of debauchery" with Mike. He and Katie had flirted endlessly in college, and they were both excited to finally sleep together. He had a long-distance girlfriend, and at first that was fine with Katie—she was after sexual exploration, not love. She described the appeal: "I wanted to know how it all worked, and how to make it feel good. And we were comfortable enough with each other to talk about that. So that was really the beginning of me starting to feel like, 'Oh, my body is interesting to me. And even though I don't necessarily perceive it as attractive, you know, he does. And he's making that clear to me.'"

Despite the lack of a relationship or commitment, Katie felt comfortable with Mike and began to feel curious about her body when she was with a partner. Alone, she could explore her own body and knew what to do to reliably bring herself to climax. But Katie did not feel particularly at ease exposing her body and its pleasures to a partner. Mike and Katie's time together was explicitly focused on sex, which early on felt like a welcome relief to both of them. Having no emotional complications appealed to both Katie and Mike. But as they continued to spend time together, she began to want a relationship with him, and was disappointed that one didn't develop.

When she was twenty-three, Katie met Jim, and they fell hard for each other. He worked in the same lab that she did, and they spent the first several months they knew each other denying the sparks between them because Jim had a girlfriend. Katie was immediately drawn to Jim physically, and she loved his thoughtfulness and self-reflection. Jim's relationship with his long-distance girlfriend was "very complicated." He purportedly wanted to break up with her, but he didn't want to interrupt her progress on her dissertation. Meanwhile, Katie waited in the wings. Yet Katie's relationship with Jim was groundbreaking for her. It was the first time she had fallen in love, it was the longest relationship she'd had to date (four months), and it was the first time she felt really sexually intimate and could orgasm with a partner. Finally, Katie felt secure in a relationship, confident that Jim was interested in her and cared about her. This security allowed her to let go of insecurities about her body and her worries about whether Jim was enjoying himself in sex. She described sex with him as fun and exploratory: "And we would just say, you know, 'Let's go.' And I think if I wanted to switch positions or whatever, it was all kind of just very happy, playfully, 'Let's do this.' And it felt very comfortable to just express what I wanted, and when. And I think he definitely felt comfortable, too, doing the same thing . . . moving each other, just physically placing each other's hands in different places, whatever. So, just communicating through words and through movement." Because of the security and comfort she had with him, Katie felt confident that Jim would break up with his girlfriend and that they could build a committed relationship together.

As Katie's departure for graduate school in California drew near, things began to fall apart with Jim. While Jim said he wanted to choose Katie, he worried that his girlfriend would be lost without him. Katie and his girlfriend eventually learned that he was lying to them, and he lost both of them. Katie felt deeply distressed that she had trusted him so much, and that she had believed that he would leave his girlfriend for her.

Having had a relatively serious relationship helped Katie to feel secure, but also showed her some of what she missed when single. She begrudgingly came to see that she actually wanted a man in her life, and that having a relationship could have a generally stabilizing influence on her. Katie expressed the sense, or perhaps the hope, that she'd feel better and more secure about her career and academic choices if she had a relationship as an anchor in her life.

Despite this realization, once in California Katie found herself having conflicted sexual contact with Dave, who, like Jim, had a long-distance girlfriend. This time, although it felt difficult to control, Katie tried to extricate herself from the situation. Dave was smart and attractive, and Katie felt an instant rapport with him. They talked well together and clicked physically—it was difficult to deny the attraction and the potential for a relationship. But he had a girlfriend on the East Coast, and Katie already had a string of relationships behind her in which she'd been the other woman. Dave seemed to need Katie, which made it hard for her to end it. He made half-hearted statements about their relationship being wrong, but somehow they'd end up in bed together. Katie would then stop in the midst of having sex and say, "What are we doing? This can't happen." If things were to end for good, someone needed to be firm, and it wasn't going to be Dave. Finally, Katie put a stop to their relationship. She felt sad to lose Dave and disappointed in herself for getting involved with him in the first place.

Katie repeatedly chose to form relationships with men who already had girlfriends. But what had started as a strategy for gaining sexual experience—being a Sexual Woman who avoids relationships—became increasingly frustrating and unsatisfying. By being with unavailable men, Katie ensured that she didn't develop an ongoing connection with someone with whom she could feel secure. She was struggling to transition from keeping relationships at bay to prioritizing relationships, and she felt herself to be woefully unprepared to do so.

WHY UNAVAILABLE MEN?

One might conclude that Katie chose unavailable men because of her father, who cheated on her mother, and her stepfather, who was emotionally unavailable and had limited involvement with his wife or stepchildren. And that may be the case—it may be that Katie merely followed the models available to her. Or it would seem that Katie found only men who acted in ways that confirmed her mother's fears about men. While her mother did remarry, Katie grew up regularly hearing her mother's warnings about men's fundamental unreliability and sexually aggressive nature. In cheating with her, Katie's partners proved themselves to be worthy of wariness. In effect, they showed her that her mom was right. Or Katie may have been unconsciously acting like the men her mother had warned her about by doing her own cheating, thus seizing some power in a situation in which she felt powerless. But I had the sense that there was more to Katie's choice.

It seemed to me that Katie not only didn't want the closeness and interdependence that accompany a serious relationship, but actually feared them. She admitted that early in her relationship history, "I didn't really want to be in a relationship, and so it was kind of just like, 'Well, we have this play relationship, and it's never gonna go anywhere, it's not that serious, and it's kind of like having my independence but [also] having someone to kiss.'" She came to recognize that she got something out of *not* being someone's girlfriend—she kept her independence. And she deeply feared that this independence would be compromised by a relationship. She desperately feared becoming a Relational Woman, lacking sexual desire and, more important in her eyes, independence.

We can understand some of Katie's determination to maintain her independence when we look at her mother. Katie was so resolute in her efforts not to be like her mother that perhaps she avoided committed relationships with men altogether. Although Katie felt close to her mom, she wanted a life very different from hers.

> In creating who I am, I definitely try to avoid the things that I feel like [might predispose me] to be who my [mom is] . . . losing sight of your own goals in life, and just things that you find interesting, when you have children. And if I have children, I'll definitely . . . make [an] extra effort to keep my own personal life going on as well, with hobbies or career or whatever. Which my mom didn't do at all, and now she's kind of, her career was us. And now we're gone, basically, and she's left with "What do I do now?" And she can't think of anything.

Katie's mother had not maintained a career or even independent interests while raising her children, and for Katie this served as an object lesson about how to live, or not to live, her own life.

Katie's fierce attachment to her independence gave me some important insight into her struggles. Half of the women I spoke with shared her strong concerns about compromising their independence when they were in a relationship. Of course, independence and autonomy matter to all of us—we need to be able to think for ourselves, make decisions for ourselves, and take care of ourselves. But many of the women I spoke with were subject to an ideal of radical independence that holds that invulnerability, safety, and control are important to maintain at all times. This ideal, however, is based upon a fear of closeness, vulnerability, and interdependence.[8] So it is not surprising that Katie didn't like to admit her desire for a relationship, feeling that such a desire made her weak and dependent. This seemed to be one key to her being with unavailable men: as long as she was never someone's girlfriend, she could continue to be radically independent.

Katie felt ashamed of her desire for a man in her life on whom she could rely: "Women feel like they want to reach for their goals, and yet they can't admit that they want to be in a relationship. And women who want to be in a relationship more than reach for their goals are seen as weak and spineless. . . . I think for years I've never wanted to admit that I wanted a relationship." In Katie's social context of young and aspiring women and men, she felt as though it were disappointing to prioritize a relationship with a man. This is a new cultural message that goes against the grain of centuries of female socialization. Historically, women have been encouraged to value relationships, often at the expense of their own aspirations. Much of feminist scholarship has focused on understanding and sometimes trying to change this apparently distinctive aspect of female psychology.[9] Katie is part of a new generation of highly educated women who are, of course, still socialized differently than are men, but who feel they ought to focus on their career goals, potentially at the expense of developing a relationship, at least in their twenties. All the women I interviewed felt this encouragement, and many, like Katie, expressed shame at their desire to prioritize a relationship.

This shame seemed to be at the core of Katie's continued involvement with unavailable men. Her choice allowed her to have emotional and sexual relationships with men but keep them at a distance. She did not, and in fact could not, put them at the center of her life—they remained at the periphery. This ideal of radical independence was so powerful because it matched up with Katie's fears: men leave and men are unreliable, so she'd best avoid closeness, vulnerability, and interdependence with them.

INTERNAL CONFLICT AND SPLITTING

Katie's dilemma—being with men who were taken yet desiring relationships—signaled her internal conflict about being in a relationship at all. Her desire was tempered by her fears of losing her focus on career and herself.

But instead of just being conflicted and acknowledging her mixed feelings about both relationship and career, Katie split the two desires. She set them up as mutually exclusive in her mind, and therefore made their coexistence seem impossible. This kind of splitting is the basis of much helpful categorization of the world—past and present, you and I, here and there. These are the building blocks of the mind's organization and distinguish people with a healthy orientation to reality from those with a disturbed orientation to reality. But many otherwise healthy people also use splitting as a defense against complexity and uncertainty. When someone such as Katie splits rather than acknowledges her internal conflict, she neither recognizes her complex desires nor opens herself to the uncertainty and vulnerability inherent in desiring seemingly paradoxical things. By splitting, Katie solved the problem of uncertainty and vulnerability, but she also didn't get the relationship or sex that she tentatively wanted.

Katie followed a path trod by many women in her generation—she doggedly pursued her career goals and achieved success by being aggressive and competitive. She was smart and accomplished in her work but had trouble finding as much success in her love life. She approached the latter mainly by keeping it at bay. To prioritize relationships felt embarrassing and slightly humiliating, and could also have threatened her identity. But the identity that Katie was so fiercely defending was based in part on splitting.

We all have internal conflicts—over whether we want to be in a relationship, over whether we want a career. It's when we turn these conflicts into splits that we run into trouble. When we make our conflicts categorically true, we're likely to have difficulty achieving our desires. For example, we might assert: "I can't have a relationship and a career at the same time." Splitting deprives us of the opportunity to know our complicated feelings about our desires.[10]

Katie was able to talk about and identify these conflicts, which was hopeful, as she tried to sort out how to fulfill her desires. But the conflicts were more solid than fluid, more external realities in Katie's mind than complex internal experiences. Katie imagined commitment to career and commitment to relationship to be mutually exclusive and felt guilty for wanting a relationship. This split goes a long way toward explaining why Katie tended to be with unavailable men.

Katie split for a variety of reasons, both personal and social. For Katie, and for many women, the vulnerability that characterizes relationships was difficult to tolerate. Katie's solution to managing her vulnerability and internal conflict was to split and to develop a version of radical independence. At the same time that she wouldn't depend upon a man financially, she wouldn't need a man emotionally, either. In this way, she maintained her invulnerability.

Personally, Katie worried that wanting a relationship made her too much like her mother, a woman who gave all her energy to her family and children. Katie worried that desire for a relationship made her "weak and spineless," unintelligent, and dependent. She was concerned that if she prioritized her career, she would be unable to have a relationship with a man because that is not something that intelligent and strong career women do. She was left feeling shame over wanting and valuing a relationship. By being involved with men who were already taken, Katie resolved her conflict and ensured that she did not become like her mother.

In addition to being personal, Katie's splits also followed cultural and social norms. Women (and men) in contemporary U.S. society are generally offered two choices: be relational, dependent, passive, privately oriented, and feminine, or be autonomous, powerful, assertive, publicly focused, and masculine.[11] To succeed at being a relationship- *and* career-oriented woman is quite an individual accomplishment, one for which society does not give women much help or guidance.

The split between career and relationships felt natural to Katie—it *is* difficult to be successful at both. In Katie's chosen career, academia, women who achieve tenure are more than twice as likely as their male counterparts to be single twelve years after earning their PhDs. And women who are married when they begin their faculty careers are much more likely than men in the same position to divorce or separate from their spouses.[12] Katie accepted that these social realities would naturally translate into deeply felt personal conflicts. But in fact these personal conflicts were not inevitable—many of the women I spoke with also felt conflicted about their commitments to relationships and career, but not all of them did.

As a feminist sociologist and a woman striving to develop both a career and a relationship myself, I understand the power of splitting at a cultural level. I have seen countless women deny the significance of their personal relationships in the workplace, not wanting to ruin their chances for career advancement—one colleague deliberately didn't mention her daughter in a job interview out of fear that being a mother would make her seem less serious and committed.[13] And we see women regularly downplay their professional and financial successes in order not to threaten potential male partners: the *New York Times* published a front-page article on successful young women in New York who date less successful young men. The women often deliberately obfuscate their financial and professional success in order not to scare men away.[14] Katie was not alone in thinking that career success might come at the expense of a relationship, and vice versa. These cultural splits can powerfully affect a woman's ability to even acknowledge, much less to feel, the full range of her desires.

So what would it mean for Katie to have identified the personal split between relationship and career as central to her dilemma? And why was it difficult for her to identify it? It challenged her identity as a strong and independent woman—one who locates these conflicts outside, in the culture, but who has trouble locating these conflicts within herself. If these splits were held in our personal selves, perhaps we would have complicated feelings about both relationships and careers. Perhaps part of us sometimes wants to run wild with our desire for a relationship, putting all of ourselves into it even while we fear such abandon. On other days, throwing ourselves wholeheartedly into our careers, which may feel so much more within our control than messy relationships, can seem both appealing and scary. These may have been frightening desires for Katie to acknowledge—frightening because they threatened her identity as a modern woman.

CHAPTER THREE

The Bad Girl

Jayanthi

One of the apparent advantages of being a bad girl is that it's supposed to be fun. Being a bad girl may be a bad deal in other respects—it gains a woman social condemnation and ostracism, and leads to others' assumptions of limitless availability for sex; the list goes on. But at least it should be fun. There can be pleasure in defying others' expectations, breaking the rules, and upsetting tradition. And there can be pleasure in having no messy emotional consequences, no attachments, no settling down, and no guilt about sex. There is also appeal in the drama and excitement of having crazy stories to tell and creating a history for oneself, especially if one's history previously has been defined by others' expectations of what a woman should be and do.

However, I found that the real-life experience of being the bad girl was often not so much fun. Instead, this approach sometimes left the women I studied feeling unhappy and numb. Particularly for women with fragile senses of self, the bad-girl strategy seemed to provide a strong identity. At the same time, it ostensibly protected women from losing track of their identities in a relationship by never investing in one emotionally. But rather than feeling strong and protected, some bad girls were left feeling alone and vulnerable.

Jayanthi, a twenty-nine-year-old second-generation Indian American woman born in 1974, spent her early twenties rebelling against her upper-middle-class, traditional but moderately religious Hindu family, doing everything she could to be "bad" in their eyes.[1] Jayanthi spent years casually hooking up with men, and she enjoyed some of it, but often felt "played" and used by them. She would then retreat from men and sex and be a "goody-goody girl" who toyed with her parents' offers of an arranged marriage. But eventually she'd swing back to being bad.

Having lots of sex felt like both a way to rebel against her parents and a way to assert her sense of herself as a strong woman. But while the sex helped Jayanthi to define herself in opposition to a stereotypical good girl, she didn't get much pleasure or a solid sense of herself out of it. She felt more confused than ever about whether she was good or bad, Indian or American. And even as she eventually figured some things out about how to have an orgasm, Jayanthi confided anxiously that she worried about losing herself in relationships with men. She imagined that in a relationship, she'd get swept up into her partner's world and lose track of her identity and things that mattered to her.

I heard this fear of losing track of their identities again and again from women in their twenties. Self-help books call out to them to "focus on yourself," "make yourself happy," and not to "lose yourself in a relationship." But without a solid and reliable identity, these intonations rang hollow for women such as Jayanthi. This chapter explores why Jayanthi so feared that she would be subsumed in a relationship with a man. Why did a woman with such passionate interests of her own fear that she would lose track of herself and her desires in a relationship?

TENTATIVE IDENTITY

Jayanthi, a dancer and teacher who was tiny in stature, spoke very quickly and seemed to have boundless energy. Her enthusiasm for life, for dance, and for political causes was palpable, and she expressed strong opinions about the things in life that mattered to her. I was surprised, then, when Jayanthi confessed that she worried about being overwhelmed by a relationship, concerned that she'd quickly lose her own identity in the other person. It was difficult to square her fear of disappearing into someone else with the forceful personality before me. I came to learn that Jayanthi's strength felt very tentative to her, and was not something that she could count on when faced with the prospect of close emotional and physical ties with a man.

Jayanthi's early sexual experiences profoundly shaped her expectations of men and their trustworthiness. She had her first kiss and sexual experience in college at eighteen, and it was passionate and fun. They didn't have intercourse, but experimented with almost everything else. It turned out, however, that Jayanthi had greater expectations of a relationship than the man did. She later felt the man had "played" her—he was dating other women, and she was disgusted and put off by that. In that first experience, she felt devastated and too emotionally involved. She vowed not to be played by a man again. So to avoid being either played or too involved, Jayanthi spent the next decade bouncing back and forth between being good and being bad. In both cases, she distanced herself from the men she was involved with, either physically or emotionally. While being a good girl, Jayanthi remained both physically and emotionally removed from men. And while being a bad girl, Jayanthi was physically close to but emotionally distant from men.

When employing the good-girl strategy, Jayanthi entertained her parents' offers to find a suitable Indian partner for her. On a few occasions, she met men whose families her parents knew as a way to anchor herself amid the "craziness." Or she would troll listings on Indian matchmaking websites, consoling herself that she might find some clarity and certainty about the entirety of her life if she had a secure partner who met her parents' and community's expectations of her. "When I got confused, I would freak out and feel, 'I need to settle down. I need to find a partner, and I'm not seeing anybody now, so I better do it my parents' way, through family friends or meeting people online.' . . . It was like, you marry somebody and that problem of what you're gonna do with your life disappears." Being a good girl gave Jayanthi some clarity and purpose, but it didn't feel like an identity of her own.

THE BAD-GIRL STRATEGY

Being a bad girl, on the other hand, gave Jayanthi a strong sense of identity. Particularly for women from families with traditional ideas and teachings about sex (for example, some immigrant families and conservative religious families), being a bad girl can enable them to feel independent and "bad-ass," and to separate from the parents and traditions that may have felt restrictive to them while they were growing up. Tired of being a good girl who met all her parents' and community's expectations, Jayanthi began casually hooking up with men after college, often meeting several in one night.

> I was twenty-one and hadn't had that many experiences in intimacy, didn't know what it's about, really. I was still a virgin, I went to a women's college. I'm my mom and dad's ideal child—what is that? Fuck the standards, fuck the expectations of what I'm supposed to be. I'm just gonna break them. So I just broke them. So I ended up really going crazy. . . . I was just like, "I don't want to be the poster child, so the other extreme is this." It was like the Virgin Mary or the ho. And I was going to the other side. And I just didn't like that. And I was like, "Okay, I'm not gonna do this anymore." I'd try not to do it and then it'd be the other extreme. I wouldn't find anybody meaningful. I'd try not to associate with that group of people, and then I'd be having a really, really sheltered life again and I'd be like, "Fuck this, I don't want to do this," and I'd go and freak out again.

She was aware now that she had been feeling insecure at the time, and that she had been seeking out attention and affection. She reflected that she loved part of it, but also felt lucky for not having gotten STDs and not having been raped or killed (although, as we learn later in this chapter, she was in the process of redefining a specific encounter as rape, one in which she "kind of gave my body without giving my mind; I didn't really want it to happen"). At the time she had longed for a sexual history, for stories that would make her feel real and alive.

> [At the time I was] in one box or another box, and in both ways I had censorship. I was censored on this really sheltered side 'cause it was limiting what I wanted to do. And when I was doing everything, I was censoring myself, 'cause I didn't know what . . . I wanted. I kind of knew what I wanted, but I wasn't able to really express that. I wasn't able to really say no. I wasn't able to be honest to myself, [to say,] "Jay, what are you doing to yourself?" . . . I would just give in. So both sides had censorship. Both sides had limitations, and [on] both sides

I felt I was being trapped in some way. So I felt like, "God, this is shit, this is terrible." So basically what happened was . . . by the beginning of '98 I realized I was being played by a lot of different guys. I was being manipulated. I was given fake affection. I was silencing myself. I was putting myself in hard situations, dangerous ones, risky ones, not even pleasurable situations at times. But it wasn't all bad. Otherwise I wouldn't have continued on with it. I also liked the drama, I liked the excitement, I liked the fact I was having stories, I liked being bad. And then there were some people I actually loved having sex with and I loved the intimacy with. So it all came in a package. I don't want it to come across as all negative. Otherwise it makes no sense as to why I stayed there and did it, okay?

When I asked how she made sense of it at the time, she replied:

What I was thinking at the time was, "I'm liberating myself, this is liberation, I'm getting myself out. I've been repressed for so long, and I'm just gonna let it out. I don't care." So that's what it was. . . . I look back and I'm like, "Damn, I should have cared a little more about protection." But at the time I was like, "I don't care, I've been so repressed, this is all about letting it out." That's what was going on at the time. . . . "I want to party, I want to meet people, I want to hook up, I want to have stories, I want to have a history." I didn't have a history, so I wanted to create a history. I don't want to be naïve.[2]

Jayanthi worked hard to give herself a history that differed from her family's expectations—she needed sexual experiences and crazy stories about sexual exploits to create that history. Prior to her crazy time, she felt herself to be meeting all her parents' expectations of a good Indian girl. She went to a women's college, was not sexually promiscuous, did traditional Indian dance, and cooked Indian food. Releasing herself from the repression she felt as her parents' daughter allowed her to feel more her own woman.

The bad-girl strategy also appealed to Jayanthi because prior to college, she hadn't felt attractive. Growing up in a predominantly white town in the Southwest, she found that the attractive and popular girls were always white, and Jayanthi felt that boys didn't find her pretty. On top of not feeling desirable because she was Indian American, Jayanthi felt sheltered by her parents, who would not allow her to date. Embracing the bad-girl strategy highlighted for Jayanthi the degree to which she actually was considered desirable and attractive.

Being a bad girl allowed Jayanthi to control her identity, rather than having it controlled by either her family or the men she encountered. With American men, Jayanthi had felt stereotyped as naïve, passive, innocent, shy, submissive, and virginal because she was an Indian woman. Indian men also expected her to be a nice, virginal girl whom they could bring home to their families. By having extensive sexual experiences, Jayanthi could feel herself to be different from these stereotypes.

Being her own woman in charge of her identity, however, didn't automatically translate into her enjoying sex. Jayanthi never had orgasms during the "sexual frenzy" time: "I didn't really express much desire, I just took whatever was given. It wasn't about how I liked it. No one had any interest in making me come, and I had no interest in coming 'cause it wasn't even about me." She also says that 30 percent of the time, she had sex because she felt obligated to do so.

A turning point in Jayanthi's bad-girl era came one night in India. It was only recently that she was able to recount fully this experience.

> I used to go and dance at this one club a lot. There was this one African person there, 'cause a lot of West Africans, East Africans come do some studies in India 'cause it's cheaper for them. So there

was this one; I think he was from Sudan. He—I forget his name. He was kind of cute. I was like, "I don't mind fooling around with him." And I didn't have a car, so had to depend on these guys to take me home. I wouldn't sleep at my place 'cause my mom was so mad at me at the time for doing all this. She was just like, "If you're gonna do it, you have to come back in the morning. I'm not gonna open up the gate for you." So I'd have to sleep at other people's places. So I decided one night, he asked me to come home with him. I was like, "Sure, I'll come home with you." But he stayed with three other African roommates. So we get home around five in the morning after dancing at the club. Me and him are fooling around, then we start talking, and we have sex, and I'm okay with it. Not that I really want to have sex with him, but whatever, I'll do it. Then we went to take a shower. He stepped out for a minute, and then his friend came in and took a shower with me, finished up with me. And I didn't know what to do. 'Cause, again, I'm in this unknown place. I don't want to be like, "What the fuck are you doing? Get the fuck out!" I didn't know what to do. I was like, "I guess I'll have to be cool with it, have to pretend like I'm cool with having a shower with his friend." After the shower with his friend, his friend wanted to have sex with me. And I think I had sex with him too. And then he was lying down with me for ten minutes and then he got up. I was lying there [thinking], "Oh, my God, I need to get home." I didn't know what to do. Then his other roommate came in, and he wanted me to have sex with him. I didn't have sex with him. I just kind of gave him oral sex, which I didn't really want to do. By this time, I was like, "This is so crazy." And then the fourth guy came in. By then I was like, "I'm not doing anything." I just got up and was like, "I'm just gonna go home. Can one of you help me get a taxi or something to get home?" I still had to be nice to them 'cause I needed their help to get a taxi. That's the powerlessness I felt. . . . It was only recently, literally recently, Leslie, that I thought back on it, and I was like, "Oh, my God, that actually happened to me. Oh, my God, what was that about?"

She had now come to understand and describe this experience as a disturbing version of sexual exploitation. Earlier it had felt like another in a series of crazy antics—something that was annoying, but not exploitative and devastating. Jayanthi now felt saddened and disturbed by the experience, angry at the men who pressured her to have sex with them, shocked that they could be such "assholes," and sad that she felt so starved for attention that she allowed herself to be in such a vulnerable position. Over the course of the interviews, she reflected that perhaps she reacted against such experiences of exploitation by later using men as sex objects and playing them.

After this experience, Jayanthi's strategy shifted from being a bad girl who was "up for anything" to being a bad girl who was in control. She began to use men for sex and became the player herself, by which she meant being a smooth talker, acting and talking as though she cared about the men with whom she was involved. But when playing men, she was just after sex and had no intention of becoming emotionally involved. She felt that she had been played by men earlier, but from those experiences she herself learned how to play, so she began juggling people and having sex with multiple partners without becoming emotionally involved. She used men for sex and dumped them when they became too serious or emotionally engaged. And she successfully avoided being hurt herself by steering clear of any emotional connection to the men she slept with. One of the ways in which she remained untouched emotionally was by hooking up primarily with African American men. These men became a solution and a part of her strategy—they weren't white men, who oversexualized her, and they weren't Indian American men, who undersexualized her. But they also weren't "relationship material," according to her family or herself, so this strategy "protected" her from the possibility of developing an emotional connection with the men.

When doing the playing herself, Jayanthi began to feel more desire and pleasure, and more able to say no to things she did not want. Being a player allowed her to be the subject in sex, the one calling the shots instead of the object responding to another's desires. When she shifted to being the player herself, she began masturbating and discovering what she liked sexually, and she felt free to pursue her desires when she wanted or did not want to have sex. She would tell partners to stop if she did not enjoy an activity. And she began having orgasms, both through masturbation and with partners. At first she worried about what would happen during an orgasm—would she be scared; would she be loud? She challenged herself to masturbate in as many places as she could without being noticed: in an airplane seated next to people, while driving, or while in bed at relatives' houses. She felt "bad-ass" about being able to do it, and it excited her at the same time that it relaxed her.

Being a bad girl did open space for Jayanthi to experiment sexually and to be with many sexual partners, despite her conservative upbringing. And it helped her to establish an identity independent of her parents and community. But with some distance, she reflected that those experiences were not driven by desire, and did not give her much sexual pleasure. Later, when she was doing the playing and felt more in control, Jayanthi began to figure out what she wanted sexually, when, and with whom. And she protected herself from harm by remaining emotionally distant. She later worried that her sense of independence and her knowledge of her own desires, so hard won during her "crazy time," could be endangered by emotional attachment to a man.

STRONG IDENTITY
VERSUS RELATIONSHIPS

Jayanthi found it difficult to be in an emotional and physical relationship with a man without losing her identity. In relation to men, she sometimes felt overwhelmingly emotionally connected to them and almost overtaken by that connection. Or she had dissociated experiences of sex in which she was not present. Or she had experiences of sex in which she was physically present and enjoying herself, but the personhood of the man was irrelevant or disregarded. The idea of both herself and a man maintaining strong identities[3] seemed impossible—either they merged into one, or only one of them was a subject and the other the object.[4] In order to be sexually active, Jayanthi managed this difficulty by alternately being a goody-goody girl who didn't have sex but considered arranged marriage proposals from her parents, and being a very bad girl who had lots of casual and risky sex.

Jayanthi, like all of us, experienced a great deal of internal conflict—over her desire for intimacy and her fear of intimacy, over her desire to please her parents and her desire to rebel against them. Rather than feeling these conflicts and acknowledging the presence of contradictory desires within herself, Jayanthi saw her available options in mutually exclusive terms—she could have a strong identity or have a relationship. Socially and psychologically, we all have trouble imagining closeness in tandem with separateness; we have difficulty conceiving that we can maintain individuality and subjectivity at the same time that we are close to another person.[5] As anyone who is in one can attest, feelings that arise in close relationships are intense and can feel threatening to a person's independent identity. In an intimate relationship, one is likely to feel needy, attached, and invested in and dependent on someone else. But twenty-something independent women are schooled that such feelings are undesirable and unseemly. Jayanthi wished that she could be light and breezy about relationships, and not so affected by them. She wanted to be a Desiring Woman, but without any fears of losing herself and her identity. She feared that by desiring a relationship, she would become a Relational Woman, without sexual desire and lost to herself.

Jayanthi and her fellow twenty-something women, many of whom also fear being overwhelmed and overtaken by relationships, live in a new social landscape in which they can spend their twenties choosing whether to be in a relationship and hearing new edicts about how personal development should happen (on one's own, not in a relationship). Building a strong identity through being in a relationship is, among some high-achieving twenty-something women, no longer seen as possible. And Jayanthi was no exception—her model for developing was to go it alone, and only once she felt "complete" as an adult could she be in a relationship.

At the same time, the social and cultural expectation that a relationship with a significant other—after they've "found themselves" and "figured themselves out"—will be the centerpiece and a primary accomplishment of women's adult lives persists. Developing oneself within a relationship used to be the only path to follow and was restrictive to women. But now, twenty-something women are expected to form intimate relationships in their late twenties and early thirties, having spent their college years and early twenties assiduously avoiding them.

Reconciling these competing and contradictory messages is confusing and sometimes painful, particularly for women whose early family relationships did not lay the groundwork for a strong identity. Some had mothers who were withdrawn or checked out. Some had fathers who were physically or emotionally unavailable. Others, such as Jayanthi, had parents who distanced themselves from her as she entered puberty, at precisely the time that she needed strong and reliable relationships to help her develop her own identity.

Once Jayanthi entered junior high school, her mother would spend lengthy periods of time in India. She had been unhappy about their move to the United States, and once the children were young adolescents she took every opportunity to stay on in India following their summer family holidays there. Instead of featuring an overinvolved mother prying into her affairs, Jayanthi's adolescence was characterized by her mother's absence. Tellingly, I heard less from Jayanthi about her mother than I did from any other interviewee whose mother was still a part of her life.

At the same time, Jayanthi's father, who had been close to her when she was a young tomboy, became uncomfortable and remote around her when she went through puberty. He began to withdraw emotionally from her, and she longed for the paternal attention that her brother continued to receive. Jayanthi felt that as she developed a more obviously female body, her father was no longer available as someone with whom to identify. This is an all too common experience among girls whose fathers are not able to tolerate their daughters' sexuality and so, in an effort to be appropriate or chaste or to spare their daughters discomfort, withdraw from them.⁶ This usually has damaging consequences for girls, who then read their sexuality as dangerous, threatening, emotionally distancing, and not something to which men can relate. When, in her early twenties, she confronted her father about his withdrawal from her, he replied that he did not know how to relate to an adult daughter who was sexually mature. She challenged him to try, and their relationship subsequently became closer.

Learning to become a woman with a solid identity is not something Jayanthi felt she had much help in doing. Her mother could not bear to tell Jayanthi about menstruation, and asked her father to do so. An awkward conversation ensued, and the message that Jayanthi took away from it was that transitioning from girlhood to womanhood was unappealing and embarrassing, not meaningful in the ways that becoming a man were. She found evidence for her beliefs about becoming a woman versus becoming a man in the differing coming-of-age ceremonies for boys and girls in India:

> For boys, when you're between nine and fifteen, you get this special ceremony about becoming a man that's actually meaningful; you have these special challenges, you have to learn this stuff, you're being inducted into adulthood and the culture. And it's really great. I remember, when my brother was ten and I was nine, being really jealous he got to have this, because there was a big party, all this attention, it was great. . . . Once I got my period, there was this party and celebration, but it was just my family, not big like they had for my brother. And people talk about how you're a woman now, but it means all these things, like you now can't be in the kitchen when you're menstruating because you're considered unclean. So there's this kind of celebration, but really you're entering this terrible status of having to be unclean every month from now on. So I hated the attention for something like that. I just felt embarrassed and didn't want everyone to know.

Jayanthi's culture did not celebrate becoming a woman in the same ways that it did becoming a man. And her parents reinforced this sense of shame about being a woman through their avoidance of and discomfort in talking with her about it.

While Jayanthi's parents seemed unavailable to help her develop through adolescence, her brother served as a source of support in her life. Her relationship with him provided a model for how development could occur within a relationship, and not merely on her own. They were very different—he was a doctor, while she was an artist—but they shared the same politics and values. She always looked up to him, and wished in many ways to be him. While she envied her brother, he also felt like an anchor to Jayanthi when she felt confused by her own life. He was always very focused academically and knew what he wanted, but was supportive of the choices she made to figure out what she wanted from life.

Jayanthi's brother repeatedly expressed his concern about her sexual behavior in her twenties to her. She was open with both her parents and her brother about much of her sexual activity as part of her effort to tell the truth and not keep things hidden, which she had found was common among many Indian American families. While this caused her parents to judge and condemn her sexual behavior, her brother showed primarily concern. He was worried about both her mental and her physical health, and she described his involvement as important in her shift to focusing on her own desires rather than indiscriminately sleeping with people. Her brother questioned her behavior and encouraged her to pursue more meaningful relationships. "He was like, 'What is this? You meet someone at the gym and you sleep with them that night, then that's it? What does that person mean to you?' . . . My brother kept pushing, challenging me to get something where I was mutually vulnerable with somebody else, mutually emotional with somebody else."

And because her brother was available as someone with whom she could be vulnerable, his advice was delivered inside a relationship that served as a model for how to be close to someone and yet remain firmly herself. At the time of our interviews, Jayanthi was still struggling to apply her experience in the relationship with her brother to her intimate relationships with men.

RELATIONSHIPS AND IDENTITY

Being a bad girl may seem to be a perfect twenty-first-century strategy for a twenty-something woman to get fun, good sex, empowerment, and diverse experiences on which to build an identity. Sounds ideal! The bad-girl option really does represent tremendous advances for women, who are increasingly free to be players who use sex for their own ends, as men have done for years. And the option to develop one's self and sexuality outside of intimate relationships is unprecedented for women.

Young women run into trouble, however, when they use the bad-girl strategy defensively, as a way to avoid the hurt and vulnerability that necessarily accompany relationships. In this case they are left not empowered, but isolated and scared.

Jayanthi used the bad-girl strategy to develop an identity ·independent of her parents and culture. But she also used it, somewhat ironically given its inherent risks, to remain safe from emotional hurt. Once she was ready to move on from the bad-girl strategy, Jayanthi found herself at a loss. Just heeding the edict to focus on herself and be the architect of her own happiness didn't provide Jayanthi with much help in figuring out how to maintain a strong identity within an intimate relationship.

The identity that Jayanthi built through her bad-girl days didn't help her to navigate relationships.

Jayanthi's struggle was a reflection of her individual family and history, but it also demonstrates a problem in our current thinking about relationships and identity. Ambitious young women are now schooled in the notion that a strong identity is built independent of relationships, not within them. In fact, I heard many young women describe encouragement from their parents to delay relationships until later, after they'd accomplished their academic and career goals. Relationships might distract them from their professional ambitions, so should be put on hold until they were older.

This is an interesting shift from earlier academic thinking and folk wisdom about women and relationships—that women are naturally relationship oriented, and that women develop in relationships more than they do independent of them. Some psychological theories of second-wave feminism, such as self-in-relation theories, with their focus on the development of identity as it occurs within relationships, served as an important corrective to earlier male models that focused on the development of identity separate from and independent of relationships.[7] But some of these models smacked too much of essentialism, with women portrayed as being basically more oriented toward relationships and connections than are men.[8] Later poststructural theories of gender identity and development and feminist psychoanalytic theories of gender identity and development provided important correctives to this tendency toward essentialism, arguing that dichotomous thinking about men's and women's more or less related natures is in fact essentialist and doesn't allow for the ways in which men also develop in relationships and women also strive toward identities independent of relationships.[9]

With critiques of second-wave feminism's models of female development and new strategies such as the Sexual Woman, the pendulum has swung perhaps too far toward underplaying the importance of relationships in the development of identity. Strategies of the Sexual Woman variety provide women such as Jayanthi a fantasy alternative to being played by men—if she could focus on just expressing sexual desire, she'd never get hurt. For Jayanthi, a strong identity and relationships became split, as did commitment to career and commitment to relationship for Katie. But the split didn't solve the problem of how to maintain a strong identity in the context of closeness to another person—it merely shunted that problem to the side.

As Jayanthi began to want a relationship, she feared that her identity was too fragile to survive the closeness, intensity, and dependency that characterize intimate attachments. In some sense, Jayanthi faced an old dilemma for women: how to maintain her self and not get lost in a relationship. But she was not contemplating old-fashioned relationships in which her desires and needs would necessarily be neglected. In fact, she was facing a *new* dilemma for women: how to maintain a strong sense of self at the same time that she allowed herself and her development to be affected by a partner. She hoped that she could figure it all out with the support of her brother and friends, but wasn't confident about her ability to either maintain a strong identity or survive hurt in a relationship.

CHAPTER FOUR

A Pill to Kill Desire

Claudia

Sexual desire, when it shows itself full force, can come as a surprise to some twenty-something women. After many years of being (or hoping to be) the object of others' desires, feeling themselves to be the subject of their own desire can be exciting, but also potentially frightening. Sexual longing and wanting can feel as though they have come alive, unbidden and powerful, in spite of some women's attempts to tamp them down. And sexual desire and its attendant emotions and sensations cannot always be as effectively controlled as other aspects of women's lives— their education, their careers, or their bodies. Several women I spoke with who experienced intense sexual desire as a driving force in their twenties expressed surprise at its power. They did not always welcome it with open arms.[1]

The strength of Claudia's sexual desire frightened her because she worried that it kept her from developing relationships with "suitable" men, and because it came into stark contrast with her Mexican Catholic family's values and ideas about sexuality. She wished that she could "take a pill to kill [her] desire." Claudia was a "good girl" for a while—she delayed having sex until college, and had it for the first time in a committed relationship. But then she grew exploratory about sex and started really enjoying it, both with committed and with casual sexual partners. While she took a lot of pleasure in sex, she worried that her level of sexual desire was abnormally high for a woman and would "get her into trouble," potentially alienating her from her family and from men who were "relationship material." Claudia tried to rein it in, but would find herself going for booty calls with what she termed "unsuitable" men who were not interested in relationships. In recent years, following her sexual instincts alone seemed to lead her to men who were not interested in relationships. If her sexual desires were not as strong, she imagined that she would be attracted to a different kind of man. At the same time, while she professed a wish to kill her sexual desire, in recent years Claudia had worked hard to kill her desire for a relationship.

On the one hand, we can see progress in the fact that a woman such as Claudia could feel her intense sexual desire at all, that she was not repressed or out of touch with her body. And Claudia was very much enlivened and animated by her desire. But at the same time she wished she could take a pill to kill her desire—not a ringing endorsement for sexual progress.

Despite having a strong identity, knowledge of their sexual desires and desires for a relationship, and experiences of both intimacy and good sex, some twenty-something women still split and conclude that they can have only sexual desire, not fulfilling relationships. This chapter explores why Claudia, who'd had at least one committed relationship in which she'd expressed her strong sexual desire, concluded that it could never happen again. Why did she see one-night stands as her only option?

KEEPING THE MOTORCYCLE

Claudia, a Mexican American woman born in 1976, had a hip haircut and clothes and fashionable glasses, and she lived in a trendy neighborhood. A postdoctoral researcher in the social sciences, she'd come a long way from her poor roots. Her immigrant parents worked in manual labor and had six children by the time they were in their thirties. At twenty-eight, Claudia had a PhD, had lived on both coasts, had traveled extensively, and hadn't been in a committed relationship for the past few years. Her freedom was unencumbered.

As a young girl, Claudia imagined that she would be like the women around her—married with children at a young age, and working. She foresaw that she would drop out of high school at sixteen because then she could work to help her family and have spending money for herself, which she never had in her poor family. From her traditional Catholic family, she learned that sex outside of marriage was wrong, that hard work was valuable, and that marriage and children were her most important aspirations. Claudia thought that marriage and babies would come easily and naturally once she was ready. But even as a girl, there were indications that Claudia might be different from her sisters and cousins, who mostly did marry and have children young. An academic success from early on, Claudia was encouraged by several teachers throughout her schooling to pursue higher education and to aim high. She did so, and succeeded wildly. Her success inspired pride in her parents, but it also distanced her from them, given their very different opportunities and values.

While Claudia didn't particularly identify with her mother, whom she described as more traditional than herself, she saw her mom as having been forced into a traditional role. Stories about her mother's youth, in contrast, were full of spirit and adventure:

> I feel I get a lot of my spirit from her that was squelched in her life early on. Just from stories she's told me from when she was younger. She told me when she first got married and had my sister, she was still living in Mexico and my dad was in the U.S. She wanted to buy a motorcycle. She thought, "Oh, I have a daughter, I'll buy her a little carriage thing." She was going to have a motorcycle with a little seat on the side for my sister. And my grandmother was like, "What are you thinking? You're married now! You can't go around riding a motorcycle now." She was like, "Oh, okay," and that was it, end of dream. Whereas me now, I'd be like, "So what? Give me that motorcycle." But she had that sense of adventure; it's still in her. She kind of dreams, "Oh, wouldn't it be nice to go do this? Go to this exotic island?" Whereas I tend to do those things, which is probably why I'm not married still [laughs]. She's just kind of accepted at some point [that] that's not in her realm of possibilities because of financial stuff, but also [because of] responsibilities as a wife or mother. But I feel I get that [adventurous spirit] from her.

In part because of her mom's experiences, Claudia feared that a relationship would require sacrificing her sense of adventure and her ambition. It seemed that these were incompatible, that she would have to limit herself in order to be married. In fact, she imagined that one reason she was not married was that she had not given up her sense of adventure. Giving up the motorcycle was a powerful metaphor for what marriage and committed relationships meant to Claudia.

Claudia struck an uneasy compromise between keeping the motorcycle and remaining close to her family. Early in her dating life, before the advent of her strong sexual desire, she employed a good-girl strategy of desire and had a long-term boyfriend with whom she delayed intercourse, making her a

Relational Woman at the time. Theirs was a traditional relationship in the sense that he had had many sexual partners while Claudia remained a virginal good girl. For several years of the relationship, they did not have intercourse because "he thought I was too young for him at the time, but [he] cared about me a lot and liked me, so I think he was trying to save me for later. But he didn't want to let go meanwhile. But he also didn't want to coerce me into something I didn't want." Later, in high school, Claudia "gave in" to sex with him: "When we finally had sex, it wasn't under good circumstances in the sense that I didn't want to. And I just kind of finally gave in because I knew it was something he really wanted. And he—it was technically an open relationship—he dated around a lot, and I didn't necessarily." Claudia's desire did not propel her into sex, so in some sense she remained a traditional good girl whose behavior was acceptable to her family.

While Claudia sometimes enjoyed sex with her boyfriend, it was not great. She did not feel much sexual desire or pleasure, and sex was simply an activity they did together, but not something she particularly wanted. Again, Claudia remained a good girl in that she was having sex according to her boyfriend's desires, in the context of a long-term relationship. After she got older and went away to college, he became increasingly jealous and possessive, so she broke up with him in her senior year of college.

The first pleasurable sex Claudia had was with a friend whom she didn't want a relationship with, but they both wanted sex with each other. She felt her own sexual desire for the first time with him, and continued to feel that same level of desire ever since. With him, she expanded the repertoire of what she enjoyed sexually and had much more fun than she had ever had with her boyfriend. She attributed this to the lack of pressure, the absence of a relationship, the lack of commitment, the end of college, and the sense of freedom all those circumstances engendered. Through this experience, she started down a road of not being a good girl any longer. She felt her own desire, enjoyed sex outside the context of a relationship, and felt sexual pleasure strongly.

She then had a relationship with a man she really loved and with whom sex was great. For a period, then, she had it all: an intimate relationship *and* good sex. She described sex with him after not having seen him for a few months because they were in graduate schools in different cities: "I can remember one night he came, after [we] hadn't seen each other for several months. I remember being with him the whole night, just trying a lot of different positions, just wanting so much, so badly to be with him, that even while he was there [I was feeling], 'I can't believe you're here!' [I remember] not wanting it to end, but wanting to do everything at once."

She broke up with him after two years. He was older and wanted to get married and start having kids. He wanted Claudia to transfer to his graduate school so that they could be in the same city, but she was unwilling because her school was more prestigious and competitive, and such a move might limit her professional opportunities. Claudia was very clear about her commitment to graduate school, and while she wanted to have kids with him later, she was not interested in having kids while still in school—she didn't want to give up the motorcycle. After she broke up with him, he quickly dated and married someone else and had kids with her, which indicated to Claudia that she was not the one for him.

The outcome of this serious relationship seemed to confirm Claudia's fears—that she could not maintain her ambition and independent desires and sustain a committed relationship at the same time. The relationship ended four years before we talked, and since then Claudia had had casual and generally short-term sexual interactions with men. She characterized them as flings and booty calls—with people she knew but did not want a relationship with, "for whatever reason." She enjoyed them and found them fun: "I liked having this understanding of not having an emotional investment in him." These would be interrupted by occasional experiences of "really liking" a man, which meant wanting more than a fling.

> I moved up here and after a couple of months met somebody I really liked. We started spending time together. . . . [T]hree weekends in a row we went out, group stuff, and he'd stay at my place, but I wasn't really sure if he liked me or he was just friendly, or if he liked me as a friend but not sexually. [Three weeks into it] he ended up kissing me, and then we ended up having sex for a couple of hours. After that, anytime we went out, he'd come over and we'd sleep together. But that didn't last very long, about a month. Then he had to leave on business. He was gonna be gone for six weeks, and I had just moved here. As he was leaving he was trying to clarify, "What's going on between us?" I was like, "I don't know. I like you, but you're leaving." I just thought, "Why don't we figure it out when you come back if I'm still interested, you're still interested? 'Cause I might meet somebody." He ended up being gone for over two months. He had a long trip to Europe and met somebody there who he's still dating. That was the last person I was involved with.

Claudia experienced this as a rejection: he met someone while in Europe and so didn't choose her. Claudia had a few experiences like this one: wanting more than a fling with someone, and

feeling rejected. She then began to develop a new set of fears—
that she couldn't attract men who were relationship material.

LOVING SEX, AND HER FAMILY

The night before our first interview, Claudia had a one-night
stand that highlighted some of her complicated feelings about
her sexual desire. She enjoyed the experience, but felt somewhat
ashamed about it. It provided us an easy way to start talking
about her strong sexual desires and how she felt about them.
Claudia felt that her sexual desire was beyond her control and
was something that could get her into trouble. When I asked
whether there were ways she wished she felt differently about
sex, she responded: "I wish I weren't so horny, so I didn't need to
go out and get it so much. I wish I could take a pill to kill my
desire. I wish I weren't attracted always to younger men—that
seems bad because they're not as interested in a relationship. I
worry I'll be older and still attracted to the same-age guys."

Claudia worried that her desire, in the absence of a relationship, made her go out and get sex from possibly unsuitable men.
The implication was that she might jeopardize her chances of
finding a relationship because of her need for sex. Following her
sexual instincts alone seemed to lead her to men who were not
interested in relationships, and she imagined that she would be
attracted to a different kind of man were her sexual instincts not
so strong. She worried that if women's sexual peak occurs in
their forties, she would be even hornier then and, if not in a relationship, more likely to pursue one-night stands with inappropriate men.

Claudia wished she could take a pill to kill her desire, but at
the same time she enjoyed sex—a lot. More than most of the

women I spoke with, Claudia described loving sex and feeling a great deal of pleasure in different contexts, both committed relationships and more casual encounters. She loved sex with her long-term boyfriend because she enjoyed him so much as a person, felt so loved and cared for by him, and liked everything he did:

> I was so in love with him—I really thought he was a great person in every way—that anything I did with him felt awesome. It was just an incredible feeling that never went away. "Wow, I can't believe you picked me. This is so awesome!" He really liked me and who I was. And so that was definitely just . . . the greatest feeling. . . . It was also one of those things I felt I could never get enough [of]. I really enjoyed being with him, . . . I just liked him so much. . . . [I] liked everything, the way he touched me, the way he kissed me.

And she loved sex with someone she dated casually because she was so attracted to him, loved pleasing him, and was so drawn to him physically:

> And other times, . . . this guy I met at a conference from San Luis Obispo. Him, it was definitely purely physical, sexual, although not purely 'cause I liked his personality, too. And we had practically the same background in terms of family and stuff. I felt I could totally relate to him, but just also had a really strong physical reaction that I can't shake . . . off. Every time I see him, oh, my God! . . . There's something about him. I'm so attracted to him every time we're together. Somehow it doesn't matter how flaky he is or how much of a jerk he is; I'm willing to forgive it when I'm with him. I don't know what it is about him. That physicalness. He's my body type I like. I like tall, skinny guys. He's muscular on some level in a way I'm not accustomed to. But still, I'm so attracted to him physically, I just can't get enough. Sometimes when I'm masturbating, he's one of the images I go back to. And because I didn't like oral sex for a long time, it just amazes me how much I liked going down on

him. I just can't get enough. I really enjoy it, and I know he really enjoys it too.

She enjoyed both receiving and giving pleasure with committed and casual partners. When she was with someone with whom she had really good sex, Claudia would often feel she could not get enough sex. Relative to the other women I spoke with, Claudia felt a great amount of sexual desire and pleasure, and was able to articulate it quite clearly. So it appears on the one hand surprising that she would have so many negative feelings about her sexual desire. Many of the other women I spoke with struggled valiantly to feel as much sexual desire and pleasure as Claudia seemed to possess naturally. But the strength of her desire also starkly contrasted with her family's values and ideas about female sexuality.

Claudia worried about being a "ho," which for her mainly had to do with "having, wanting, and needing sex when not in the context of a relationship." Claudia learned in her traditional Catholic family that women do not have intercourse before marriage, do not have multiple sexual partners, do not (and should not) have strong desires for sex in the way that men do, and should not be concerned with sexual pleasure. She felt that her sisters followed these rules, as did her female cousins, and that she disobeyed all of them. Claudia had the sense that she had had too many sexual partners and had gone over the number that qualified her as a ho. When I asked what she imagined her family's reaction might be were she to tell them this, she replied: "From my parents? Huge disappointment. Devastation that this isn't who they brought me up to be. Among my sisters, I think they'd be pretty shocked. I don't think they would cut me out. But I think it would be probably a big deal and then never talked about again. . . . I think my family fear was always there. Only now it's become more numbers, so it's more present." Claudia's sexual history not only differentiated her from her family; in her mind it also distanced her from them because they would disapprove of her behavior and not understand it.

Her family was able to tolerate some experiences of premarital sex, but not those in which Claudia engaged:

> Even though as Catholics we were raised with that message of "no premarital sex," a lot of my cousins have had babies before they were married, so it's obvious they've had premarital sex. Even within that, there's this idea that "now you're gonna marry that person" or "that's the only person you're gonna be with for the rest of your life, or maybe one other if you don't get married." It's still this idea that "well, you really loved that person, so maybe you jumped the gun, but it's still just that one." So I definitely have this internalized feeling of "Ugh! I've gone way over that limit."

Claudia's traditional family could accept premarital sex if it led to babies and potential commitment from the male partner, but they had more difficulty accepting female desire and sexuality apart from reproduction and love. "I grew up with this idea that you shouldn't even have these desires, really. And that you should only have sex if you're gonna have kids. So even though it's not something I believe or buy into, it's something I carry in how I think I'm gonna be perceived by my family." Her family's stance toward female sexuality certainly contributed to Claudia's feelings about sexual desire, worrying her in terms of how she was perceived by her family, and distancing her from them because she was so different from them.

At the same time, Claudia also contended with stereotypes about "sexy" Latina women that contributed to and complicated her negative feelings about her sexual desire.

> I've often had encounters with people where I feel like they're judging my sexuality by my ethnicity. When I go dancing at clubs, often

I've had guys who are like, "Ooh, Latina." Like it's some big, foreign, exciting thing. Or . . . people who I think perceive me as being very sexualized just because of my ethnicity. When I speak Spanish, that whole thing, I mean, they've commented on my voice or my accent: "Oh, that's so sexy!" Whatever, it's just how I talk, and it's not any more exciting or less exciting than anybody else. I find those things annoying. . . . So I think that in terms of my own sexuality, when I've been with guys who aren't Latino, . . . [they] might find me to be more exciting than what I'm putting out there.

Claudia experienced some of her sexiness as imposed upon her by virtue of her being Latina, not as something she tried to communicate. Not only was her sexiness linked to her ethnicity, but her level of sexual activity was interpreted differently, because of her ethnicity, than was that of her white peers. "Sometimes I get stereotypes about being a sexy Latina, particularly at work. I work with an all-white group of people who have had similar sexual experiences as me, the same amount of sexual activity, but because I'm Latina it's assumed and read to be more, and slutty. I react against that by not wanting to fit into the stereotype. So then sometimes I'm perceived as a prude."

Claudia's public presentation of sexual desire and longing was influenced by her peers' reception of her as a sexually active Latina woman. She contended with not only the general ways in which sexually active women are received by society—as alternately titillating and worthy of condemnation—but also with the specific ways in which sexually active Latina women are received: as extratitillating and slutty. It seems likely that this public reception of her sexuality made her strong sexual desires feel particularly problematic to her.

Claudia straddled the traditional family from which she came and the modern and educated world she inhabited with her peers. She was the most educated child of her immigrant parents, and her education, opportunities, cultural capital, and values set her apart from her family. One-night stands, while acceptable in Claudia's current world, were abhorrent in her family's world. But she also felt like something of an outsider in her predominantly white cohort of highly educated peers. Claudia wished that she could manage to feel fearless about sex—without guilt or negative feelings about sexual desire and pleasure. But her family of origin's values conflicted with her own. Claudia came from a loving and stable family from which she didn't want to distance herself. The gap between her own behavior and her family's values was a source of profound unease and discomfort for Claudia, who wished to please and remain close to her family at the same time that she pursued her career ambitions in her modern social milieu.

THE NONCOMMITTAL STRATEGY OF DESIRE AND ITS DISCONTENTS

With the advent of her strong sexual desire, Claudia grew afraid of alienating herself from her family by being sexual outside committed relationships. This fear, combined with the conclusions she reached about her suitability for committed relationships, placed Claudia in a quandary when it came to sexual desire. She was supposed to express sexual desire only in the context of a relationship, but Claudia understood committed relationships as limiting her ambition and adventurousness. If Claudia acted on sexual desire outside the context of a relationship, she was going against her family's and culture's expectations of her, but her ambition and adventurousness were preserved. Claudia reluctantly concluded that she could live with a split life in which her family didn't know the extent of her sexual experiences. But she still had to manage the conflicts she felt among ambition, adventurousness, independence, and committed relationships. Rather than tolerating this conflict, Claudia split sexual desire, ambition, adventurousness, and independence away from committed relationships.

This split led Claudia to pursue two strategies of desire, albeit unconsciously. She had one-night stands with men whom she knew but who were not relationship material. She also pre-emptively cut short relationships before they could develop into something that may have required her to compromise her ambition and adventurousness. This strategy of desire allowed her to have sex without risking a relationship that might limit her. Both of these strategies of desire maintained Claudia's sexual expression and independence, but she bemoaned the fact that it had been difficult to develop lasting relationships.

And Claudia did not understand these to be strategies that she was pursuing. She perceived men as rejecting her, when in fact it was often she who imposed limits on her relationships. For example, with her long-distance boyfriend, she had not wanted to sacrifice her career in order to move to be near him. But she perceived him as rejecting her because he wanted someone willing to start a family at the time. Similarly, with her recent month-long relationship, the man expressed interest in defining their relationship as something to invest in, while she suggested that they wait and see. But in both of these situations, she experienced herself as being rejected and not as the rejecting party. Framing herself as the injured party severely limited Claudia's options and left her feeling powerless to do things differently.

A conscious strategy of desire that Claudia reluctantly adopted to deal with her strong sexual desire was masturbation.

Masturbation was linked for Claudia with the absence of a sexual partner, and was something she hoped not to have to resort to for protracted periods of time. Since she had spent so much time outside of relationships, however, it had become one of her primary modes of sexual release. Claudia did not masturbate until late in college, and she did not even realize that women could masturbate until late in high school. She felt mixed about masturbation, on the one hand describing herself as pathetic for not knowing about it earlier and not masturbating until after college. On the other hand, she felt sad about having to resort to masturbation because there was no available sexual partner: "It's something I enjoy when I'm actually doing it, but I always have this feeling of 'I'm so pathetic, I can't get a guy, so I have to rely on masturbating.' Then there are other times I feel like, 'At least I know how to take care of myself.' But I definitely would prefer to have a man. So I don't know." She was in something of a predicament here, feeling pathetic for masturbating so late in life, but also berating herself for needing to masturbate because of the current absence of a sexual partner. Similarly, she considered using toys in masturbation to be sad and desperate: "I have that feeling of, 'If I do use them, then it's because I'm that desperate.' And that I imagine it isn't gonna be the same as having a guy, so why pretend?"

Claudia hadn't imagined that it would be so difficult to find a partner. She thought that one would come easily to her, as partners had to her sisters and cousins. Having so many uncommitted sexual experiences was not part of her vision of her life:

> At an earlier time in my life, I didn't think I'd have so many sexual partners. I always thought I'd be in a sexual relationship and it would be easy to find somebody to have a relationship with. After I hadn't found somebody to date for a while, after my second

long-term relationship, I went through a long period where I couldn't find somebody I actually wanted to be with. But I had sexual desire. That's when the concern started to become a prominent thing: "Damn, I can't just go have sex because I want it." If I had a relationship, I knew I could have some regular sex and that there was safety, and I could have my needs met regularly. But once that ended, I couldn't have my needs met, and it was taking longer to find people I was attracted to or interested in.

It was upsetting to Claudia that it was so difficult to find a partner, but she portrayed herself as quite passive in this dilemma. And once in the quandary, she worried about her unmet sexual needs and what they might lead her to do.

According to Claudia, her intense sexual desires led her to pursue one-night stands, inappropriate men, and masturbation—all options that came into conflict with her family's ideas about sex. But Claudia framed committed relationships as exclusive of ambition and adventurousness, so she cut them short. She managed to have good sex and control of her life, but didn't get a committed relationship or closeness with her family. Nor could she manage to control her sexual desires.

Claudia seemed to have an amazing opportunity to "have it all." But sadly, in her mind, her dilemmas would be solved by taking a pill to kill desire. Then she wouldn't seek out inappropriate men for one-night stands. She imagined that if her desire weren't so strong, she would be able to wait for an appropriate man and would comfortably build a relationship with him. In considering this strategy to kill desire, however, Claudia conveniently covered over her other serious conflicts about being in a committed relationship.

Had Claudia belonged to an earlier generation of women, she might never have discovered her strong sexual desire

independent of being in a relationship, so might have remained
untroubled by it. Nor would she have had as many educational and career opportunities and a long, socially sanctioned
time to pursue them before settling down to marriage and
motherhood.

Her reaction to an instance of nonconsensual sex highlighted
the ways in which Claudia's investment in control kept her from
developing a realistic appraisal of herself and of situations.
When I asked about unpleasant experiences of sex, at first she
did not remember any instance of nonconsensual sex, but she
later did: "Oh, it's funny I don't remember this one so easily. I
block this one out. I fooled around with a guy, we were drinking,
he was pushy, and I'd told him I didn't want to have sex. I passed
out and when I woke up he was on top of me. I didn't want to feel
like it was rape, so I went along with it. I didn't want it to be
traumatic, so I acted along with it. It's funny that I block
that out."

Given that it was difficult for Claudia to pursue her subjective desires—for sex in the context of a relationship because it
felt threatening to her ambition and adventurousness; for sex
outside a relationship because it went against her family's and
culture's values—it makes sense that it would be difficult for her
to be clear about her own desires in an exploitative situation.
She maintained a strong awareness of the potential physical
dangers involved in casual sex: "The times I've had one-night
stands, it's always with people I've known for a while. The reason I haven't had more random ones is 'cause I'm always concerned about my physical safety or infection. It's just not worth
the risk." She worked hard to maintain control in her sexual
experiences, and in this instance she worked to reframe what
was happening as being within her control. This is in keeping

with Lynn Phillips's finding that young women often redefine sexually assaultive and exploitative experiences as within their control in order to maintain an autonomous sense of self.[2] This experience didn't fit in with Claudia's efforts to maintain control, so she had trouble remembering it. This is another of the costs of employing the noncommittal strategy of desire: Claudia didn't allow herself to acknowledge ways in which she didn't always have control.

Claudia worked hard to cast herself as in control on the one hand (faking it even when a man forced himself on her), but not in charge on the other hand (rejected by men who chose others over her). The noncommittal strategy of desire allowed Claudia to maintain this control, and to preserve her sense of herself as subject to her own strong desires and men's whims at the same time.

WHAT'S THE PROBLEM WITH DESIRE?

Many women I spoke with shared Claudia's fears of their desires leading them to people and places they would rather have avoided. They, like Claudia, sensed that following their sexual desires would put them in conflict with their families and with their own desire for a relationship. They learned from anachronistic-sounding (but extremely popular) dating guides such as *The Rules* and *Why Hasn't He Called?* that they'd better keep their desires in check or they wouldn't get the kind of men they wanted.[3] These guides encourage women to play hard to get, not to say "I love you" first, and essentially to be the objects of men's desire but not the subjects of their own desire. And they learn from church, family, and culture that only limited expressions of sexual desire are acceptable—within marriage, for procreative purposes—and that if they venture outside that realm, they risk ostracism and alienation.

I heard the fear from many women that assertively expressing too much sexual desire would result in rejection by partners and by society as a whole. They feared being perceived as demanding women whose needs and desires were insatiable. The specter of the whore and the slut continued to loom large in the minds of the twenty-something women with whom I spoke.[4]

This old dilemma, risking being perceived as a whore by expressing sexual desire, has plagued young women even in the new millennium. By adopting a noncommittal strategy of desire, women seem to be immune from this dilemma, but Claudia shows us that they are not necessarily safe. Sexual desire isn't all about a being a powerful she-devil, but is a vulnerable experience on multiple levels. Being sexually desiring does not always involve feeling in control. In fact, it often involves feeling out of control, subject to strong and deeply felt yearnings that may not always be satisfied or received positively by others.

As a solution to this new problem, the vulnerability that expressing sexual desire in relationships creates, Claudia split relationships from strong sexual desire. This split led her to reject and turn away from possible long-term relationships—resigning herself halfheartedly to hooking up with unsuitable men.

There is much collective hand-wringing over the phenomenon of hooking up, in which Claudia routinely engaged.[5] Much of this concern is centered on young women's lack of agency in the type of hook-ups in which they engage. Essentially, educators, commentators, and researchers are concerned that young girls are allowing themselves to be used, as Jayanthi was. Claudia illustrates that the problem with hooking up may not necessarily be victimhood at the hands of others, but women's defensive use of the hooking-up strategy as a way to avoid getting close to partners and keep themselves invulnerable.[6] This strategy of desire keeps young women such as Claudia seemingly in control, but her desires kept manifesting themselves, showing her to be more human than she might have liked. Claudia then kept wishing that she could just take a pill to kill her desires, rather than using those desires as a guide to get what she wanted.

PART II

The Relational Woman

CHAPTER FIVE

The Good Girl

Alicia

Despite its limited charms, being a "good" girl ought at least to protect women from harm of various kinds. If young women follow the rules for being good, it seems that they should emerge from college and their twenties unscathed by the emotional and physical damage that afflicts women who explore and experiment with sexuality.

Alicia was a very good girl. A twenty-eight-year-old Hispanic woman raised by her Catholic grandparents, Alicia didn't have sex until after college, and then protected herself from unplanned pregnancies, which were common in her working-class family. When she finally did have sex, in committed relationships, being a good girl didn't protect Alicia from STDs—she contracted gonorrhea from one partner and genital warts from another.[1] Nor did being a good girl ensure that Alicia had satisfying and committed relationships. Alicia was frustrated that she'd ostensibly done the right thing but still ended up with two STDs, and without a lasting relationship.

This chapter explores why Alicia, who worked so hard to protect herself from harm and the dangers of pregnancy, was so profoundly hurt by partners. How did a woman who escorted her friends to Planned Parenthood as a teenager wind up having so much trouble keeping herself safe?

GOOD-GIRL REBEL

Alicia became a good girl as a way out. A way out of poverty. A way out of teen pregnancy. A way out of conforming to low expectations. To be a good girl in her working-class Hispanic family was, ironically, to be a rebel. Particularly for women from impoverished and working-class backgrounds, being a good girl is often a mark of distinction from their peers, many of whom are sexually active early but don't use birth control and so sometimes become parents as teenagers.[2] Being a good girl gave Alicia an alternative to the well-worn path of teen pregnancy, sexual exploitation by older men, and dropping out of school that many of her peers had followed. Women such as Alicia, who are determined, as she said, "not to become a statistic," may delay sex "because no form of birth control is 100 percent effective." Following the good-girl strategy buys some poor and working-class girls the time for education and development that middle-class and upper-middle-class girls claim as their birthright. And being a good girl did work for Alicia as a strategy to get an education, get out of poverty, and separate from her family of origin.[3] Being a good girl, for Alicia, was only partly about delaying sex. It also involved doing the right things academically and socially.

Spunky might be the word to describe Alicia, a petite and pretty businesswoman with spiky salt-and-pepper hair, although it doesn't fully capture her mix of strength, humor, and sadness. Born in 1975, she was funny and warm, combining sarcasm with a dose of sweetness so that she didn't come off as harsh or embittered. She described herself this way: "I'm a good little girl. However, I do have my mind and my mouth, and I use them."

In some ways Alicia's family molded her into being a good girl—as noted, she was raised Catholic, and her father forbid her from dating in high school. But at the same time that her family encouraged her use of the good-girl strategy, Alicia also adopted it as a way to separate herself from them, to prove that she was different from them by not becoming a teen mom or a high-school dropout. So during high school Alicia didn't date at all. And during college she dated a bit, but never for longer than a few months. Many girls in the same circumstances, including her cousins, asserted themselves through rebellion by having sex early. Alicia's rebellion was to succeed academically and to be different from her family.

In Alicia's family, sex was either bad—she would end up a "ho" like other girls in the neighborhood if she had sex, or pregnant like her cousins—or it was the good and unspoken part of romance with a man that would lead to a relationship and marriage. Alicia recalled that her family addressed sex obliquely, never directly: "It sounded like this great thing, this indirect great thing: 'You're going to find a man who's going to respect you,'" and sex would then follow naturally. Alicia did not learn about the mechanics of sex from her family, nor did she learn a great deal from her Catholic school. Most of her information came from friends. She was determined not to be "irresponsible," as she saw several of her friends being—having unprotected sex, becoming pregnant, or contracting STDs.

Alicia's choice of partners was another way in which she rebelled against her family. Her primary relationships were with African American men of whom her family didn't approve. She described wishing there were "eligible" men from her own culture, but found it difficult to meet "educated Hispanic men." There are indeed more college-educated Latina women than there are college-educated Latino men in the United States, but educated African American women also often bemoan the lack of eligible, educated African American men.[4] And yet Alicia seemed to find educated African American men easily. She felt that they were able to bridge the two worlds she inhabited— they often had an understanding of the neighborhood and inner-city culture in which she grew up, they knew what it was like to feel like an outsider, and they had access to and valued education. At the same time that they understood her and the world she came from, they served to further distance her from her family of origin.

Although Alicia's grandparents raised her, she also sought out other parental figures in friends' parents, teachers, and people for whom she babysat. While she professed gratitude to her grandparents for having raised her, she felt alienated from them because of her ambitions and their acceptance of her abusive father. She avidly sought role models outside her family, and was determined not to repeat her family's patterns: early marriage and pregnancy, lack of education, low income, lack of "culture," alcohol and drug abuse, physical and sexual abuse, lack of "responsibility" and "respectability."

The families and women Alicia did want to model herself after as a child were Caucasian and middle or upper-middle class, and their race and class were important parts of what made them different from her and her family. The person she most wanted to emulate was a "lovely woman" with "beautiful green eyes" and blonde hair for whom she babysat. For Alicia, she was the epitome of a lady. She drank milk with her tea. She spoke in a very educated and correct manner. She dressed nicely, sometimes wearing scarves. Her house was tastefully decorated, with pictures each in their own frame and not stuck in the corner of existing frames, as they were in Alicia's home. She was a great hostess and knew how to make people feel comfortable and welcome. And she had a loving relationship with her husband.

Another woman Alicia admired deeply was the mother of her childhood friend Christine. The mother came from a white working-class background and worked hard to build a successful family and life. At the same time that she provided a good life for her three children, she was also generous to those less fortunate than she. She opened her home and family to Alicia, who spent a lot of time with them. Alicia told a poignant story of the kind of devotion this woman had to her husband and children, which Alicia wished she herself had experienced.

> At times I used to think, "Your mother's a slave to your father, Christine." And she'd say, "No, that's just how you do it." I remember her waking up at four in the morning to pack his lunch 'cause he didn't want her to pack it the night before, 'cause it wasn't as fresh. Deirdre [the mother] would get up and pack his lunch, make coffee, and they would sit on the couch. I remember being asleep in Christine's bedroom, hearing them have their coffee in the morning and him saying, "Well, momma, I gotta go to work now." And she'd say, "Okay." And I remember waking up to that . . . [soft, slow], so it [teary, she pauses and whispers] . . . that's what I wanted. And when I have a husband, that's what I want. . . . I wanted to be in Christine's family so bad. And to have a mother who cared, and who was there

when she was sick. And to have a dad and a mom to go camping and have fun on the weekend.

The stability, structure, and love of a traditional family seemed to afford all of the experiences Alicia herself lacked in her upbringing. A traditional family became the solution to the problem of instability in Alicia's mind. And being a good girl was the strategy Alicia adopted to enable her to have a traditional family. By being a good girl, she would acquire a good man who would treat her well, want to marry her, and build a "respectable" life with her.

Through her receipt of scholarships to private schools beginning in elementary school, Alicia managed to assume middle-class values about education and opportunity (e.g., that education is a valuable investment and worth delaying pregnancy for).[5] Alicia willed and worked her way out of her working-class background through academic accomplishment and abstinence.

ESCAPE FROM THE PAST

By being a good girl, Alicia wasn't only escaping her working-class background. She was also trying to protect herself from the dangers of men to whom she was close, who early on proved themselves undeserving of her trust.

I heard less about Alicia's family and their role in her life than I did from most women with whom I spoke. Alicia seemed determined to convey, to others and to herself, the degree to which she had gotten over her family's impact on her. She wanted to have a sense of control over her life, and minimizing her family's perceived influence on her was one strategy to do so. Her parents divorced when she was four years old due to her father's physical abuse of her mother and his drug abuse. Her mother raised Alicia and her brother as a single mom for one year. And then "she dropped us off for an overnight stay at my grandparents and she never came to pick us up. Now she did come when it was convenient for her, when she needed kids in tow for work functions or family functions on her side." Alicia's father lived in the house with her, her brother, and her grandparents, but Alicia did not consider him her parent.

> My paternal grandparents raised us. My father was in the household, although he was pretty much not employed at times. [He was] alcoholic. I knew he was my father and he lived in this house, but I didn't understand why he did the things he did. As I grew older, I feared him. As I grew older, I . . . saw who he was and knew I didn't want to be that. Now we don't talk, and we haven't spoken to one another since probably '93. . . . Because I believe when people act certain ways and do things to children, they lose their parental rights. And at times he touched me, he kissed me, he put guns to my head. And after that I said, "I can't no more." . . . So I've chosen not to speak to him, chosen not to deal with him. However, when I go to my grandparents' house, because the parasite still lives there, I see him. He'll walk out of the room, he'll go in the backyard, he'll go in the bedroom and close the door. We don't talk.

As a preadolescent child, Alicia was kissed and touched sexually by her father. She was loathe to discuss his behavior's impact on her development, although she knew it to be profound. She sought to cut him out of her life and therefore minimize his current impact on her.

Alicia's early sexual experiences reinforced the notion that men she was close to were dangerous and would hurt her. Her first intercourse was a date rape with someone she saw briefly after college when she was twenty-one. She said no and told the man to get off her, but he persisted and had sex with her, and they stayed the night together in bed, with him kissing her good-bye in the morning. Even at the time we spoke, she did not think about having been raped, although she knew that technically that she had been. After the rape, she did not want to be intimate with or touch anyone for a very long time. She was not scared of sex, but as she said, she "had no desire to have a penis near [her] vaginal area." While fluent in Spanish, Alicia still did not know the Spanish words for sexual body parts. In discussing the rape, this was the one time in our conversations that she used the word *vagina* and not "downstairs" or "down there"; in this one clinical and angry description, she used the word itself. She understood this trauma as not unlike the rest of her life, which had been difficult. Her mantra was "You gotta move on. Get up, go forward, come on." Alicia willed herself not to be defined by this experience and did not consider the rape her "first time" having sex. She thought of herself as a virgin until she first had consensual intercourse at age twenty-five.

Alicia was able to be a good girl but still play with sexuality with men to whom she wasn't close. She could be quite flirtatious, and was particularly bold with someone she knew she would never see again. She was very comfortable flirting, particularly when she knew someone found her appealing and attractive. She enjoyed knowing that she looked good and took pleasure in it. She did not feel threatened at work by her sexuality, as did other women with whom I spoke. They worried about being sexualized by coworkers in ways that were defining and limiting. But Alicia actually enjoyed flirting at work when she knew it was safe. She recounted an incident with a man at work whom she knew to be looking down her blouse. During meetings she would purposefully drop things and make sure he saw her pick them up, or tease him by touching his leg under the table. When it came to men she was not close to, Alicia was able to play with her attractiveness and sexuality in a way that was unique among the women with whom I spoke. This seemed safer to her than sexually focused interactions with men to whom she was close. The more distant a man, the safer he felt to her.

GOOD GIRLS IN THE NEW MILLENNIUM

Good girls in the new millennium share some similarities with their good-girl foremothers—delaying sex, focusing more on academics than on boys while growing up, and not pursuing boys. But while their predecessors may have quickly settled into marriages in their twenties that seemed consistent with their good-girl roots, today's highly educated women who were good girls in high school and college now face a decade or more of an in-between period of early adulthood during which to reconcile their good-girl strategy with being sexually active and unmarried.

Using the good-girl strategy to solve some problems—in Alicia's case, avoiding teen pregnancy—can lead to other problems later in women's lives, because good girls no longer get married right away. While being a good girl, women such as Alicia gain much experience in assertively saying "no" to sex, but little experience in voicing or even knowing what they *do* want. Through Alicia's story, we can see how the good-girl strategy left her, in her later years, unprepared to be assertive in her relationships with men.

So what's a good girl to do? The one form of assertion open to a good girl in relation to men is to say no. But what happens when she starts wanting to say yes? And what if she wants to say yes some of the time and no some of the time?

Alicia's spunkiness seemed to go underground with men in relationships. At the same time that she spoke her mind clearly in the rest of her life, in sexual relationships she described herself as "so not what I am." She felt unsure and insecure in sexual relationships and didn't assert herself in matters of sex—or anything else, for that matter. Being a good girl didn't prepare Alicia for sexual relationships, because she had avoided them until she was safely accomplished in terms of education. She carefully steered clear of situations and relationships that could "get me into trouble."

The problems with Alicia's good-girl strategy began to show up once she started dating. Her first significant relationship was with a man she loved, but who was selfish and called all the shots in their relationship. The entire relationship was conducted on his terms. "He was self-centered, selfish. I didn't ask a lot. I didn't ask anything." She rarely initiated sex because she felt he had all the control in the relationship. "I felt that I couldn't do anything. I felt he had control, from sex to the restaurants we ate at, to when we saw one another, what movie we saw. And sex was the top of the list." Sexually the relationship was quite unfulfilling to her, with no communication about sex, her desires, or how sex felt. And he had little to no regard for her experience of sex, which was painful and unpleasant. She remembered on multiple occasions "hanging out there [during sex]. I just wanted him to come, 'just come.' 'Cause at times it would hurt. . . . [I would be thinking,] 'If you don't hurry up and come I'm gonna kick you!'" It did not occur to Alicia that she could ask him to stop.[6]

Alicia later had pleasurable sex and felt freer to express her desires in a relationship with a man she loved. They had a fulfilling and loving relationship in which she felt very cared for, attended to, and taken into account. He was attentive sexually, asked her what felt good, and helped her to figure out that they needed to use lubricant to have intercourse. She did have orgasms with him, but not every time. She had the sense that sometimes she did not let herself climax because she did not want sex to end, and sometimes she worried about making noise. And when I asked for clarification about her orgasms— "It doesn't happen every time you have intercourse?"—she responded, "Oh, God, no. Do other people say it does? Oh, my God. I want to meet them. No. No. I wish." Even though she had fulfilling sex some of the time, Alicia was somewhat passive in her acceptance of only occasional orgasms.

Alicia was also passive in accepting the limited commitment that her second boyfriend offered. While in Alicia's mind they had become engaged during their relationship together, after about five months it became clear that he didn't see it that way. They had never had an explicit agreement about marriage, and he was ready to move on at that point. Over the course of my conversations with Alicia, I could see how such a misunder-standing might have occurred between her and a partner. As Alicia herself said, she had a mouth and would use it, but she was still a good little girl—she talked clearly and forcefully at times but was often indirect, leaving lots of room for confusion.

Alicia's fantasy life revealed a great deal of her conflict about asserting herself. A fantasy she wanted to enact with her most recent partner involved her dancing naked in front of him, then climbing on top of him and making him happy, kissing and touching him, not being assisted, and his not doing anything or telling her what to do. This fantasy involved her being in control and him loving it. This stood in contrast to experiences in which she often felt inexperienced and maneuvered by her partners, who were big men, while she was a small woman. "He was strong. He'd kind of sling me around like a rag doll. And we'd end up here or there. And he always kind of orchestrated it." But Alicia didn't live out these fantasies with her second boyfriend. "My fantasy is that I would be in control and he would— I think that was another reason I didn't do it. I would always fear that he wouldn't like what I did." She relegated her aggressive desires for control to fantasies of a man who enjoyed her assertion.

Alicia also fantasized about having a purely sexual relationship with a man she met through work, who was funny and attractive, had a great body, and was someone with whom she knew she would not want a relationship. But she did not know if she could just have sex with someone, get up, put her clothes on, and say, "Bye." Could she leave and not care whether this man called her that night or the next morning? "Could I not get attached? Would I consider myself trashy?" She played with this idea in her mind, but couldn't imagine actually enacting it.

While she felt confident and sure of herself in both work and social situations, it felt difficult to try new sexual experiences with a partner or to feel confident that she would please him. In sexual activity in general, Alicia tended to be passive, which gave her pleasure but also felt constraining. She enjoyed being able to relax and have her partner do all the work. Not surprisingly, she did not particularly enjoy masturbating, in large part because she wanted someone else to pleasure her, not to have to do the work herself. Yet she sometimes felt that her passivity came from a lack of confidence, not so much from a desire to be acted upon. She wished that she could feel more confident with partners, that she could feel comfortable calling the shots for a change.

Alicia contracted STDs from both of her long-term consensual partners. In the first case, her partner had been sleeping around during their relationship and caught gonorrhea. In the second case, her partner had genital warts and failed to tell her about them. Although she had waited to have consensual intercourse until she was twenty-five and was often the person who advocated using condoms to her friends, she did not use condoms with either partner, both of whom assured her that they had been checked out for STDs. She had learned about the genital warts just a few weeks prior to our first interview, and sex in general seemed quite unappealing to her at the time. She also felt foolish for not having used condoms with her partners. These experiences added to her sense of feeling duped by men, who seemed not to have her best interests in mind. "I'm a virgin until I'm twenty-five and I get friggin' gonorrhea that my doctor hasn't seen in fifteen years? What the hell is this?" It felt profoundly unfair to have been so good and to be hurt so badly.

Alicia struggled, in her recent relationships, with being as assertive sexually as she was in other areas of her life. Until the past few years, being a good girl had been an assertive stance that facilitated Alicia's development and educational and career advancement. She remained a good girl in order to avoid the dangers that befell many of her family members and friends. And it paid off: Alicia became comfortably middle class and avoided an unwed pregnancy. But as Alicia worked to build adult sexual relationships, she had difficulty advocating for herself and being as assertive as she would have liked—both sexually and in terms of securing a commitment. Being a good girl bought her time and protected her from being with a sexual partner, but it did not give her particularly good training in self-assertion and self-protection once she was with a partner. It also did not protect her from sexual trauma in the instance of the rape in her twenties.

HOW CAN A GOOD GIRL
BE ASSERTIVE IN RELATIONSHIPS?

Had Alicia been a member of an earlier generation, her good-girl strategy might have worked (sort of). She might have avoided pregnancy during her teens, gone to college and met an educated man from a different culture, married soon thereafter, and had children. Her difficulties with assertion might have persisted inside her marriage, but she would have succeeded in acquiring some of the stability for which she longed. Instead, she had a decade in which to sort out what she wanted from sex and love and how to get it, and had to do so on her own. And she had no idea how to begin to assert herself in relationships. Women such as Alicia, unlike those of earlier generations, have the sense that they *should* be assertive after having been such good girls. No longer do good girls only feel clear prohibitions on certain behaviors. They now feel pressure to be assertive, but receive little training in doing so. As Alicia's experience illustrates, it's difficult for women to learn assertion just through avoidance and saying no.

The good-girl strategy, with its focus on self-protection, recognizes what *is* true for many of the women with whom I spoke: that sex can result in emotional hurt. The good-girl strategy attempts to mitigate the potentially harmful effects of sex by encouraging it only within a relationship characterized by love, trust, and commitment. But at the same time, it portrays only sex outside of relationships as dangerous and vulnerable. It doesn't acknowledge the ways that sex *inside* relationships might also feel dangerous and difficult.

The good-girl strategy that Alicia adopted is based in part on splitting safety from sexual desire and assertion. With this split as her guide, it's no surprise that Alicia found it challenging to be assertive in her sexual relationships in her twenties. According to this thinking, to be sexually abstinent and passive is the only way to be safe. Alicia's experiences with STDs reinforced her concern that with sexual activity comes danger. And with an estimated 50 to 75 percent of American women infected by an STD in their lifetimes, her fears were not unfounded.[7] But in fact, it was Alicia's lack of assertiveness, not her sexual activity, that put her in danger. Alicia's confusion over this point led her to draw incorrect conclusions about the dangers inherent in sexual desire and assertiveness.

The cultural split between good girls and bad girls also makes it difficult for former good girls to assert themselves in relationships. If good girls are passive and accommodating in relationships, then bad girls are assertive and demanding—domineering bitches and shrews. And perhaps most important for Alicia, whose greatest wish was for a traditional family, being too assertive and risking being perceived as a bitch or a shrew might mean that she couldn't have that family. Alicia worried about how a boyfriend might receive her attempts at assertion, and rather than risking a negative reception, she remained passive.

Alicia felt stuck—she'd done "the right thing" but had been hurt and was left without a relationship that might lead to a traditional family. Good-girl handbooks such as *The Rules* might advise her to stay the course—delay sex, don't let on how much she cared about a relationship—and she'd be both safe and on her way to a traditional family.[8] But the rules of old no longer apply in the world that Alicia and her peers occupy.

Alicia was a fireball of determination who directed her energy toward making a different kind of life for herself than the one from which she came. I found myself rooting for her, hoping desperately that she would get what she wanted. But Alicia needed more than me cheering for her on the sidelines. She needed help in learning how to assert and protect herself, and to be open to the vulnerability inherent in assertiveness and desire at the same time.

CHAPTER SIX

On Not Having It All

Phoebe

For a woman to concede that she cannot have it all seems, on the one hand, to be a realistic assessment of life: we can't always get what we want. But on the other hand, abandoning the hope of getting what we want too early may foreclose possibilities that could otherwise exist.

Phoebe almost managed to get what she wanted. She moved through periods of being in committed relationships and then playing the field, having good sex in either case. But Phoebe then found herself in a relationship that seemed likely to lead to marriage—he was financially stable and committed, and took good care of her. The problem was that the relationship lacked passion. The sex was not great, and there wasn't much emotional intensity between them, either. But at twenty-six, thirty loomed large for Phoebe, and thirty meant marriage and children. The freedom and fun of her twenties would be behind her. Unlike many other women with whom I spoke, Phoebe had spent her twenties having good sex and relationships, but as she got ready to settle down, she found herself tentatively ready to settle.

Phoebe believed that she wouldn't be able to "have it all": good sex, a satisfying relationship, a successful career, and kids. On the one hand, this might have seemed a realistic assessment, given how little workplaces have responded to the needs of families, continuing inequities in the degree to which men share responsibility for housework and childcare, the relatively small percentage of women who regularly enjoy sex, and the degree to which relationships require compromise.[1] But on the other hand, Phoebe seemed to be selling her future short before she had even embarked upon it.

This chapter examines why, at the age of twenty-six, Phoebe was willing to settle for less than satisfying sex for the rest of her life, when earlier in her twenties she had enjoyed and embraced passionate sex. How did a confident girl become willing to settle? Why didn't she think she could find a committed partner she loved deeply and with whom the sex was good?

A CONFIDENT GIRL

A tall, long-haired redhead born in 1977 who exuded self-confidence, Phoebe didn't seem to be the kind of woman who would sell herself short. She talked of how easy it had been to pick up guys in her early twenties—"Basically, you talk to them." And she'd spent her college years and early twenties either in relationships she enjoyed or playing the field when that suited her.

As a young girl, Phoebe seemed on track to have it all. Phoebe was a "kick-ass" girl who didn't care what boys, or girls either, for that matter, thought about her. She played multiple sports and was confident about her body and what it could do.[2] She sometimes felt uncertain of her attractiveness to boys in high school, but mainly she was too interested in other things to bother with boys. Her life was full of extracurricular activities at which she excelled, and her extroverted nature made her very successful socially.

Unlike many of the women with whom I spoke, Phoebe had parents who were both active, loving, supportive, and nurturing parts of her life. And although they divorced when she was a young child, they worked very hard to prioritize their parenting over any disputes between the two of them, so that the divorce itself was not particularly traumatic in Phoebe's life. The reasons behind the divorce, however, affected her profoundly. When Phoebe was four, her father came out as gay, and her parents separated shortly thereafter. She later came to learn that her parents' sex life had been, understandably, "terrible" from the start. Apart from their own troubled sexual relationship, her parents continued to be sexually unfulfilled following the divorce. Even though her father had a long-term partner whom Phoebe considered a stepfather, her father remained uncomfortable with his sexuality and with sex in general throughout her childhood. He couldn't talk with her about his own sexuality, much less hers, except to say that she should avoid sex. Her mother did not date at all during Phoebe's childhood, and seemed to Phoebe to have little confidence in herself sexually. In Phoebe's mind, her mother gave up on sex and relationships and focused exclusively on her kids and career.

Phoebe's involvement in a conservative Christian church while growing up didn't inhibit her sexual development and confidence in the ways that it does for some women. She did not feel that her sexual behavior or desires were constrained by her family's involvement in the church. Phoebe described her mother's membership in the church as based mainly on a desire for community and connection. Her father professed to follow church doctrine, but to Phoebe that stance seemed hypocritical, given his divorce and homosexuality. So she didn't feel the judgment about sex that so powerfully affected Claudia (chapter 4) or Alicia (chapter 5). She had a lot of room to explore her sexuality, free from shame.

Phoebe's close relationship with her mother fostered her confidence. Her mother nurtured her, believed in her, and served as a role model in some areas of life. She was very involved with her children and was physically and emotionally present for them, which Phoebe hoped to be for her own children as well. But at the same time, her mother was divorced, was ambitious and successful in her work, and had no romantic relationships following her divorce while Phoebe was growing up, so in Phoebe's mind she was not a good model of how to have a relationship or sexual fulfillment. Phoebe reflected on her mother: "She's really independent, probably too independent. She focused on her career and her kids. I don't think she made time for dating or really ever thought she was very beautiful or desirable. She just had this singular focus. So she's really successful and was really into us. Those were the choices that she made. That was her life." Her mother, said Phoebe, explained that she "purposely didn't have men around, in order to shield the kids from what might be a traumatic experience of her dating." Phoebe wanted to be more relationship focused than her mother, and she spent her early twenties defining herself in opposition to her mother, involved in passionate relationships and sexual encounters and not terribly focused on her career.

PASSION AND DEPENDENCY

Phoebe's early sexual experiences linked passion and dependency in relationships in important and defining ways. Phoebe's college boyfriend was her "first love," and they had what she described as "great and passionate" sex. Her relationship with him profoundly shaped her notions of what good sex was like. "He was my first boyfriend. I was so smitten with him, so head over heels. All five years we had this incredible sexual relationship. It was just really charged. I was young, we were both young. . . . It was just a really positive relationship. I was really lucky 'cause my first relationship was really great. . . . We had this intense emotional bond and he made me feel sexy and attractive, all those things." With him, her first experiences of sex and intimacy were fun and exploratory. He was similarly sexually inexperienced, and they developed together. But her boyfriend's dependency on her was also a defining feature of their relationship. He was from another country and so depended on her in basic ways to help him navigate through life. While they relied upon each other emotionally, she was definitely the one "in charge" of certain aspects of their lives.

At the time of our conversation, Phoebe's favorite sexual experiences thus far had been with her first boyfriend—they felt well matched sexually in terms of desire, passion, and intensity. She imagined that they would get married, and so she was devastated when, after college, he moved to his home country. Breaking up seemed the only option at that point, given that neither wanted to build a life in a foreign country.

Phoebe later had another passionate, eight-month-long relationship with an older man, but it felt anomalous to her. The man was an unusual partner for her in that he was very passive, feminine, and physically smaller than she. Prior to that time, she had enjoyed being with men who were larger and more dominant than she. She and the older man had an emotionally tumultuous relationship but had what she described as great sex.

> The sex was amazing, but the emotional aspect of the relationship was so shitty, and that's why the sex was so good. Because we were constantly driving each other crazy. By the end of that I thought, "If I were gonna be in this type of relationship for my whole life, I'd die young." It was so draining. We would fight all the time. People who talk about make-up sex or angry sex, that's what our relationship was. We were always fighting, and then always sex was the thing that brought us together. It was really unhealthy, but the sex was really amazing. Looking back, I don't care about that kind of sex. I'd rather have intimacy and stability.

They had an unequal relationship in which she was the lively and passionate person whom he needed:

> He was very, very needy. . . . He would always talk about how I was amazing. He was kind of a dead person, and he would fulfill his sense of aliveness through me. He had this feeling that I was giving him something, and that's where sex was so incredible. He had so many issues. There was so much psychologically [that was] so fucked up. I was saving him, or we were always—I don't know, it was really weird. It was just a very intense experience. He was one of those people who was always like, "You're so amazing, you're doing this." It was almost a feeling that someone's obsessed with you. That's what I felt like: he was obsessed with me.

She was relieved when she finally ended it, but she was left uncertain about how to have passion in a stable and equal relationship.

SEX AND CONTROL

Between her first and second relationships, Phoebe had a series of encounters that linked casual sex and control in significant ways. Her friends referred to her life at this time as "so *Sex and the City*." She described herself having sex relatively quickly, after dating someone for two weeks or so, because sex was important to her and she wanted to know whether it was going to be a deal-breaker. For a time she serially dated, but relationships would last for less than a month, so she had several sex partners over a one-year period. Phoebe felt good about having lived "like a guy" during part of her twenties. She felt pleasure in pursuing her desires, being comfortable in her body, and enjoying sex. These experiences also gave her a new experience of sex, one characterized not by dependence, but by independence. She felt in charge, in control, and "like a man."

Phoebe, along with several other women with whom I spoke, described having casual sex as acting like a man. She was less disturbed by this idea than were other interviewees. She referred to her behavior as like a man's, not in a disparaging way, but as a value-neutral description, and I did not find myself feeling worried about her in the ways that I did about Jayanthi (chapter 3) when Jayanthi described her "sexual frenzy" phase. Phoebe felt like a man in that she was "figuring herself out" by sleeping with various people and having lots of experiences. She saw behaving like a man as helping her to discover what she wanted and liked and what was important to her. In contrast, other women with whom I spoke expressed shame at behaving like men in their sexual interactions.

During this time, Phoebe did not consider herself to be slutty or promiscuous, but she knew that her behavior would lead some people to categorize her as such. The reception that she got from friends who were more traditional and conservative than she was one of envy: they wished that they could be like her and wished that they did not care so much about their own behavior. In Phoebe's mind, she was making conscious choices about having sex and feeling okay about it. She knew herself not to be "promiscuous" because of what she described as her conservative core, and instead she experienced that time as really fun and free. "My friend and I . . . we don't consider ourselves to be slutty or promiscuous, but we weren't holding back. If we were guys, no one would even think twice about it. But being women, if you're sleeping with all these different people, somehow you're a slut. At the time we talked about that a lot and how ridiculous that is, 'cause we were making our own choices and not feeling particularly slutty."

Phoebe felt empowered by her behavior—she was in charge, calling the shots, figuring out her desires, and enjoying herself. What Phoebe defined as slutty and promiscuous were women who had lots of sex but who were actually looking for a relationship and were consequently hurt by men's lack of interest in one (like Jayanthi when she was being played). She thought that people were perceived as slutty because they were unhappy and not in control. There was a sadness about the slut, at least in this definition, that Phoebe did not have. During this time, being the Sexual Woman was not just a strategy—Phoebe was living the dream. She was sexually confident, felt no guilt about having sex, enjoyed it, didn't particularly care if sex led to a relationship, and felt invulnerable.

SETTLING FOR STABILITY

While Phoebe felt free to be sexually exploratory and passionate in her twenties, as she approached her thirties she felt more concerned with building a stable relationship likely to lead to marriage and children. But rather than sustaining an interest in passion, she began to settle for stability over passion. And in fact, she began to split stability from passion in her own mind, convinced that she couldn't have both.

With her current partner, Mark, Phoebe felt taken care of, but wished that he were more assertive and sexually passionate. He did not initiate sex much, and when he did it was verbal rather than physical initiation, which felt less passionate to her than she would prefer.

> He's a little more of a talker. "Oh, you want to have sex tonight?" That is always so foreign to me. I laugh 'cause that seems so planned. I'd want it to be a little more spontaneous. But it doesn't. Obviously once things get going, it's totally fine, but the whole process of initiation is something still totally weird for me in this relationship. I expect it to be more natural. That's why I see this one as good, 'cause we're equal. Neither of us idealizes the other. In that there's a realism that takes hold: "Oh, this could be forever, but it's never gonna be those other things." But I guess that's kind of good in a way.

She expressed ambivalence about their lack of passion, convinced that it signaled maturity, but felt disappointed that things seemed mundane.

Phoebe moved in with Mark after they had dated for two months. Doing so surprised her, but it was something he wanted. She talked about marriage in a similar way, as something that he wanted but as something about which she felt uncertain. She felt that Mark was an anchor who provided her with safety and security, and that was something she never saw her mother have as a single parent.

> The relationship in general is good. We've struggled a lot. We've only been together a year and a half, but we moved in together after two months. And so our first year was really rough. We almost broke up six or seven times. I don't know why I jumped into it. Usually I'm a person who thinks things out. So it was sort of weird. Looking back, I don't know why I did that. I think I just felt like he really wanted to, and he's this anchor. That's been the great thing in the relationship—he's the strong one, having a lot of resolve and knowing what he wants. And I've always initiated the wanting to leave.

She felt that she was coming to terms with the fact that she could not have the strong sexual charge of her first relationship, in which she had what she characterized as "I need you" sex, but she felt sad at the loss of that intensity. "The intensity [was] great. I wish that's something you could have in the kind of relationship Mark and I have, but I don't think that's realistic. Some people might have that, and that's great, but I can't imagine how we would have that and have the relationship that we have, 'cause we're both really mellow together." This conflict manifested itself clearly over the course of our three interviews: in the first interview, she said that her sexual relationship with her current boyfriend was great, but by the third, she expressed disappointment in and dissatisfaction with it. By that third interview, she indicated that she was committed to her boyfriend, who wanted to get married, and she appeared to be moving toward the same decision, albeit ambivalently.

Phoebe was working very hard to make her relationship with her boyfriend be what she wanted.

> I have really great memories of sexual experiences with my ex-boyfriend [from college]. That has actually been in a way detrimental

to this relationship. A lot of issues we had were really hard because of that. Just those moments where you're just consumed with that euphoria of being with another person. Those are really good times . . . just that freedom and sense of possibility that was attached to it. . . . I've had some really great moments with Mark, but I think that it's different somehow. I don't know, that's kind of hard. Not necessarily in a bad way, but in more a kind of—I don't know. It is different. I think it's that thing about idealism or romanticism. In my own mind, I tend to romanticize the past; those memories are really good. But that's not to say that ten years from now, memories of now won't be more prominent. I think it's just proximity. It hasn't been that long. Those are ideal sexual moments just because of the feelings around them.

Phoebe felt conflicted over her desire for the intensity of her first love and her desire to be taken care of—she saw these as irreconcilable wishes because her first love had been quite dependent upon her. Now she had someone on whom she could rely, but who did not need her as much, so the sex was not as passionate. She was trying to reconcile herself to a different kind of sex—not "I-need-you-type sex"—with her current partner. With her first boyfriend, they were both young, they did not live together, he was needy, and the sex was great. And with the older partner, their emotional relationship was horrible, he was needy, and they had passionate make-up sex and angry sex. She said that she did not care about that kind of sex now, that she would rather have intimacy and stability, but she still felt conflicted about it.

Phoebe characterized herself and her boyfriend as not idealizing each other. Neither of them was on a pedestal, which made their relationship feel realistic, but also less exciting. She liked feeling that she could relax and let someone else worry about things that would be her own problems were she alone. "My first boyfriend was very needy, and I took care of him, and in return what I got from him was his clinginess. And that in the bed was great, and outside in the real world was totally not great. What I have now is someone who's not needy, which is great 'cause I expressed that I love how he takes care of me and all these things. But [how] it manifests in the bedroom is that he doesn't cling to me. He's not needy. Argh!"

As she reconciled herself to the limits of her current relationship, Phoebe concluded that passion was not possible without an intolerable level of need and dependence. And in her mind, that level of need and dependence signaled immaturity and instability, qualities that she hoped to shed as she looked toward her thirties.

THE NEED TO FEEL STABILITY

Phoebe felt the pressure of powerful cultural messages in her twenties. One proclaims that the twenties is the time to get married if you want a guarantee of security. The other asserts that the twenties is the time to be free and experimental, but that you had better fit it all in before marriage in your thirties. Phoebe felt a limit on the period during which she was supposed to be free and experimental, and thought that at age twenty-six or twenty-seven she should worry about having a boyfriend and getting married before she was thirty, or else she would be in trouble.

> So there's this weird thing. I don't know if it's a backlash. My generation—so many of my friends have divorced parents. Everybody wants the stability they didn't have when they were younger. They want to get married, make it work, have a family, have stability. Then this other segment of the population, we're free, we want to

experiment. There's this age range, twenty to twenty-six to twenty-seven, where all that stuff is great—experiment, do a lot, be free, have sex, whatever—and then twenty-six, twenty-seven, hurry up, get a boyfriend, you better get married before you're thirty 'cause [otherwise] you're fucked. I'm totally experiencing that right now, and it's totally crazy 'cause I'm not even twenty-seven yet. I feel all of this peripher[al] pressure . . . like, "Get married, what are you doing?" . . . It's both things, this clamping down on the one hand and freedom of expression on the other hand. I think there's definitely a lot more opportunity for women, but I think no doubt there's still that pressure: get married before you're thirty.

She talked about friends who recently had breakups at ages twenty-six or twenty-seven, which felt very scary to her. She worried about what it would mean to break up with her boyfriend at twenty-seven and start over. "I'm at that point: I'm either gonna dig in and fight it out and make it work, or I'm gonna make the choice to let it go and move on to something else. So I'll probably dig in [laughs]. I think I've sort of already made the choice." She didn't want to settle, but she didn't want to "chase the dragon and wait for the perfect guy," either. She felt acutely the limits of time and did not want to be the last woman standing, unmarried at thirty and therefore unable to build the life that she wanted.

Phoebe cited what felt to her to be cautionary tales about women who waited to get married and have children until late in their lives. She heard stories from her mother about women who were unhappy because they were forty, had never married, and had sacrificed the potential to be in a relationship for their careers.[3] She felt some envy for women who opted to focus on their careers, and saw that they did something she was not strong enough to do. When she was in college, she imagined that she would be more successful in her career than she became, but she also felt content that her work did not dominate her life. She imagined that women who were primarily affiliated with their jobs sacrificed their personality and parts of their lives for their career, and she did not want work to be her identity.

In Phoebe's mind, there were career women and family women. She believed that women chose between a career-oriented path and a relationship-oriented path, although she caught and corrected herself as she said this, saying that maybe women could have both. She had decided, somewhat ambivalently, that she was a woman who focused on relationships and children. When she talked about this, there was a great deal of confusion and contradiction in what she said. She was not sure why she felt so pressured to get married, because she thought of herself as someone who believed that women could do whatever they wanted. But she also enjoyed and craved the support that she got from her partner, support that her mother never had. She did not want to be out there braving it on her own in the way her mother did. Phoebe had concluded that there were four aspects of life—career, relationships, passionate sex, and children—and that she could have only two out of four, as did her mother. Her mother had career and children, and Phoebe saw herself having children and a relationship. My sense in speaking with her was that she would actually like to have all four aspects but felt that was too much to hope for.

Much is made of young women such as Phoebe, poised to have it all, yet opting out of intensive careers in favor of family life.[4] She, like others of her generation, had lived through her own mother's disappointments and didn't want to make the same mistakes. But Phoebe's individual solution of "settling" was socially located in a world only half changed by feminism.[5] She was coming of age at a time during which intensive work demands,[6] superinvolved parenting,[7] and limited changes among men predominated. Through Phoebe's story, we see that she paid a significant price for living in this half-changed world.

WHY SETTLE
FOR LESS THAN HAVING IT ALL?

Phoebe was unusual among the women with whom I spoke in that she didn't feel inhibited in her desires for either sex or a relationship. She didn't feel like a bad girl for having casual sex in her twenties—instead she used the experiences as opportunities to figure herself out. And she didn't use the good-girl strategy to keep herself safe. She knew the power of her own attractiveness and the allure of her sexual desire, so she could be sexually assertive and receptive. Nor did Phoebe feel either shame or fear about desires for a relationship. She knew that she had a strong enough identity to survive relationships, so she didn't avoid them. And she did not fear the interpersonal vulnerability that comes with being in a relationship—she had multiple experiences, both with her family and with partners, of people tolerating her needs and vulnerabilities.

What did scare Phoebe was the instability that might come with passion in a relationship. She wanted the safety of a relationship and didn't want to risk disturbing that safety with passionate sexual desire. She could tolerate both her desire for a relationship and her sexual desires, something that was difficult for many of the women with whom I spoke. But she did split the possible outcomes into passionate and unhealthy relationships or staid and stable relationships.

So why did she sell herself short and adopt the strategy of settling for a stable relationship that lacked passion? Why did she split stability and passion? She'd had passionate sex in relationships in her twenties, but they featured men who depended overmuch on her—for material guidance and help in navigating a foreign country in the one case, and for vitality in the other. This dependency yielded passion, but was unlikely to produce the stable relationship she sought to obtain the safety and security her mother lacked. Her other model for passionate and good sex was casual sex, in which she felt strong and in control. This was also an experience that didn't translate easily to the "mature" relationship she sought to build for her thirties and beyond. From her experiences of committed and passionate, then casual and in-control sex in her twenties, Phoebe knew clearly what passion and desire felt like, but she wanted to steer clear of them in her late twenties out of a desire to remain in control and safe. While Phoebe may have looked like a modern woman in her twenties, she was looking to become a traditional woman in her thirties.

Phoebe desired a relationship, but a relationship was in open conflict with two of her other desires: sexual passion and pleasure and career success. She had a sense that, for a woman, her goals were not compatible with each other. Phoebe felt as though these desires must be split—into different women, or at least into different periods of one woman's life—because they were mutually exclusive. In her mind, women must choose the desires that will predominate in their lives once they approach thirty and confront marriage and children. After all, her own mother served as a cautionary tale for Phoebe. A successful career woman and mom, she had neither good sex nor a satisfying relationship. But rather than feeling her life to contain more potential than her mother's, Phoebe concluded that, like her mother, she wouldn't be able to "fit it all in" either. Phoebe tried to be realistic about the possibility of having it all. She didn't want to chase the dragon and wind up with none of what she wanted in life.

Phoebe didn't want to risk the safety that she had worked for and that her mother lacked. So she sought that safety in a relationship, as though it could protect her from being vulnerable. And in some sense, she hit upon the perfect solution: Her current partner was so emotionally contained that neither of them emotionally needed the other. And she could rely on him materially, which was a welcome change from her earlier relationships, in which she was more responsible and competent than her partners. But Phoebe seemed to conflate emotional vulnerability with material vulnerability—her current boyfriend was a good provider who owned a home, had a high-paying job, and was skilled at managing the details of life. He was fully capable of protecting her from material vulnerability. But his lack of emotional engagement meant that their relationship lacked the emotional vulnerability that could make passion possible. The price of protection, safety, and control was passion, dependency, and vulnerability.

Phoebe saw her twenties as a time for growth, development, desire, and passion. She envisioned her thirties as a time for maturity, stability, and not having it all. She enjoyed the modern twenties, but then was thrown back to an earlier generation's message when she thought about navigating her thirties: "Don't try for too much, because you won't get it." Her individual solution, in the context of this half-changed world, was to settle and split passion from stability so that she could get at least some of what she wanted.[8]

PART III

The Desiring Woman

CHAPTER SEVEN

How Does She Do It?

Maria and Susan

Despite the challenges of mixed messages, and lacking a road map to follow in their twenties, some women do manage to get what they want from sex and love. Maria and Susan did so in their late twenties, after both struggled in their teens and early twenties. They progressed over time from using defensive strategies of desire to using productive strategies of desire. Although they still felt conflicted about their desires, they found compromise solutions to their conflicts and succeeded in pursuing sex, love, and pleasure.

During her twenties, Maria developed the ability to give up some control and began to express her desires more assertively at the same time that she made her vulnerable longings known to partners. But independence and vulnerability had not been easy for Maria to balance in the past. She lived "like a guy" during high school and college so that she wouldn't get hurt by men. She was callous, unattached, and unaffected. She made sure that she was always in control emotionally, which meant that she didn't let anyone know what she wanted.

Susan spent her twenties learning to let go sexually and emotionally and abandoning some of the control she had held so dear earlier in life. For many years, Susan had been unable to express sexual desire in an emotionally vulnerable way. She spent her high-school and college years keeping men emotionally at bay, and she prided herself on her ability to be "good in bed." While Susan knew what would please her, she never let men in on it. Being in control of sexual situations, and never losing control herself, felt like a feminist act.

Maria and Susan, in contrast to the women discussed in earlier chapters, clearly expressed their multiple and sometimes contradictory desires for sex, control, independence, and intimacy in their later twenties. They recognized the complicated desires that they felt and acknowledged the vulnerability and absence of control that inhere in expressing desires. And they didn't split these desires and conflicts, but instead felt them all as parts of themselves. Maria and Susan both began to get what they wanted after being unable to voice desires and feel pleasure, and being frightened of desire for both sex and relationships, in their teens and early twenties. The sixty-four-thousand dollar question is: How did they do it?

FROM NO DESIRE TO PLEASURE: MARIA

Maria, a twenty-eight-year-old woman of Latina and Filipina descent born in 1975, wore her strength and vulnerability comfortably. Tall and pretty, she had bright eyes and an easy smile that was warm and inviting, but her face could harden when she was determined or angry. A strong girl who didn't abide weakness, Maria had been privy to some scary experiences as an adolescent. Revealing neither sexual nor relational desire was a logical outgrowth of these early experiences. Yet Maria became a woman capable of independence, emotional intimacy, and sexual pleasure.

Just by looking at Maria's background, we might not conclude that she would develop a capacity to get what she wants from sex and love in the new millennium. Her traditional Catholic family provided her with many things—love, stability, and structure chief among them—but it didn't provide a model for women to fulfill their desires. Maria's father, a first-generation Latino immigrant, was a domineering presence in the family and parented according to the school of hard knocks. He dominated the family and insisted that everyone live by his rules. Maria wanted to be nothing like him. At the same time, she identified with him because they were both strong-willed, determined, and stubborn. Not surprisingly, they butted heads frequently. Maria's mother, a first-generation Filipina immigrant, was a passive, feminine, and "traditional" woman. Never an advocate for herself in the family, Maria's mother was not a model for getting what a woman wanted.

A Scary Adolescence

As a young adolescent, Maria was party to many experiences that felt dangerous and risky to her, although her friends were in more danger than she was. She linked these early experiences to her later concerns about safety and her defensive attitude toward boys. By seventh grade, Maria was drinking during recess, smoking cigarettes, and popping muscle relaxants in class. And she went to a school in which many of her poor and working-class peers got pregnant before they finished eighth grade.

During seventh and eighth grades, she and her two best friends would stay all night at a motel owned by one of their fathers, trying to get picked up by young men who had just graduated from high school. One of the girls would customarily have sex with multiple guys each night, and the other had a few different partners. Maria never had sex with the boys, but saw it as her job to make sure the others were safe and did not get gang-raped.

Maria's parents hadn't given her the information and tools that she needed to navigate the dangers of adolescence in the United States. Maria was not allowed to date at all (although she did so without her parents' knowledge in high school); she was taught not to have sex before marriage; and she had no education from her parents about the specifics of sexuality. What she remembered about puberty, when sex and drugs and the dangers they posed came on the scene, was rage. She felt angry with her parents for not understanding American society, for not protecting her from the real dangers she faced, and for teaching her things that were not applicable to her life. Rather than being protected by her parents, Maria felt that she needed to teach them, educate them, and socialize them into American society.

When Maria did start dating, at thirteen, she was no longer able to keep herself safe. Her first boyfriend was emotionally abusive to her, raped her, and then stalked her to the point that she had to transfer to another school. She vacillated between thinking she had been raped and worrying that she was a slut for not having screamed when he forced her to have sex. He had pinned her with his legs and arms so that she could not move, despite knowing that she did not want to have sex, and then penetrated her. This was her first time. Her parents did not know that she was dating him because she had been forbidden to date, and she told no one about the rape. When she broke up with her boyfriend, he began threatening suicide, punching walls, and following her until her school principal got involved and said, "He's destroying himself over you. What are you gonna do about it?" Maria's parents, who had advanced from working class to middle class by this time, moved her to a private school after this incident, although they ostensibly moved her because they began to see how many of Maria's peers were already pregnant in the eighth grade. She described this first relationship as "good and bad in a way. 'Cause I certainly learned a lot from it at a young age." She interpreted these early experiences as providing her with a rough exterior that she needed to get through high school.

These experiences induced Maria not to "give a shit about boys." In our discussions, she expressed some longing for a more positive early experience with a boy-next-door type, but she quickly moved on to discuss the ways in which she had made sense of the experience, ways that were in fact protective:

Maybe it was helpful in the dating world, 'cause a lot of my friends would have sex, feel guilty about it, cry over guys. And my policy was like, "Hey, I don't give a fuck, why should you?" I just had this "Oh, well, I'm gonna hurt you if you hurt me" kind of thing. I was never the type to sit home and cry by the phone and wait, 'cause I never gave myself enough chance to be vulnerable. So maybe it was helpful in a way. I look back . . . and realize I've grown so much in terms of how I think about sex. . . . The whole low self-esteem thing, I never had it. "If you don't like it, if you don't like me, you can kiss my ass." And that was my attitude. That really helped me. Everyone was like, "You don't care, that's so great." And I'm like, "That's 'cause I've been stalked for the last two years." What it did was made me mature very early, and that was a good thing. And in that sense I was able to help a lot of people. Who knows why this stuff happens to you?

Maria seemed self-possessed and unaffected by others in high school, but that self-presentation came from being deeply affected by her abusive relationship with her first boyfriend.

Maria's early traumatic experiences of sexuality, along with what she learned culturally in her family—that she should never be too forward with men—contributed to her caution in approaching and dating men. In her twenties, Maria was still uncomfortable with taking the initiative in dating. She wished she had dated more in her twenties, which she felt she should have done to gain more experience and practice at being assertive. Flirting came naturally to her, but she waited for the man to ask for her number or come on to her in some way. She was envious of friends who were able to go on Match.com without feeling embarrassed, or who could go up to someone and ask for a date. She wished she were willing to take more risks, be more open to people, and be more approachable.

While Maria was uncomfortable with being forward in dating, she customarily behaved "like a guy" both in relationships and in one-night stands. She recalled behaving "as guys do," with an attitude of "don't let the door hit your ass on the way out." She presented herself as invulnerable, unaffected, and uncaring. In those circumstances, she participated in what she termed a power play, in which she held the power because she did not care about the other person or about what happened. While she may have had power in these relationships, she wasn't having good sex. It wasn't until a boyfriend gave her a homework assignment to masturbate that she realized what she'd been missing.

A Helping Hand

Maria began to experiment with masturbation when she was twenty-three, after her college boyfriend suggested that she needed to get in touch with her body to discover what she did and did not like. His suggestion came out of his frustration that she was so uncomfortable with sex, was afraid to look at her vagina, and kept her sexual feelings a mystery to herself and to him. Prior to this time, she had thought that masturbation was disgusting for both men and women.

> Finally, one time he got to the point where we were talking about masturbation. He was like, "I'm in a long-distance relationship [with you]. I've gotta do what I've gotta do." I was just like, "That's disgusting. How could you do that?" He made it a homework assignment for me. He was like, "I feel like you're not in touch with your body, you feel a lot of shame, and I think you need to start doing this to really know what you like done. You're so afraid to look at your vagina, I don't think that's right. I think you need to start figuring out what that looks like, what that feels like. I think you need to stop making it such a mystery. Then maybe it won't feel so bad." So I did. And I was like . . . , "I know exactly what I feel when I do this and that." That was the first educational thing, that homework assignment. I was already twenty-three, so that was the first time [I really masturbated and got to know what felt good to me]. . . . I think that was really good for me.

Maria then had further experiences in relationships with partners who cared about her pleasure, which felt like a revelation to her.

> [I had one relationship] where he felt it was all about how happy I was sexually; that was his main goal in our relationship. Everything else in our relationship could be falling apart, but he felt as long as that was taken care of, then everything was great. That was the first

time I had felt like, "Wow, people care about stuff like that? That's an issue for you?" I thought it was really bizarre. But it really made me think about that, and how important it was, and how I never had thought about it before. That was a very significant relationship.

After this relationship, Maria had a one-night stand in which she felt no power exchange, had an orgasm, had a great time, and did not feel guilty or pained.

> I finally met this guy. He was kind of a meathead, but really a good person. He was nice, a friend of my roommate's. We all went out one night. He's a teacher, which is incredible, wanting to give to society. I was living in Silicon Valley at the time, so to me it was the most impressive thing I'd heard forever. So we got together that night, and it wasn't dirty at all, there was no power exchange. . . . I felt comfortable enough to have an orgasm. I was like, "Wow, this is totally not how this was before." That was after this whole home-work period, and then I really started to think differently about sex. "Wow, this is great, I could do this and not feel I need to hide myself for another two years." Before, every time that happened, I needed to get away for a while and think about how painful it is. That was the first time it was like, "This is great, and it was great to meet you, and I'll see you later [laughs], and I don't feel bad." That stands out in my mind, where I'd reached a point where I thought about it differently.

At the time of the interviews, Maria was in a relationship in which she was comfortable expressing herself sexually and talking about sex, which was a big change from earlier times, when she could not talk about sex at all and hated sex. She could now "let go and let a lot of control out, to say I like something. To me that's huge. It's been a huge change." She told her boyfriend what felt good to her and suggested that they have sex. This was in contrast to her earlier experiences, in which she would never say anything about what she wanted and would hope that her partner picked up on it, read her mind, and wanted the same thing. She now felt less guilt and shame in relation to sex, and more able to let go. This was related to her own comfort level and to her boyfriend's sensitivity—he made it a point to be concerned about her desires and pleasure, whereas in other relationships that did not feel like the point. She now felt that she deserved to have pleasurable sex and felt that she had selected someone who cared about her pleasure. "I had to spend lot of time dispelling a lot of feelings I had about sex from when I was younger, and a lot of things that happened to me when I was younger. It took a lot of mental breakthroughs, and a lot of . . . maturing and thinking, 'Okay, in my life I deserve this.' I was also saying, 'Sexually, I deserve this too.' Because of that growth, you naturally select people who can care about what it's like for you."

As she considered it, it occurred to Maria that the quality of her sexual experiences depended more upon where she was mentally and developmentally in her life than it did on the relationship she was in. So from about age twenty-five onward, regardless of the context, she enjoyed sex. Expressing her feelings about sex finally did not feel trashy to her, and she was in relationships in which she could be both emotionally intimate and sexually expressive. When I asked if there was a difference she felt between sex in a relationship versus sex in a one-night stand, Maria responded:

It doesn't depend on the relationship, it depended on where I was in life. So even when in a relationship, when I was younger, sex sucked. I hated it. I had to get motivated for it. I started to like it a little bit more. I convinced myself, "Yeah, this is great." I think it was the type of people I was with, too, not giving. I got older and started to think, "I deserve to have good sexual interactions like everyone else." I started to take hold of that and say, "I don't understand what all this hype is about, because I'm certainly not enjoying this." Even instances I had when I was about twenty-five, even one-night stands, I'd feel like, "I'm enjoying this, I like this, and I'm with someone who I just met two days ago, but I trust this person and I know what I want out of this." There's less guilt, less shame in it, and more me letting go. That really wasn't dependent on a relationship or not; it was just that by the time I was twenty-five, I just had a different concept of what sex meant to me. It was more about me.

In describing what was distinctive about her twenties in terms of sexuality, she stated: "My sexuality in my twenties is more about me. It's more open, less shameful, more pleasureful, more mature, more intimate than before." When asked how sex had changed over time, Maria responded:

I think what's happened was I was afforded good experiences throughout relationships from college, and even ones not so good, good things I learned about myself. I was able to test a lot of theories I had from before when I was growing up. When I was growing up, I thought all these things about relationships and sex, and in relationships I was able to think about whether those made sense or not, knock them down slowly, and then build up other ways of thinking about sex. One thing that came to mind: when I was in the long-term relationship when he said I need[ed] to masturbate, that was the best gift he could give me. That got me excited; I can explore this. Maybe . . . I was expecting something I feared, but really now I'm thinking this can be different. After being in a couple of fairly healthy dating situations and healthy relationships, that's really been extremely beneficial. And some good dating situations, too. I have to say, of all the one-night stands, the one I had where I felt he was respectable really helped me. It wasn't just sexual, it was a very safe situation. He was a very safe type of person, no power exchange, no struggle with after. That helped 'cause it didn't feel bad afterwards. There was always something bad afterwards in my mind, but that didn't happen. There was nothing bad, it was so great, and that made a big difference.

However, at the same time that Maria developed comfort with feeling and expressing sexual desires, some of her old fears persisted. "A remnant of the past is a heavy amount of distrust. I'll distrust somebody up until the second year of a relationship. I always have an out. Me and my boyfriend now, I always have an out just in case I need to bail. I'm always a little distrusting towards anyone I get close to. That's the remainder. I need to have an out in case things get unsafe at all. That's how I'm wired still." And she imagined that sex with women would be free of this danger and fear:

> One thing that's different, I always view women as more trusting. I'm a girly girl. I would trust a girl more. Maybe things would just be—dating would be a safe thing all the time. There would be no preconceived notions 'cause I trust women a lot more. Dating to me would be free, actually safe. I'd feel I could be the aggressor, would feel less pretense, would feel dating wouldn't be a power thing. "You call me, you do that," not like one has to initiate, "then I'll evaluate what's going on and see if that's good enough." There wouldn't be any of that. Just really straightforward. I think it would be different. So, yeah. I hope you don't think I'm some raging man-hater, I'm really not [she seems really worried].

In talking about being with women, Maria spoke very freely and easily; when discussing other topics, she had not seemed so relaxed. She believed that trust would be easier to achieve with a woman. Maria still had fears about safety, both emotional and physical, which felt very linked to gender for her—men could hurt her in a way that she imagined women could not or would not.

Maria felt encouraged to live it up in her twenties, and some of those experiences helped her to further her development. She had one really good instance of casual sex that was pleasurable and that allowed her to experience sex differently. But she was principally sexual in the context of relationships, and worked toward having more satisfying sex, toward discovering ways in which sex and emotion would not be so split within relationships. She felt challenged, primarily by partners, to be both more expressive about her desires and more vulnerable in relationships.

For a time, Maria had seemed to be acting "like a man"—uncaring, invulnerable, and unaffected. She cared about neither relationships nor about the person she was in a relationship with. But she was not enjoying sex; she was not expressing her desires, nor was she climaxing. The problem with taking such a defensive stance is that it denies the fact that the expression of sexual desire and pleasure is often vulnerable, that their expression involves the admission of need, and not just wantonness. Merely being bold and callous in her pursuit of sex did not guarantee that Maria would get the sex she wanted—that would have required some vulnerability on her part.

Maria attributed her "hardness" to witnessing and experiencing sexual dangers as an adolescent. She responded to these dangers quite differently than did Jayanthi (chapter 3), who continued to put herself in dangerous situations following traumatic sexual experiences, or than did Alicia (chapter 5), who withdrew from sex and became a good girl to avoid danger. Maria continued to be involved in sex and relationships, but she withdrew emotionally from them. While this distance was perhaps protective for a while, she later recognized the ways in which it kept her removed from partners and from herself. Maria ultimately made use of these life challenges to further her development rather than limit it.

Maria expected that her thirties would be a logical outgrowth of her experiences in her twenties. She had used her twenties to focus on herself, and she viewed that as progress toward being able to focus on commitment and compromise in her thirties. She anticipated being able, in her thirties, to reap the rewards of the growth she had accomplished in her twenties.

FROM NONCOMMITTAL
TO MUTUAL: SUSAN

A "momma's girl" who struggled to be independent as a child, Susan became a radically independent woman in her early twenties. Susan herself was surprised at the degree to which she had been able to enjoy independence, commitment, vulnerability, and sexual pleasure in her later twenties. A twenty-eight-year-old white woman born in 1975 who was short and cute, with curly hair, Susan could barely contain her enthusiasm for my project, and for the prospect of letting go of the control that had kept her safe but also held her back.

Susan, like Maria, didn't necessarily look like a woman destined to get what she wanted from sex and love. Her upper-middle-class parents provided stability and training in independence, but little training in managing emotional vulnerability. Her father's alcoholism left everyone in the house "walking on eggshells" for fear of setting off his rage. And Susan recalled her mother as emotionally detached, leaving Susan and her sister to fend for themselves emotionally. While Susan was a momma's girl in preschool and kindergarten, she quickly learned from her parents that that level of attachment was shameful and wasn't encouraged. Susan made it her task in first and second grades to be more independent. She learned from both her mother and father that dependent and scared feelings were not acceptable— she needed to "snap out of it," "get a handle on things," and "move on." Useful lessons for independence and control, but not for vulnerability and mutuality.

The Ideal Partner

Until recently, Susan had used an elaborate schema to manage the vulnerability of sex, and it made her the "ideal partner" in some ways: sexy, undemanding, and focused only on her partners' pleasure. She could easily perform oral sex on a man for whom she didn't have any feelings. But she would have intercourse only with men she loved. There was something sacred about vaginal sex, and the connection that was possible through it, that she reserved for people she loved. And she was loathe to let a man perform oral sex on her under any circumstances. It felt too vulnerable to tolerate either in a relationship or in casual encounters. As long as sex was not really focused on her pleasure (which she managed by engaging chiefly in fellatio), she was able to manage her vulnerability. She was very sexual, but wasn't having good sex.

Fears of being labeled a slut kept Susan focused on her partners' desires and not on her own. Growing up, she learned that she should "make yourself attractive so people will look at you, but be a tease and don't give it up." But Susan *did* have sex with her first boyfriend, and *was* aroused by him. Although she and her boyfriend had intercourse when she was fifteen, she vehemently denied it for years. Susan felt subject to a double standard that prevailed at her high school: girls should not be proud of having sex, but guys should be. She was determined not to be considered a slut in high school. Those who did have sex and were open about it had that reputation. She feared that she might be labeled a slut if she were "too public about it." But even as she followed the rules of her high school and had sex only with her boyfriend, whom she loved, Susan *felt* slutty for being sexually active at all.[1]

Additionally, Susan kept her sexual desires under wraps from the boys with whom she was sexually active, even though she knew what would have felt good to her. "There was internalized discomfort around, 'No, do it this way, do it that way. No, stop.' I never felt comfortable expressing this, and I think that could be an internal stereotype about how women are supposed to be, which is not very expressive or direct with what they want or need sexually. That was internalized for me, even though I had a sexually active sister and it was expressed in my family." While her family had always been very open about sexuality—her mom playfully reminded her to bring along condoms on a college trip to South America—she consistently felt uncomfortable with saying, "Do this because it makes me feel good." She grew up feeling as though she were not supposed to be expressive or direct about her sexual desires and needs.

Another way in which Susan managed her fears of being a slut was to excel at pleasing men, but inhibit herself from feeling and expressing pleasure of her own.

> It was like, "I can have sex, but no demands for pleasure." . . . Sex to me was something that was about male pleasure, not about me getting off. It was about him getting off, for years. . . . And then I tried to say, "Well, I get pleasure in getting him off" [silly, whiny voice]. . . . "And I'm in control here. And I give great head. And I'm so cool

because I can get these guys off and it's a power trip for me." And there's something erotic about that. But it wasn't about me getting any kind of . . . climax . . . , or . . . real physical [pleasure. It was] almost more of a mental pleasure. But it wasn't something I was supposed to experience. It wasn't about me, not in that way. . . . I didn't even think so much about my pleasure. . . . My partner would be like, "What do you like?" And I'd just dodge the question.

While a few partners expressed interest in her pleasure, most did not. This fueled Susan's sense that the sex wasn't about her enjoyment. There was a certain eroticism Susan felt in being able to provide her male partners with pleasure. And her ability to please them made her desirable to men in a way that she could control. Both her male partners and she contributed to the lack of attention to her pleasure—they asked about it infrequently, and she avoided discussion of it even when they raised the issue.

Susan experienced eroticism in providing her partners with pleasure and being in control, but she also gained a sense of invulnerability by not expressing sexual desires and needs. Earlier, while she knew what would have felt good to her, she never told her male partner about it, and climaxed extremely infrequently. With her long-term boyfriend, "It's interesting because near the end of our relationship, Joe was starting to ask, 'What do you want? What do you like?' He'd even lay it on the table for me. It's still, it wasn't comfortable for me to say, 'This is what I want.'" Nor was she comfortable having orgasms with Joe. "[If I did climax with him, I would do] it in a way that it's not obvious and more like . . . the movement of my body is doing it, not anything he's doing. He happens to be the body that's next to me. Allowing somebody to make me have an orgasm other than myself was kind of a big deal. I wasn't comfortable with orgasm until two years ago, and I've been sexually active since I was fifteen." It felt vulnerable to Susan to climax *with* a partner, to expose herself to a partner in that way, and to make clear to her partner and to herself that he had a role in bringing her to orgasm.

Similar to the vulnerability of orgasm, Susan also felt that to have a man perform oral sex on her was extremely exposing, and almost intolerable.

> It was too vulnerable for me. I would have vaginal sex with Joe all the time, a lot. But oral sex, no . . . I didn't know my vagina well enough. "I don't know her, you can't know her." I never would have articulated it then like that. I think, "Well, shit, that makes sense to me now." . . . I didn't know myself that well. It put me in too much of a vulnerable place, even with someone like Joe, who I was with for eight years. And there wasn't—it's not like I had all these guys who wanted to and I was like, "Stop." They were okay with me doing it and not having to do anything afterwards. It's interesting . . . because I very much remember the first time anyone went down on me, and I loved it. I was in high school. It was Mark, he was my very first boyfriend. We were in a park at night, and I was ripping out the grass. I was loving it. It was really interesting. And I didn't let him do it all that often either. But the very first time I was like, "This is wonderful." But it didn't . . . manifest in "Oh, therefore I'm not gonna let people do this." [I had a good experience of it, not a] particularly bad experience of it. My first experience was great.

Oral sex felt exposing to Susan in a way that other forms of sex did not. Despite loving it as a teenager, the literal position felt exposing to her, and the entire experience felt too vulnerable to repeat.

Susan's other strategy for maintaining invulnerability was to be unfaithful in all of her romantic relationships. Infidelity was a way to show her partners, and the world at large, that she cared less about her relationships and was less invested in them than were her partners. In this way, despite being in serious relationships since high school, Susan managed to avoid feeling needs or desires for her partners.

With both Mark, her high school boyfriend of two years, and Joe, her college boyfriend of eight years, Susan was unfaithful multiple times, often with her boyfriends' friends. At one point, in her midtwenties, she was juggling five partners—two men and three women. Part of her enjoyed the excitement of having so many partners, but part of her began to feel overwhelmed. She started having panic attacks and had trouble sleeping. At that time she began to see a therapist and learned about the ways that she was detached from her body and her emotions. She learned to accept that she had complicated feelings and began to communicate them to others. Earlier, she had worried that a focus on herself and her feelings would make her selfish. She came to see that that was not the case.

Susan began to understand that she had been avoiding vulnerability in her sexual life in her teens and early twenties. She had focused on being desired and took pleasure in being good at making men climax, but had avoided letting someone else give her pleasure because it felt too scary to her.

> I was like the ideal: "She'll go down on you; she won't even ask for anything." I can't imagine that wasn't going on. I held this huge kind of pride about it. Almost as if I thought it *did* make me a feminist because I *was* in control and I wasn't going to let anyone control me. I wasn't letting myself be vulnerable. . . . [But] I'll never forget this. I had a guy, it was the same situation. I knew he wanted to have sex with me, vaginal sex with me, and I was doing my little thing, and I started inching down like I was gonna go down on him. And he said, "You know what? If you're just going down on me to

avoid having sex with me, you should stop right now." I was flab-bergasted. And I stopped and we didn't do anything. I could not believe it. At first I thought, "This guy's an idiot. Oh, my God, he's an idiot." Then part of me was like, "Whoa." And after the fact, I was like, "He so called me on my shit." He was the only guy who saw the game completely. That was the game. And no other guy had come even close to pretending like he saw it. And he was, point blank, "If you're just doing this to avoid having sex with me, you might as well stop." That floored me. But it didn't therefore change me.

Susan managed to play her game for years, keeping men at bay by focusing on them and not admitting her own desires. And most of the men she was with happily "played" with her, as they seemed to get a good deal, but neither she nor her male partners had experiences of mutuality, as Susan absented herself and her desires from the equation.

An Independent Woman with Needs

In her late twenties, Susan became much more comfortable talk-ing about her sexual and emotional needs, and she felt as though she had a right to have those needs met. She also developed a new version of independence that did not involve the absence of needs, but the honest expression of them.

Like Maria, Susan began masturbating when she was older—it did not occur to her until late in college that she could mas-turbate, that a man who skillfully stimulated her with his fingers and hands had the same equipment that she did, and that she could do it to herself. Also like Maria, beginning to masturbate marked a turning point for Susan in coming to acknowledge her desires. For a while, Susan felt ashamed about masturbation, as though it were something not to be proud of, but to be hidden. She then got angry that it was so forbidden for women and so accepted for men. She began talking with friends about it and learned that some had been doing it for years, although quietly and secretly. And she practiced more, so she learned what she could do to please herself, and what others could do to pleasure her.

Between her mid- and late twenties, Susan learned more about her sexual desires and developed greater ease in expressing desire without feeling ashamed and guilty. This took the form of increased knowledge of her body, gained through masturbation and through having partners who cared about her pleasure and desire. In therapy she learned to tolerate more of her feelings and needs so that she could express them to partners. She also became increasingly confident about how her desire would be received by others—that others would not shame her, would act responsively, and would match her vulnerability. Being with her current female partner was important to Susan's development because she felt more able to tolerate vulnerability and exposure with a woman, and because her sexual activity with women was necessarily more mutual than that with men. She was not able to "play the game" as easily with her girlfriend, who was interested in Susan's pleasure and whose relatively less strong sexual desire allowed Susan to more acutely feel her own.[2]

It is important to note that Susan's experience of what psychologist Lisa Diamond terms "sexual fluidity"—that is, moving between male and female partners without much identity transformation—was not unusual among the lesbian, bisexual, and queer women with whom I spoke.[3] Only five out of ten had what might be described as "traditional" coming-out stories, in which they struggled in college with their sexual orientation, both internally and in relation to others, and then came out definitely as something other than straight. The remaining five, and three other women with bisexual experiences who identified as straight, may have had sexual experiences with both men and women during college and later and been thoughtful about their sexuality, but they did not experience the identity transformation characteristic of traditional coming-out stories. My findings echo those of Diamond, who found that young women are increasingly unlikely to have a traditional coming-out experience and are more likely to experience sexual fluidity than were earlier generations of women.

Susan, unlike Maria, may have looked like a sexually liberated woman in her teens and early twenties: having sex with multiple partners, experimenting sexually, being sexually skilled at pleasing her male partners, and having casual sex. She was also well versed at being sexually desirable to men, and she made sexual encounters happen easily. But her experience of sex was devoid of pleasure for herself, was characterized by fear of exposure and vulnerability, and lacked a focus on or expression of her desires.

For Susan, letting go sexually and emotionally were inextricably linked—both were instances of vulnerability in her mind and experience. She came to understand that her early sexual experiences had been attempts to stay in control, not expose her needs and vulnerabilities to a partner, and avoid mutuality. Susan didn't tell her partners what she wanted and needed because it felt too exposing, scary, and vulnerable to do so. And she kept her long-term partners at a distance by cheating on them. By committing neither to her desires nor to her partners, she kept herself safe. Her noncommittal strategy maintained her invulnerability, which was her primary goal in her teens and twenties. But her strategy began to fray at the edges, and the safety and control she'd worked so hard for became elusive as she moved through her twenties.

Susan still had questions about the degree to which her current experiences of sexual desire and pleasure were tied to her relationships with women. So many of her earlier prohibitions on desire were based on gender: she had felt inhibited from and ashamed about her desire because she was a woman, and desire seemed to belong to men. In relationships with women, for there to be any sex at all, desire must reside in women, not only in men. So it made sense that with women, Susan would have to feel her own desire. But Susan was reassured that in her experiences with women, she also experienced emotional vulnerability and exposed herself. She gave up some control, which previously she had feared in general, not just in relation to men. She now was able to feel desire and need in relation to her partner, but she still wondered how that would work with a man.

PLEASURE AND MUTUALITY

Maria and Susan represent different yet characteristic paths to developing pleasure and mutuality in the later twenties. Both overcame earlier defensive stances in which they maintained control and invulnerability. Maria's defensive stance grew partly out of early traumatic experiences, and Susan's came, to some extent, from early lessons in independence.

Maria's development benefited from relationships with men who were interested in her pleasure, who insisted that she figure out what she did and didn't like. Over time, she also gained confidence in her ability to survive hurt. She learned that her adult identity was stronger than her adolescent identity and that she could bear the risk of vulnerability that came with emotionally trusting men.

Susan's development was aided by relationships with men and women, and by work with a therapist, all of whom were interested in knowing more about her needs, feelings, and desires. Susan came to understand that her insistence on staying in control and meeting only her partners' needs was not actually strong but self-denying, and a perversion of the feminism she held so dear. She began to see her habitual infidelity as similarly defensive.

For both Maria and Susan, later experiences of partners positively receiving their sexuality were particularly important in developing pleasure and mutuality. For Susan, experiences with female partners were also important, as so much of her earlier experience had to do with gendered expectations of pleasure— "He deserved it; I didn't." At the same time, both Maria and Susan did have some earlier experiences in which partners expressed interest in their desire and pleasure, which they discussed as remarkable, but not as fundamentally changing their experience. It was only later, when they were developmentally ready, that they were able to make use of their partners' interest in and positive reception of their sexual desire and pleasure.

This developmental readiness was related, for Maria, to an increasing sense of safety in relationships with men, as she had experiences with men who were respectful, interested in her, and mature. It was also related to a growing awareness that she could enjoy sex, which she began to feel as she experimented with masturbation. For Susan, developmental readiness had to do with an increasing tolerance of vulnerability—of knowing her own desire, and of mutual expression of that desire with an equal partner. And as with Maria, it also had to do with learning about her own desires through masturbation.

Maria and Susan both also developed new understandings of mature relationships involving both independence and needs. They had previously thought of independence alone as a marker of maturity. But their extensive training in independence did not serve them well in achieving satisfying sex and relationships. They were both left to their own devices—hard-won through relationships and therapy—to develop the capacity for vulnerability and desire. They came to understand that needs and vulnerability could also be important aspects of maturity.

Throughout the book, we have seen multiple instances of women's conflicts over desire and needs. Susan and Maria too felt conflicted about their desires, but they managed to find compromise solutions to their conflicts. They figured out ways to feel pleasure, sexual desire, and relational desire in the face of cultural and psychological pressure to be radically independent and invulnerable. They still felt frightened by these vulnerable feelings, but they were able to tolerate them and fulfill more of their desires sexually and in relationships. Such fulfillment did not mean the absence of conflicts. Rather, it involved active engagement with conflicts so that they did not solidify into splits. In this way, they became independent women who valued and respected their needs and desires—a hopeful starting place to build satisfying sex and relationships.

CHAPTER EIGHT

Maybe She's Born with It

Sophia and Jeanette

Some twenty-something women whom I interviewed didn't need defensive strategies of desire to achieve satisfying sex and relationships. They didn't overvalue control, independence, and safety. Nor did they avoid intimacy, need, vulnerability, and desires. So they weren't prone to split. This meant that they didn't feel the uncertainty and fear about sex and love that many other women with whom I spoke did. This freed them to pursue sexual and relationship experiences that furthered their development and allowed them to know clearly what they wanted and to pursue pleasure and mutuality.

What set these women apart from the other twenty-something women with whom I spoke was that they had parents or caregivers who psychologically prepared them to deal with the freedoms and constraints, contradictory messages, and ideals that characterize the new developmental period of the childless twenties.

Sophia and Jeanette were two women who got much of what they desired from sex and relationships, more than did other women with whom I spoke, and they didn't feel especially conflicted about getting it, either. Both had possessed a strong knowledge of themselves and their desires since childhood.

Sophia had a solid identity that included both strength and vulnerability—they didn't feel like contradictory characteristics to her, but parts of her whole identity. Since high school, she had felt comfortable with her desires both for sex and for relationships. And vulnerability didn't frighten her. It didn't threaten her identity; instead it facilitated growth.

Jeanette, like Sophia, felt equally at ease with her desire for sex and relationships. She didn't feel her independence to be threatened by intimacy, and instead felt confident about her personal strength regardless of her relationship status.

Sophia and Jeanette may have looked like they were born with confidence and solid identities. But like other women with whom I spoke who made it look easy to get what they wanted, they had parents or caregivers who had facilitated their development in important ways.

VULNERABLE AND STRONG: SOPHIA

Sophia, in contrast with Maria and Susan (chapter 7), had been able to fulfill her desires in sex and love from early on in her development. Through the course of her twenties, she developed through her sexual and relationship experiences, but she started the decade with a strong identity and stable sense of herself as capable of connection with others. Her twenties had been a time to further this development.

From the outside, Sophia didn't look so different from twenty-something women who struggled to get what they wanted. But as I talked with her, her confidence and ease gave her away as different. Sophia, a twenty-five-year-old mixed-race woman born in 1978, had short, cropped hair that was somewhat boyish, but in all of our interviews she wore stylish and fitted athletic clothes that showed her toned and curvy body. She was pretty and energetic, and was enthusiastic about the interviews, as she felt this was an exciting developmental moment to explore her sexuality. She grew up in California in a working/middle-class, nonreligious family, although she attended Catholic schools. Her mother was white and her father black, and she grew up with her mother and white stepfather, having no contact with her father after her parents' divorce when she was two. Her biological father died when she was eleven, but she developed ongoing relationships with a few paternal aunts and cousins after his death.

While she had no relationship with her father, Sophia's mother and stepfather were both consistent and loving figures in her life who modeled various qualities with which she could identify. Sophia identified strongly with her mother, who was an "independent, strong-willed, strong-minded woman." As a girl, she imagined she would be like her mom, whom she described as masculine, a machinist by trade. But at the same time, her mom insisted on cooking, declaring the kitchen to be her domain. Sophia worked to be "independent, strong, comfortable with [her]self and who [she is]," but in recent years she also had begun to emulate her stepfather, who was calmer, more passive, "less emotional and aggressive." She began to feel that she did not want to be an angry and aggressive person, which was how she sometimes perceived her mom. She did not make a conscious decision to move away from her mom, but she noticed that she was heading closer toward her stepdad in certain ways.

While Sophia had resented her stepfather's presence in her family as a child (her mother began dating him when Sophia was four), since late adolescence, she had felt close to her stepfather. She characterized him as very loving, although in a less overtly emotional way than was her mother.

Sophia had a relatively straightforward and uncomplicated puberty experience that afforded her with confidence in and knowledge of her body and its desires. She linked this to her experience as an athlete, in which she consistently felt good about her body. She also gained a great deal of self-esteem from her success at athletics. In addition to these positive athletic experiences, Sophia's mom was very tactful and straightforward about everything in relation to puberty so that Sophia did not feel embarrassed about what was happening—needing to get a bra, buy deodorant, and get tampons. As her body began developing, Sophia felt excited to be growing breasts. But she was also comfortable with her girl's body—she was a late developer and recalled comments about her being flat-chested. But she thought, "Well, I guess that's a problem for *you!*" Once she was fully developed, she remembered her mom saying that she was jealous of Sophia's body because her mom had always wanted to have bigger breasts. Hearing that her mom liked her body made Sophia feel good.

Sophia appreciated many aspects of being a woman—she loved her body and what it could do, loved the way she could think and express herself as a woman, loved that she could cry and not be looked down upon, and loved that she could be emotionally intimate with other women in ways that men were not allowed to be with other men. And she appreciated what she characterized as the masculine parts of herself—wanting to take care of people; showing strength physically by helping people to move and carrying heavy objects. Sophia had had the sense, since childhood, that her body was useful, pleasurable, beautiful, and capable of great things.

In addition to her confidence and solid identity, Sophia felt relatively unconflicted about being close to people and being emotionally intimate with those with whom she was sexually involved. She had a four-and-a-half-year relationship through college and the first year afterward with a man to whom she was still close, and with whom she had had a loving, mutually vulnerable, and exploratory relationship. Sophia identified as queer and was currently involved with a woman, but most of her sexual and relationship experiences had been with men.

Sophia's confidence in herself extended to her ability to attract men. "With guys, [I think,] 'Of course you like me, I'm attractive, let's move on.'" She also felt confident initiating sex with male partners because she knew they would be receptive. "With men, I know I can get you off and can tell when you come because it goes all over."

Unlike many of the women with whom I spoke, Sophia's induction into sex was motivated chiefly by curiosity, not by anyone's actual or perceived pressure. "I was ready for sex. Bring it on! What is the big deal?" She wanted to see what sex was all about, so went out on a few dates with someone in her senior year in high school and then slept with him, but she was explicitly not in a relationship with him. She was, in fact, surprised when friends asked if she would go to the prom with him. It had not occurred to her that she should or would want to date him. She never wanted a relationship in high school, and described sex then as an "amusement ride, a neat, new adventure to try." From her senior year of high school through her first year of college, she was in a phase during which she felt, "'You're interesting, you're cute. Let's see if you're any good.' It never felt like an image issue or that I wanted to be sexy. It was more 'I want to see what *you're* about.'" While she enjoyed these experiences of casual sex, she had begun to tire of them by the middle of her freshman year. "During freshman year, at one point I said, 'Okay, I'm done with that. The next person I want to have sex with is someone I want to be in love with. I'm tired of sleeping with random people just to do it.'"

Sophia had a significant boyfriend in college, Rashid, who was her first love, and with him she had sex with someone she cared about for the first time. They were together for four and a half years. Her relationship with Rashid developed slowly and carefully. "He and I dated, and it was six months until we had sex. It was very significant. For him, it was the first time. For me, it was the first person I actually cared about. That was completely monogamous. We were very innocent; we were both really young. We thought, 'We're gonna get married, we're so in love.' First love. I really care[d] about him. And it was great knowing he really cared about me." Sophia could comfortably move between her desires for sex with casual partners or committed partners. She saw them all as valuable and didn't judge her desires for one or the other.

> With Rashid, it was about sharing my entire self. It was very different from any other guy. With Michael [a casual sex partner who followed Rashid], it was all about having *fun*. How many places can you have sex? Where? How many positions? There wasn't so much learning and sharing. It was more about having fun. With Margo [her current girlfriend], it's been a mix. Being with a woman, I'm really wanting to share, and that emotional aspect comes on a lot faster. It feels new. Then there's the sex that's pure curiosity—those

are always really fast, they're over quickly. I never saw the big deal until Rashid: "Wow, this can be really good!" Also with Margo, I felt, "Wow, I'm really feeling enmeshed with this person and wanting, feeling I can't get close enough." Being so involved in it—not that I black out, but nothing else exists. That's what makes sex with people I love *much* more enjoyable. Then there's just curiosity.

While she enjoyed sex more with people she loved, she also saw the fun of casual sex.

As she had recently become involved with women, Sophia's confidence had begun to feel more complicated: "If she looks like me, does she want to date someone exactly like her? . . . When we're too much alike, it doesn't work." And when initiating sex with women, she was less sure of herself because the outcome was uncertain. And her female partner's satisfaction was more difficult to measure. "With Margo, I can't tell. There's no noise; was it good? . . . I expect the same reaction from women as I have because we're the same gender and have the same bodies," but it didn't always work.

Yet because Sophia felt so comfortable with her own desires, and so enjoyed sex that satisfied and pleased her, she also took pleasure in making her partner feel good.

I want to make the other person feel completely lost and out of their realm, with nothing they *want* to focus on. . . . This person in front of me is the only thing I see, the only thing I'm experiencing. I have knowledge that something else is out there, but I really don't care. It's really far out there and far away; this is the only thing. And it's not just about how I feel. This person is here at the same time. I can't be close enough. I can't quite get what I want, but I'm getting it all at the same time, too. Nothing else exists.

Sophia took pleasure in a high degree of mutuality, but could also enjoy sex that was primarily about her partner or herself.

"Sometimes . . . it's all about me. But sometimes I just want to make the other person feel really good."

Sophia's most prominent recent fantasy involved meeting a woman who identified as a switch, who could act as both the aggressor and the receiver. This meant that Sophia could experience everything and even use toys, maybe a double dildo. She liked to receive but also enjoyed giving, and that was not possible with her most recent girlfriend, who was allowed to penetrate Sophia while Sophia was not allowed to penetrate her. Perhaps somewhat ironically, Sophia felt more freedom to explore being both the aggressor and the receiver with men than with women. This may be because she had dated principally butch women who had more rigid sexual practices than had her male partners.

Sophia imagined a future progressing fluidly from her experience in her twenties. Her sexuality in her twenties was principally about her individual development, but she envisioned her sexuality in her thirties centering around her development in a relationship. "After my twenties, I think that in my early to mid-thirties, my sexuality will be more about the relationship I'm in—it will be intimate and close to one person, not just for now. It will be an ongoing thing to work on and grow together. Now my sexuality is more about myself—if I'm intimate with somebody else, it's in the present and not about building a future." She also pictured a future including children that would be progressive from her experience in her twenties. "I do want to settle down and have kids. I imagine it will be with women, though I recognize that's still very hard, especially having kids. I can't physically have a kid with another woman. I like the idea of artificially inseminating her egg into my body. . . . I see myself settling down in five to ten years. I'm not ready now. But that may change in two years. I don't know." This capacity to think clearly about the future distinguished Sophia from other twenty-something women who viewed the future as discontinuous from their twenties.

While generally free from the conflicts and splitting that characterized many of the women with whom I spoke, Sophia was not immune from the social pressures and conflicting messages that predominate for twenty-something women. Sophia described herself as a serial monogamist, even though she wished that she were not. She tended to "land" in monogamous relationships, but she wished that she could more easily date and explore her interest in various people. However, Sophia was less troubled by falling short of the new "standards" than were other women with whom I spoke. She may have longed for an experience other than the serial monogamy that came naturally to her, but she didn't judge or disparage herself for her natural tendency.

From her earliest sexual relationships, Sophia had been able to get what she wanted. She grew up feeling connected to and appreciated and supported by both her mother and stepfather. And she had felt her body to be useful, pleasurable, and appreciated since girlhood. She had enjoyable experiences of sex both in and out of relationships, and she felt free to explore her desires for both. Sophia had, throughout her development, a simultaneous capacity for sexual desire, a strong identity, and vulnerability. Over time, she also developed increased appreciation of intimacy, mutuality, and the pleasure she could take from her partners' experience of pleasure.

BAD GIRL/SMART GIRL: JEANETTE

Jeanette, like Sophia, had had a remarkable capacity to get what she wanted from sex and love from early on in her development. From childhood, Jeanette had possessed a strong identity, confidence, and the ability to be close to others and be vulnerable. Her twenties, like Sophia's, had been a time to further develop these capacities.

A twenty-eight-year-old born in 1975, Jeanette had always understood herself to be, simultaneously, a bad girl and a good girl. She was another "bad-ass" girl who was smart, opinionated, and talked back to teachers. But she was also a good student who didn't have intercourse in high school. Because of this solid sense of self, Jeanette felt comfortable with all of her desires.

Cursory knowledge of Jeanette's demographics wouldn't lead one to predict that she would demonstrate the confidence, comfort with her sexual desires, and solid identity that would enable her to reach her goals. Jeanette's mother was sexually promiscuous and poor, and she gave up all parental rights when Jeanette was five years old. Jeanette was then raised by her working-class father and great-aunt in California. And she grew up very religious, attending a conservative, fundamentalist Christian church.[1] Not exactly a recipe for graceful and easy sexual development.

While not providing a traditional family structure, Jeanette's father and extended family provided her with the nurturance and figures of identification necessary to develop a strong identity and become capable of getting what she wanted.[2] Jeanette's father was her primary emotional caretaker. He was the one she would go to with concerns, feelings, and needs for support and comfort. He talked with her easily and comfortably, and had "real conversations" with her. Her dad had been granted custody of Jeanette when she was five because he was deemed the more fit parent in the divorce proceedings. Her mother lived a "chaotic lifestyle" involving job instability, poverty, and unstable relationships. When she was ten years old, Jeanette decided to break off contact with her mother, and she'd had no contact with her since then. Growing up, Jeanette knew that she did not want to be like her mother, who was unreliable and irresponsible. Her father was a stable parent and loving presence who was actually available to her, as opposed to her mother, who in some sense could not be bothered with her.

Jeanette's great-aunt provided most of her physical caretaking—cooking, cleaning, homemaking. She was another stable presence in Jeanette's life who, while not particularly emotionally engaged, was reliable, loving, and supportive. Jeanette's paternal aunts were also important to her. She saw them as secondary caregivers: they took her school shopping, and she sometimes spent weekends and summers with them. And she had a female cousin, ten years older than she, who was an important role model—she and Jeanette were the most educated members of their family, shared a similar political sensibility, and had a similar experience and understanding of their extended family. With all these figures of identification available to her, Jeanette developed somewhat unpredictably but solidly.

Particularly with regard to femininity, Jeanette felt some confusion about her identity, but the absence of clear models of femininity—because she lived primarily with her father and her postmenopausal great-aunt—may have provided her some freedom to develop a female identity that felt genuine to her, rather than one that was imposed upon her. She enjoyed dresses and some "girly" things, but felt inhibited from exploring makeup, hair, and most girly clothes both because she lacked role models and because her family had so little money. She felt like a tomboy as a child and wore jeans and T-shirts most of the time. She clarified that she was not out climbing trees or playing with boys but was generally inside the house, reading most of the time and playing with girlfriends. She characterized herself as a "kick-ass girl who did not take any shit from anyone. . . . Most of my classmates thought I was slightly different in terms of my harshness. I was seen as somewhat political or outspoken. I would talk back to teachers. But because I was a good student, I wasn't a rebel or anything. It was a strange little niche I carved out for myself. Bad girl, smart girl. Something like that." While Jeanette did not have clear feminine role models available to her, she did develop strong thoughts, opinions, and an identity, which contributed to others' difficulty placing her in terms of gender.

Despite their involvement in an evangelical Christian church with strict conservative teachings about sex, Jeanette was very sexually active and experimental with her high school and college boyfriend of five years, whom she dated from ages fifteen to twenty. They did not, however, have intercourse. The two of them decided at the beginning of their relationship that they were both invested in saving their virginities for marriage, a decision that was informed by the teachings of their evangelical Christian church. He led the charge on this decision, and it came out of teachings that did not feel sexist to Jeanette—they applied equally to men and women, and stated that the best wedding gift you can give your spouse is exclusive access to you via intercourse. An interesting twist on this virginity pledge was that Jeanette then did not feel any shame about the sexual exploration she engaged in with her boyfriend—they both coded their sexual practices as "not sex," and therefore entirely acceptable. No matter what the sexual practice, as long as it didn't involve intercourse, Jeanette felt no shame or worry about judgment.

Jeanette felt as though she developed a great deal sexually with her boyfriend. At the beginning of their relationship, she did not feel comfortable saying what she wanted or enjoyed sexually, although she had been masturbating from an early age and knew what would feel good. After they had together for about two or three years, Jeanette began to express more of her sexual desires to her boyfriend, and he received them well, taking pleasure in her desire and seeking to please her. She felt that she could be a top and be bossy with him about what she wanted, and she felt that they could have both "functional" sex and "intimate" sex.

> With my ex-boyfriend, I feel I was, I still was more of a top for sure.... I felt more comfortable being a little bossy with him. I think it's because, for both of us, we were each our first sexual partner, and so it felt we were really on the same playing ground. It was the same experience. I felt much more comfortable being like, "Do this." Sex was a big part of our relationship, so that if both of us didn't feel like it but one of us did, we'd take care of the other person's needs and not really expect reciprocation.... There was almost a more functional nature to my sex life in my first relationship than my second. Not to say it wasn't intimate or emotional. But there was a way that it was like, "I just need to do this and you're here. I would do it on my own if you weren't here, but why don't you take care of that?" It was a little more blunt. But that could be because we were together for years. That could be part of the function of getting used to each other.

Jeanette was currently involved in a relationship with a woman that she considered to be mature:

> I've been in two significant relationships, one with a man, one with a woman. In this relationship, I'm older, I feel more mature. I feel she's much more mature. Our conflict management is much more

mature and adult. I seem to have a lot of—it's funny, I was telling a friend, I feel like in my first relationship I loved him very deeply but didn't have a lot of respect for him. Our differences were great. In this relationship I love her very deeply and have a lot of respect for who she is as a person and really value her, what she's doing in her life. I really respect it, it feels good to be part of it. I feel we're on a similar trajectory in life.

In her current relationship, she had a capacity for mutuality, for being affected by and affecting her partner: "In my relationship now, I met her as she was a fully formed adult herself. I like the person she is. Our relationship changes both of us, and we're very different. . . . Because we were young in my first relationship, I felt I could shape him into the person I wanted him to be. In this relationship, I already came in liking the person she is. That feels better." She no longer sought to control her partner, but enjoyed her as an equal subject.

Jeanette wished, like Sophia, that she could have had more casual sex in her twenties. She had been sexual only in her two serious, long-term, monogamous relationships, and she at times wished for experiences of sex that were more "slutty" and less relationship oriented. She spent her early twenties somewhat differently than did her peer group. From twenty to twenty-five, she wanted to figure out who she was by herself, outside of a relationship and as an adult, once she was no longer in her five-year-long relationship. She did not have sex at all during that time, and did not "sow any wild oats." Once she came out of her self-imposed celibate period, she pronounced to her friends that she would have the "year of the slut," the year that she slept around and had flings with cute girls. She wanted to be less relationship oriented than she generally had been. As she made that proclamation, however, she had already begun dating the woman who was to become her girlfriend, and, as she said, "Alas, she's fantastic. So at some point, many people had to say to me, 'You love her, you think she's great. Why do you want to sow your oats right now?' ... After a couple of months, I melted. She's got plenty of oats." She still wished to have a time in her life during which she could sleep with whomever she wanted, and during which she could be less relationship oriented in terms of sex. But while she felt the influence of conflicting messages about sex and relationships, and while they created some internal conflict for her, Jeanette was guided chiefly by her subjective experience.

While Jeanette had a capacity to clearly express her sexual desires from early in her relationships, her ability to be forward with strangers in situations such as flirting developed more slowly. She only recently had begun to feel comfortable flirting. Previously, when attracted to someone, she would talk to every person in the room except that person. She became, as she said, this "creepy, quiet person," which was not consistent with her naturally social self. She now understood her discomfort with flirting as related to her inability to gracefully turn people down when they expressed interest in her. "I just had no idea how to say to them, in a nice way, 'I'm not interested.' So I'd just stammer. Once I figured that out and got better at saying, 'That's so great, I appreciate it, I'm not interested,' I felt much more at ease being flirty." Before, she had worried about rejecting people, but now she felt, "That's ridiculous. It's much nicer to be flirted with and have a fun time than to have someone be kind of chilly." She now had the sense that she could be flirty without necessarily hurting the other's feelings, that she did not need to absent herself in order to be safe and not hurt people. She felt confident now that neither she nor others needed so much protection.

Jeanette had some difficulty translating the ease with her sexual desire that she developed in her heterosexual relationship to her lesbian relationship. She felt more comfortable being a "top" with her boyfriend because she knew that he would enjoy whatever she did and would always be up for sex. But she sometimes struggled with trusting that her desires did not infringe upon or hurt her girlfriend in some way. Like Claudia, Jeanette had a very high level of sexual desire, and ideally she would like to have sex four or five times a week. Her girlfriend's level of desire was different—ideally she would like to have sex once or twice a week. But unlike Claudia, Jeanette did not feel ashamed of her high level of sexual desire. Instead, she was struggling to make her desires known and not worry so much about the effect that they might have on her partner.

Among Jeanette's favorite moments in sex were those when her girlfriend asked her to do something specific for her. That was a huge turn-on for Jeanette, as she enjoyed seeing her girlfriend's desire and her willingness to be vulnerable enough to express it to her. Jeanette enjoyed receiving pleasure, but also loved being able to meet her girlfriend's needs and give her pleasure. She stated: "When she expresses a desire for something particular, I find that really sexy." One of Jeanette's favorite experiences of sex was one in which her girlfriend was more dominant than usual:

> My girlfriend and I had come back from this party, a work party for her. We were being affectionate, but it was not that sexy a party, and we came back and she was very aggressive with me, which is unusual for her. I tend to be more of the instigator, and that was really sexy, where I was like, "Oh, what's happening?" I think I tend to be the

most turned on when she is dominant. And I tend to be dominant; it's my default to do that. It might be variety, that she's doing something out of the norm.

Jeanette described here an experience of her girlfriend being vulnerable by stepping outside her regular role and taking charge, and Jeanette being vulnerable in allowing herself to let go and be dominated.

Jeanette felt that she was actively considering the future and laying the foundation for it at the time that we spoke. "With my girlfriend now—[we're] moving in together, talking about the future. It's not clear what it will be, but I feel engaged with those questions. It feels very adult. She doesn't think she wants kids, and I do. It's a conflict, and I've really worried about it. We've decided we'll see in two years how we both feel and then decide. Making decisions about potentially moving somewhere together feels adult. Having considerations about freedom and financial responsibility." She felt both open to the unknown of the future and invested in making conscious decisions about it. "I don't really want to have a sexual relationship with a man, exactly. I'm open to that in my life. But it would be disappointing. I'm much more inclined to be with women. I love the lesbian community. I feel a deeper emotional connection with women, so that's what I'd prefer. But it's not like it's out of the realm of possibility."

Children were definitely on Jeanette's mind, as she and her girlfriend had conflicting desires over whether to have them. However, unlike several examples from the previous chapters, in which twenty-something women discussed decisions about children relatively independent of the context of their relationships, Jeanette talked about her own desires as well as how those might play out in the context of her relationship. This was not a fantasy in which she alone was making decisions about a future that might involve her girlfriend—instead it was mutuality at work.

While Jeanette did not have a loving and consistent mother, she did have a stable, loving, and encouraging father and aunts who were very present in her life. She, like Sophia, developed a supportive and intimate relationship with her first boyfriend. Jeanette grew up in a very religious household, but unlike many women with whom I spoke who grew up Catholic, Jeanette was able to benefit from the structure provided by her religion and make her own interpretations of its teachings, so that while she and her boyfriend did not have intercourse, they enjoyed a variety of other sexual practices without guilt or shame. With her female partner, Jeanette was working toward mutuality at a new level, as she felt pleasure in their mutual exposure and vulnerability in ways that were different than those she'd felt with her male partner. The future for Jeanette seemed continuous with her development, and she felt it to be both within and outside her control, as she was moving toward it in partnership with another person.

CONTINUOUS DEVELOPMENT OF PLEASURE AND MUTUALITY

Sophia and Jeanette exemplified the continuous development of pleasure and mutuality. Sophia felt pleasure and delight in her body from a young age, and Jeanette possessed a strong identity from early on, both of which facilitated the unfolding of independence, closeness, desire, pleasure, vulnerability, and mutuality in their relationships.

Significantly, Sophia and Jeanette both had parents who played multiple roles in their lives: as heroes to emulate and identify with, confidantes to be close to, adult figures to rely on, disciplinarians to set appropriate limits, and workers and community figures to admire. Not surprisingly, these parents, who did not themselves split, recognized and nurtured a range of qualities in their daughters: goodness and rebellion, strength and vulnerability, athleticism and academic achievement, retiring and forward behaviors, cautious and bold ones. They didn't experience these characteristics as contradictory, but as parts of the whole that constituted their daughters. Consequently, their daughters didn't succumb to cultural or psychological pressure to split, as did many of the women with whom I spoke.

Women such as Sophia and Jeanette, who had caregivers available to them as figures of identification and who received their selfhood positively and respectfully, were more likely to feel that they were relatively autonomous from cultural ideals about sexuality. They then did not feel that they needed to be as compliant with cultural ideals as did other young women with whom I spoke. This autonomy freed them to develop their own feelings and desires about sexuality, which were, of course, still culturally influenced, but which they experienced as consistent with and integral to their identity rather than outside themselves. Other women, such as Maria and Susan, who did not have the kinds of relationships with and experiences of their parents as did Sophia and Jeanette, developed relatively greater autonomy from cultural ideals about sexuality over time.

These early experiences with caregivers translated into early relationships with partners characterized by mutuality, curiosity, and interest in each other's pleasure, need, and desire. Neither Sophia nor Jeanette struggled through relationships characterized by passivity, lack of fulfillment, or defensiveness, as Maria and Susan did.

Unlike many young women with whom I spoke, Sophia and Jeanette knew that absolute safety and control were impossible, and that independence could be had alongside need, vulnerability, abandon, intimacy, and desires. They'd had early experiences with caregivers in which independence and strength coexisted with need and closeness. And they had a great deal of internal freedom to feel desire and pleasure in their bodies, despite societal and religious messages to the contrary. These capacities extended to their sexual relationships, in which they were generally able to figure out their desires and either fulfill them with their partners or choose different relationships that provided them with what they needed.

CHAPTER NINE

Conclusion

What's a Modern Woman to Do?

Unencumbered by marriage, motherhood, and all their attendant responsibilities and limitations, some twenty-something
women's lives may look free and easy. Digging under the sur-
face, however, I came to learn that the freedom characterizing
young women's lives is paradoxical. While twenty-something
women now have tremendous opportunities to be independent
and to pursue their education, careers, and sexual and personal
development, they receive little guidance in how to navigate the
desires, vulnerabilities, and internal conflicts that accompany
these freedoms. Possessed of greater opportunities than their
grandmothers could have imagined, twenty-something women
find themselves confused, conflicted, and uncertain about their
goals in sex and love and how to achieve them. Pursuing the
strategies that have been successful in school and work is
unlikely to yield the same success in love and sex. Young women
lack guidance on how to achieve real sexual intimacy and long-
term relationships. As we have seen, this lack of information
leaves twenty-something women adrift.

Young women want help with learning to fulfill their desires in relationships, sex, and careers. I was five to ten years older than the women I interviewed for this book and was surprised by the intense interest they expressed in how I'd succeeded in building a relationship and a career at the same time. I was also surprised, as I ended each interview series, at the degree to which many women were grateful to me for talking with them about their sexuality and development.

What's so striking about all the women with whom I've spoken is the degree to which they feel that their dilemmas and the solutions to these dilemmas reside within themselves. They have little sense of the changes in the outside world necessary to facilitate their development. This places tremendous pressure on women, who hold themselves individually responsible for navigating their personal development.

In addition to this sense of individual responsibility, twenty-something women contend with a societal-level split between independence and vulnerability, with vulnerability as the denigrated category. This split holds that independence, safety, and control are valuable and important to maintain at all costs, and that anything infringing on this radical independence is to be avoided. This is not a helpful ideal to propagate to anyone. Pleasure and passion are borne of vulnerability, desire, need, dependency, abandon, and intimacy, qualities that are denigrated in this split. In this way, these young women are set up to fail. Until we offer women (and men) a developmental model that is not based on splitting and repudiation, but on true identification with complex real people, they will have to contend with contempt and scorn for the very human qualities (and the people who have them) that make possible good sex and good relationships.

The women with whom I spoke did the best they could and developed individual strategies of desire. Yet all the strategies, apart from being a Desiring Woman, fell short in providing a model for women to attain the things in life that require compromise, vulnerability, dependence, and care. Young women seem to understand that the strategies fall short. Nonetheless, they hold on to them to navigate through their sexual and romantic lives. But young women could benefit from additional help to develop productive strategies that succeed in getting them what they want. The solution is to be a Desiring Woman who wants and gets love and work, sex and relatedness. But being a Desiring Woman also involves tolerating the vulnerability, uncertainty, and lack of control that inevitably come with desire.

This requires that we acknowledge that all desire is normal and that conflict between desires is inevitable. Getting what we want from sex and relationships requires accepting and tolerating seemingly contradictory parts of ourselves—strong and vulnerable, sexual and smart, desiring and desired, relationship- and career-oriented. It's vulnerable to introduce aspects of ourselves into areas where they're traditionally hidden—showing our assertive and smart identity as well as our needy identity in relationships, and presenting our relationship-valuing identity as well as our smart and assertive identity in the professional world. If we can develop curiosity about our desires and aspects of ourselves that don't match up with those sanctioned by our culture, we may begin to build lives in which we feel more pleasure and satisfaction.

Additionally, we need to help young women to refrain from denigrating the vulnerable terrain of relationships, need, and dependency. While the pressure on college-educated women to be radically independent is historically new and may seem to be progress away from the older social insistence that women focus only on relationships, the new "taboo" on relationships can also be limiting and damaging to women. This taboo is in line with many pressures on upper-middle-class women to exert control over multiple aspects of their lives—in particular, control over their emotions and control over their desires. Relationships, as much as books such as *The Rules* would have us believe otherwise, are not so controllable.[1] And, ultimately, neither are feelings about sex so controllable, despite our best efforts to manage them. In some sense, the lack of control inherent in relationships and sex is part of what makes them exciting, but also scary.

We haven't yet evolved a way to represent attachment, vulnerability, and need as other than weak and undesirable. Taking emotional risks in relationships with others is imperative for development to occur, and requires strength, not weakness. The hurt that can result from taking risks in a relationship also does not necessarily signal weakness. But a predominant cultural discourse about relationships for twenty-something women stresses the importance of not getting played. Why isn't there as much cultural discourse about going through a bad love experience and learning from it? Why aren't there as many stories about the importance of taking risks even if you do end up feeling played? Why is being intimate with someone seen as stunting development?

Vulnerability is the underbelly of desire. We might think that desire never has anything to do with our connections and attachments to other people. It's only about ourselves. The idea that desire links us to others feels too frightening and vulnerable to consider. But desire, that most subjective of experiences, *is* fundamentally vulnerable. To desire is to be powerful and vulnerable at the same time—a paradox that will go unrecognized as long as power and vulnerability are split between different genders and different people.

STRATEGIES OF DESIRE FOR SOCIETY

Changes at the individual and cultural level can help women to integrate the splits—between independence and intimacy, assertion and vulnerability, identity and relationships, sexuality and safety, control and abandon—that currently organize much of their experience. By thinking about these as issues that are not merely personal, but social in nature, women might be relieved of individual pressure to manage it all on their own. Providing twenty-something women with help in reaching their goals in sex and love involves providing developmental models that emphasize the importance of individual and relational development, families in which caregivers relate to all children as whole people, partners who respond enthusiastically to women's desires and needs, therapists and friends who give young women honest feedback about the effect of the defenses they employ, increased opportunities for mentorship by older women, schools in which all children are treated equally and as sexual agents, unequivocal societal condemnation of sexual violence against women, workplaces in which relational concerns are valued, and media representations of women that acknowledge the complexity of women's desires. Some of these efforts are well under way, and some have further to go.

For years, feminist psychologists have been advancing the proposition that development occurs neither exclusively at the individual level nor solely inside relationships. But in public discourse, opinions have solidified around a split between advocates for independence and advocates for relationship in development. What young women need is not more splitting, but relationships in which they can develop their identities and their capacities for closeness. Relationships with people who are whole and who do not themselves split make possible solid identities that can integrate desires and will not split. Identity *does* develop in relationships, but only in relationships of the right kind—with parents who are available as figures of identification, but also value the individuality of their children; with friends who offer various models of how to live in the world and to whose struggles women can relate; with mentors who provide both modeling and advice that do not involve splitting; and with partners who positively receive women's sexual desires, pleasures, and fantasies, who are whole people themselves, and who insist that the women in their lives remain whole and not split.[2]

In our families, this requires parents to relate to girls and boys as whole and complex people who are not just caricatures: for example, girly or tough, shy or bold, docile or active, academic or athletic. Parents are in an important position to recognize and nurture the unique and seemingly contradictory aspects of their children in such a way that children come to see these parts of themselves as making sense together.[3] When parents allow their daughters to identify with all aspects of themselves, children of both sexes stand a much greater chance of becoming adults who can tolerate complexity. And when parents receive their daughters as subjects in their own right, as opposed to nascent sex objects or sexual competition, girls stand a much better chance of discovering their own desires. Women with parents who respond to them in these ways are more likely to feel relatively autonomous from cultural ideals about sexuality, and so feel freedom to develop their own feelings and desires about sexuality.

As an example, it is all too common for fathers to talk about the worry their daughters cause them. These fathers hurt their daughters' chances to develop comfort with their sexual desires by focusing on their potential status as sexual victims and their fundamental difference from boys, who are presumably worrisome in their potential status as sexual aggressors. This emphasis encourages girls to bury their sexual desires out of fear of the effect they may have on boys. Instead, a father who declares, "My daughter is an awesome soccer player! And she's stunning!" expresses his awe and appreciation of his daughter, not his fear for her based on her sexuality. A father who is involved in his daughter's athletic pursuits also makes himself available as a figure of identification, not just as a protector.[4] Responses such as this help daughters to develop a sense of competence and confidence, and leave them open and curious about their sexual desires.[5]

Similarly, mothers who compare themselves favorably or unfavorably to their daughters in such a way that one of them ends up a mere caricature do their daughters no favors. This type of competition fosters the development of stereotyped versions of gender and allows little access to one's authentic experience of sexual desire. In contrast, a friend recently recounted an exchange she had with her teenage daughter as she was trying on my friend's clothes from the 1980s. The daughter exclaimed, "Mom, you never wear this fabulous pantsuit!" And the mother replied, "Well, I never looked like *you* do in it. You look gorgeous!" She said it with much appreciation and recognition, and with the understanding that her daughter is not only gorgeous, but also funny, smart, thoughtful, and inhibited at times. A response such as this helps a daughter to develop confidence in her body and a sense that she can be separate and different from her mother without harming her, and therefore the likelihood that the daughter can know her own desires is increased.

In romantic relationships, partners who are respectful and interested in women's desires can make a big difference in helping women to get what they want. Encouragement to masturbate, when it comes from a partner, can help women discover their own bodies and desires, and develop familiarity with both sexual desire and sexual pleasure. Through such relationships, women can practice feeling and expressing desire.

An important finding from my research is that my lesbian, bisexual, and queer respondents were much more likely to use productive strategies of desire, and to fulfill their desires in sex and love, than were my straight respondents. They were much less likely to use the defense of splitting their desires than were my straight respondents. Seventy-eight percent of my interviewees who managed to get what they wanted were lesbian, bisexual, or queer.[6] Among women who used defensive strategies of the Sexual Woman or the Relational Woman, straight women predominated.[7] We may hypothesize that this is the case for several reasons. It may be that the greater barrier of coming out, for lesbian, bisexual, and queer women, pushes them to articulate and develop comfort with their desires. Or it could be the case that women involved with women are forced to initiate sex and voice their desires more than are women involved with men; they may rely more on men to be the sexual initiators. My lesbian, bisexual, and queer respondents also may have spent more conscious time and energy on their sexual development than had my straight respondents. Or perhaps some conflicts over independence and identity in relationships were mitigated by being with another woman rather than with a man. However, lesbian, bisexual, and queer women with whom I spoke did not differ systematically in the types of conflicts over sexual and relational desire they manifested. They simply seemed to have an easier time managing and tolerating these conflicts than did my straight respondents.

I regularly asked women how they imagined things would be different if they were with a differently gendered partner than usual, and I was surprised at the well-elaborated answers that I heard from many straight women. They had clearly thought about this possibility before, and generally pictured much greater comfort with their desires if they were with women, although several also anticipated missing the difference between themselves and men. Straight women might challenge themselves to see their male partners as more similar to them than different, and then to experiment with how they feel about being more assertive in their relationships. Absent a split understanding of gender in their partners, straight women might be more able to get more of the satisfaction some lesbian, bisexual, and queer women seem to get in their relationships.

In addition to romantic relationships, relationships with both friends and therapists can help young women to develop increasing comfort with their desires and to fulfill more of their desires. Intimate friendships with men and women can offer young women kind and thoughtful reactions to their use of defenses that don't serve them. And such friendships can include honest discussions of sexual desire and pleasure, and relational desire and pleasure, allowing women to hear about the various desires that all of us share. Similarly, effective therapeutic relationships can provide young women with honest feedback about the ways in which their insistence on control and their defensive use of splitting block the way toward their goals. In such relationships, young women can simultaneously experience need and strength, vulnerability and desire.

Young women could also benefit from mentorship by older women who provide both modeling and advice that do not involve splitting. Rather than the pat advice that young women often hear about "having it all" or not waiting to marry or have children until it's "too late," such mentors could acknowledge that choice involves loss as well as possibility. These models of Desiring Women don't collapse in resignation at being one thing or another. They recognize and model that maturity is characterized not only by independence, but also by a capacity for dependence and interdependence. And they acknowledge the vulnerability and risk inherent in desire and don't insist that it's easy to want.

Young women need to hear from and know women who have gone through difficult experiences but did not later avoid intimacy, because they learned from their experiences and emerged from them with hope. Such a woman practices assertion and sometimes fails at the task, but sometimes succeeds. A broken heart is not an occasion to harden emotionally to protect herself, but to seek out sources of support so that she can survive emotional hurt. This is a woman who can then express her sexual desires, who can enjoy sex and experience sexual pleasure. A woman who can communicate desires that feel vulnerable to her—for emotional closeness, for emotional distance and space, for sex that is sometimes conventional, sometimes unexpected. A woman who can take care of herself, and allow others to take care of her. Such models, unlike those offered by the rampant splitting that occurs in our culture, could help young women to know and express more of their own desires.

If successful women who are a few steps ahead, or even generations ahead, of twenty-something women can openly accept different aspects of themselves in various roles, young women might see the possibilities for wholeness and interdependence and so resist splitting quite so much. For example, a colleague of mine who teaches women's studies courses uses her experience as a mother to discuss aspects of gender. She feels her professional identity is sturdy enough to tolerate her acknowledgment of her relationship-oriented identity. Her job is also secure enough that her workplace does not question her commitment to career when she discusses her commitment to her family. And her students benefit from having a model whose professional and relational selves are intertwined and not split. For twenty-something women who long for both independence and intimacy, such an embodiment of wholeness is crucial for them to begin to satisfy their desires.

In schools, these many years after the passage of Title IX, young women could still benefit from increased gender equality and effective sexuality education. Optimal schools feature teachers working hard to give equal time and attention to girls and boys, and teachers who do not use gender as the primary way to organize and sort children. Sexist and homophobic bullying are responded to seriously in such schools, and are not treated merely as instances of "kids being kids." The kind of sex education the young women with whom I spoke need is not merely about birth control, STDs, or abstinence,[8] but *sexuality education*—a term coined by Michelle Fine to describe a curriculum that teaches students the physical and emotional aspects of sexual desire, discusses how to realize what they feel, and suggests ways to effectively communicate desire to achieve their wishes in sex.[9] While sexuality education for women could go a long way toward helping them to get what they want, as long as their potential male partners are schooled in the acceptability of sexual violence against women, young women will continue to be thwarted in their efforts. Twenty-five percent of the women I interviewed had had experiences of sexual violence, including acquaintance rape and childhood sexual abuse, which is within the range of 9 to 28 percent reported in the general population.[10] Sexuality education for men is therefore crucial to provide them with an understanding of their sexual desires and tools to non-violently express them. Law enforcement and the legal field must also continue to evolve ways to ensure that sexual violence is effectively prosecuted. Such schooling could support other efforts to help girls (and boys) to know all their desires, and know how to manage them to get what they want.

In addition to changes in family, relationships, and schools, young women could benefit from changes in the workplace. As long as it remains difficult to combine career success and family life, and as long as the work of caring for families and children remains unpaid or poorly paid, the splitting and repudiation of relationships and family from work will continue to predominate. High-powered jobs demand a level of time and energy commitment that is not easily managed with a concurrent commitment to a family.[11] The devaluing of relationships and family life that results from such family-unfriendly jobs makes it difficult for young women to consider their personal development to be as valuable as their professional development.[12]

Some solutions to the problem of devaluing relationships and family life and overvaluing jobs that are greedy for our time is to change norms about work and how many hours are considered manageable for everyone—women and men. Workplaces can begin to do so by providing options to work part time and yet continue to advance in careers, an option currently barred to most workers in competitive fields.[13] Another step involves reforming social programs so that people are not as individually responsible for providing for their economic security when unable to work—in disability, unemployment, and retirement. As long as people remain so individually responsible for their welfare when unable to work, they will be required to work for ever-more income in order to protect against financial disaster.[14] In order to increase the value placed on the work of caring for children and families, women and men who do such work for pay must earn a living wage. And men and women must be provided paid leaves to do such work as well.

These changes would make it possible for men and women to value relationships and family life as much as paid work, and so not to split so completely the qualities of care—vulnerability, intimacy, and need—from the qualities of paid work—independence, autonomy, and control. Vulnerability and assertion might then be understood as human experiences, and not located exclusively in women or men.

Some cultural solutions include increasingly complex representations of women in magazines, advertising, movies, television, and books. Various media products could wrestle with the dilemmas young women face, without resorting to pat solutions that involve heroines essentially cutting off crucial sides of themselves to achieve only part of their goals. We already see examples of such complex female characters in books by Megan Abbott, Alison Bechdel, Aimee Bender, Jennifer Egan, Miranda July, Jhumpa Lahiri, Lorrie Moore, Elissa Schappell,

Zadie Smith, and Jennifer Weiner. Female-written movies such as *Bridesmaids* and *Juno* show funny and whole women who are both strong and vulnerable. The rich array of complex female characters in television shows such as *The Good Wife* shows women wrestling with desire in a variety of ways. And the proliferation of talented female comics, such as Tina Fey, Chelsea Handler, Melissa McCarthy, Caitlin Moran, and Kristen Wiig, in recent years gives us ample evidence that women have their own desires, independent of men. These works acknowledge the complexity of women's desires, and the simultaneity of vulnerability and satisfaction of desire.

Young women are hungry for help with how to get what they want from relationships, sex, and career. We can all see parts of ourselves in Katie, Jayanthi, Alicia, Claudia, and Phoebe. At some point we've all felt afraid—of wanting a relationship, of wanting sex, of overwhelming a partner, of losing ourselves in a relationship, of being ambitious, or of losing ambition. And we've all felt uncertain about whether we'll be able to fulfill all of our desires.

Emotional and sexual involvement is inherently risky, but this is not the kind of risk we ought to avoid. This is the kind of risk that makes life worthwhile and meaningful, and that makes human connections and intimacy possible. Development, of identity and of relationships with others, requires risk taking: asserting our desires and needs, tolerating another person's vulnerabilities, risking conflict, and risking disappointment and hurt in the pursuit of our goals.

SPLITTING

The term *splitting* originated with Melanie Klein, a British object relations psychoanalyst writing in the 1940s.[1] She used the term to describe a process that predominates in early developmental stages. An early revisionist of Freud who emphasized the centrality of the mother as opposed to the father in children's development, Klein first developed the concept of splitting to account for the way that infants and young children manage the intense and complicated feelings that they have toward their powerful mothers, on whom they're absolutely dependent. She argued that infants and young children feel both intense love and intense hatred toward their mothers—intense love when their needs are being met and intense hatred when they are frustrated. Because infants and children cannot yet see people as whole—good and bad, gratifying and frustrating—they split people into two: the good mother and the bad mother.

As conceptualized by Klein, splitting is a developmentally appropriate way to categorize the world in early childhood, but an element of a rigid character structure for adults with character pathologies, and a defensive way to manage anxiety for many adults without character disorders.

Klein's thinking has influenced subsequent feminist psychoanalytic theorists, such as Jessica Benjamin, Janine Chasseguet-Smirgel, Nancy

J. Chodorow, and Dorothy Dinnerstein, who have also highlighted the centrality of the mother in children's development and argued for the ways that women's predominant role in parenting shapes both men's and women's psychological development.[2]

Subsequent theorists in the social sciences and humanities have developed various concepts related to splitting—dichotomous categories, dualities, and binaries—to describe the difficulties that people have in managing difference and complexity in their lives, and to explain the origins and perpetuation of gender, sexual, and racial difference and inequalities. They note the ways in which splitting is not value neutral and generally depends upon the existence of one valued and one abject category. Queer, poststructuralist, and postcolonial theorists such as Judith Butler, Teresa de Lauretis, Frantz Fanon, Judith Halberstam, Trinh T. Minh-ha, and Eve Kosofsky Sedgwick argue that the dichotomous categories (based on splitting) of masculine-feminine, black-white, queer-straight, subject-object, and active-passive mark our thinking about gender, sexuality, and race and require us to choose between being one thing or another, and so extremely circumscribe our capacity to be fully human.[3] While these theorists demonstrate the role of splitting in managing complexity and the ways in which splitting relies upon an abject "other," they don't necessarily focus on the role of anxiety and uncertainty in producing splitting.

These theorists argue that modern western conceptualizations of autonomy, agency, and control depend upon the existence of an abject other—woman, homosexual, person of color; dependent, passive, object—in order to maintain the fiction of absolute autonomy. Similarly, our individual psychological conceptualizations of autonomy, agency, and control depend upon our not embracing the abject within ourselves, making it difficult to know all our desires fully. See Butler, de Lauretis, Fanon, Michel Foucault, and Sedgwick for arguments about the ways in which these categories themselves contribute to the origins of racial, sexual, and gender inequalities and subject us to forms of power and domination.[4]

Contemporary feminist psychoanalytic theorists understand splitting as the basis for immature experiences and understandings of gender. Jessica Benjamin argues that absolute difference is a primary way to organize experience and is a developmental achievement for children who have worked to successfully resolve the oedipal conflict.[5] In resolving the oedipal conflict, according to traditional psychoanalytic theory, children are charged with acceptance of their biological gender and all the social and psychological "realities" that accompany it: identification with the same-sex parent, being heterosexual, being feminine if female and masculine if male, not having one's parents as one's love objects, and not killing one parent in order to unseat the other one. Benjamin and others recognize the value of oedipal-level thinking about gender, in which rigid categories and binary oppositions predominate, in children but not in adults. Here the child develops categories of thinking that organize her or his experience—male and female, black and white, can and cannot, subject and object, active and passive, and so on. It is developmentally appropriate that children should think using such categories. At the same time, Benjamin and other feminist psychoanalytic theorists critique the devaluation of feminine qualities and the overvaluation of masculine qualities by both boys and girls in the oedipal period. When adults hold to such rigid gender categories with femininity as the abject category, contemporary feminist psychoanalytic theorists contend, they rely upon the defense of splitting.

Rather than viewing the oedipal understanding of difference as the last word in development, Benjamin and other contemporary feminist psychoanalytic theorists argue that we ought to conceptualize a postoedipal developmental period during which gender is not solely an oedipal achievement, or a final arrival at a solid and fixed gender identity that corresponds to one's sexual anatomy. Postoedipal gender, in contemporary feminist psychoanalytic theory, is a true achievement. It includes the capacity to tolerate ambiguity and instability and to occupy multiple categories of gender—both the valued and the abject. Mental health in the postoedipal stage is, then, characterized by a capacity to experience oneself multiply, not as rigidly belonging to one category. But social pressure to conform to categorical ways of being, devaluation of feminine qualities, and overvaluation of masculine qualities, as well as the binary oppositions that predominate in psychic life, make it difficult for women and men to escape from splitting. While splitting may serve an organizing function for psychic and social life, Benjamin contends that to be fully human requires mutuality and the occupation of multiple positions—characteristics of the postoedipal, not the oedipal, stage of development.

CLINICAL INTERVIEWING

Both the women with whom I spoke and other researchers have described the ways in which words alone are inadequate to convey much about sexuality and relationships—that the pleasure, desire, and anxiety characterizing experiences of sex and love encompass much more than words can represent. I agree with the insights of both Lacanian feminists[1] and of social scientists such as Michelle Fine[2] that language does not do a particularly good job of representing women's embodied experiences of sexuality and relationships from their own subjective positions. This left me with the challenge of using language, through interviews, to discuss with women experiences that seem rather slippery when language attempts to capture them. I required a method of interviewing and of interpreting my data that would capture more than the mere words of the women with whom I spoke. Furthermore, both culturally and personally, sex becomes a container for, and is itself a source of, all kinds of worries and complicated emotions.[3] My research method, then, also needed to consider and identify strong anxiety and feelings at the same time that it allowed for ways to address them in the interviews themselves.

Because we lack an understanding of the sociocultural surroundings of college-educated and childless twenty-something women, and of the specifics of this new developmental period of the childless twenties, I also required a method of interviewing that would allow me not to test hypotheses, but to discover the sociocultural and psychological challenges, dilemmas, conflicts, and contradictions facing these women.

Clinical interviewing, a practice adapted from clinical work conducted by psychotherapists, provided me with access to women's subjective experiences and allowed me to identify and deal with anxieties that might have been missed using more traditional interviewing methods. Most descriptions of clinical interviewing involve its use in clinical settings, which are highly structured for the purpose of psychological treatment, or in ethnographic settings, in which the researcher's contact with respondents is ongoing and encompasses many situations. For these reasons, I developed refinements of my own in order to best meet the needs of my research. While anthropologists are more likely to use clinical interviewing than are sociologists,[4] I will argue for its particular utility in researching complex and poorly understood sociological problems such as women's development of sexual desire and relational desire in the face of confusing sociocultural conditions replete with mixed messages.

THE WOMEN

This study focused on college-educated, childless women in the San Francisco Bay Area who were between the ages of twenty-four and twenty-nine. I conducted three in-depth interviews each with twenty women, and each interview lasted approximately one and a half to two hours. The interviews took place generally once a week and within a one-month time frame. I tape-recorded, transcribed, and coded each interview. Additionally, I took detailed notes following each interview that focused on impressions and strong affective responses that I had had during the interview and other significant subjective experiences that I noticed in myself and the respondent during and after the interview.

I interviewed college-educated and childless women because of my interest in a developmental period between late adolescence and parenting that is historically new. I was curious about this period because I hypothesized that it may provide women with the opportunity to develop their sex and love lives in ways that were not previously possible. I limited the age range to the mid- to late twenties for several reasons. Women who have been out of college for a few years and who are not yet thirty are likely to be going through the developmental challenges described by adult developmental theorists: developing a beginning adult life structure, struggling with issues of intimacy versus isolation, and working toward individuation. They are likely to be psychically distanced enough from college and from their families of origin to be more consciously confronting both internal and external pressures vis-à-vis sexuality and relationships. I interviewed only childless women because motherhood seems to shift dramatically one's relationship to one's body and sexuality, and I was interested primarily in the dilemmas of sexual and relational desire of young adult women who have not yet had children. I limited my sample to college-educated women for all the reasons discussed in the introduction: they seemed likely to have the most "freedom" in their sexual, relational, and work lives.

Because of my interest in "ordinary" women, I used snowball sampling, in which I ensured that I interviewed at least ten women of color. I deliberately oversampled women of color and lesbian/bisexual/queer women because of my frustration with studies on female sexuality that focus primarily on white straight women in an effort to "simplify" experiences that are inherently affected by race and sexual orientation for women in both majority and minority groups. To find the women with whom I spoke, I asked a few acquaintances to send my recruitment letter to friends and acquaintances who fit my profile, and then asked respondents to recruit additional friends and acquaintances, and so on.[5] Given the nature of the topic and the time commitment involved in the interviews, I believed that snowball sampling would be the most effective sampling tool because women would have a prior connection with someone who had vouched for me in some way. Women were then more likely to agree to speak with me and had some sense of my trustworthiness given the personal nature of the topic. I hoped that the women with whom I spoke would have a good experience in our interviews and would be motivated to recruit additional respondents—and this did in fact occur. Using this method of recruitment, I gathered data on women who had a variety of motivations to participate, who had varying degrees of comfort in talking about sex with me and with others, and for whom sexuality was generally not an organizing feature of their public lives.

My interviewees' demographics are recorded in table 1 in appendix III. As noted, they had all graduated from college and had no children. Some were in relationships, some were not, and a few were married. Half of them were women of color and half were white; half were lesbian, bisexual, or queer and half were straight. In table 1, I use the terms for sexual orientation used by the women themselves.

In terms of race and ethnicity, I interviewed ten white women, six Latina American women, two South Asian American women, one Chinese immigrant woman, and one mixed African American and white woman. This racial/ethnic distribution closely mirrors that of the California population, which in 2011 measured 39.7 percent non-Hispanic white, 38.1 percent Hispanic, 13.6 percent Asian, and 3.6 percent mixed race.[6] The one racial/ethnic group underrepresented is African Americans, who in 2011 composed 6.6 percent of the California population. In terms of class, I interviewed four women from poor/working-class backgrounds, five from working/lower-middle-class backgrounds, two from middle/upper-middle-class backgrounds, and nine from upper-middle-class backgrounds. In terms of religion, I interviewed four women from Catholic families, three from non-Catholic Christian families, one from a Buddhist family, one from a Hindu family, one from a Muslim family, one from a Jewish family, two from nonreligious and half-Jewish families, and seven from nonreligious families. In terms of sexual orientation, I interviewed ten straight women, four bisexual women, two lesbian women, and four women who identified as queer.

I asked the women to choose the pseudonymous names by which they are known in this work because I wanted them to represent themselves. In writing about these young women, I changed the names of all the other people in their lives whom they discussed, as well as identifying information, so that the women themselves and those who know them intimately should be able to identify them, but others should be unable to do so. In some instances, I changed the year of their birth by one or two years in order to further disguise them.

While my practice includes a number of twenty-something childless and college-educated women, and while my clinical experience with those patients informs my understandings of the women I interviewed, I chose not to discuss my patients for both clinical and methodological reasons. Issues of confidentiality are of primary concern in clinical work, and given the level of specificity with which I wished to discuss young women and their lives, using patient material would have been unethical and inappropriate.

CLINICAL INTERVIEWS

Clinical interviewing borrows some techniques and areas of emphasis from clinical work with patients: a focus on unspoken communication as well as what is said; attention to the nature of the relationship between researcher and interviewee and what it may say about the interviewee; an understanding of anxiety and the ways in which it may signal something important about the interviewee; and attention to the impact of previous interactions on subsequent interactions between the researcher and the interviewee. Clinical interviewing is decidedly different from clinical work, however, in that it is not an explicitly therapeutic process. While participating in the interviews may have felt illuminating, challenging, and interesting to interviewees, my role in relation to them was an investigative one, not a therapeutic one. Clinical interviewing also differs from clinical work in that it generally uses an interview guide, with both specific questions and topic areas, to structure the interviews, while still allowing for the kind of open-ended discussion that characterizes clinical work.

Given the relationship that developed between me and my respondents over time, and given the personal and emotional nature of the material we discussed, ethical dilemmas abounded in the research and the writing of this work. Because of my training as both a psychotherapist and a sociologist, I found navigating these dilemmas to be particularly complicated. On the one hand, I didn't want the interviews to become psychotherapy, but on the other, I couldn't shut myself off from being a clinician. I didn't want to make psychological interpretations in the course of conducting interviews, but I also wanted to share my thinking with women who were interested in hearing it.

A grounding in both clinical interviewing and feminist methodology helped me to navigate these complications.[7] In conducting interviews with young women, I did not assume a capacity for objectivity on my part as a researcher, and in both conducting and analyzing the interviews, I was attentive to the ways in which my subjectivity influenced the interview itself, and what I heard from it. I listened at multiple levels, for both content and what was unspoken, stumbled over, confused, or absolutely certain. I focused on the postures, gestures, and movements that accompanied women's verbal communications. I attended particularly to moments when I thought I knew exactly what was going on for a woman and lost track of her subjectivity. I worked to listen for a woman's subjective experiences rather than imposing a sense of objective reality upon them. I attended to transference and countertransference by listening for the ways that women heard my questions and experienced me. I attended to my own affective responses to what was communicated and how it was communicated to give me additional information about a woman's experience both with me and in relation to others. I conducted multiple interviews so that I could not claim that one relational interchange had provided me with access to a woman's experience. I used empathy to try to help women to elaborate on their experiences. Finally, I attended to my respondents' and my own anxiety, noticing when it occurred and trying to make meaning of it both during the interview and in analyzing the interview. My clinical skills as a psychotherapist served me well in this endeavor.

I had originally structured the interviews to last between one and a half and two hours. After the first few sets of interviews, however, I began experimenting with setting a time limit for the interviews. I noticed that I was feeling anxious about time and about whether the women with whom I spoke perceived the interviews as too long or too short. I began to inform women that each interview would last for one and a half hours, and that we would end at a predetermined time. In psychoanalytically oriented clinical work, the structure of time provides containment for the patient, clearly delineating the period during which clinical work occurs. Similarly, in conducting interviews, I noticed that the time limit created a kind of container for the interview so that more could be expressed than in an open-ended format, in which it seemed that both the respondents and I were more anxious because it could go on forever.

Several women with whom I spoke commented on the intensity of talking about their sexual and relational development in such a condensed way. They may have had similar conversations with friends about desire, relationships, pleasure, family, and cultural influences, but talking about it all together often felt intense for respondents, and many commented that they felt they had learned something, seen something in a new way, because of the occasion to discuss all these influences and experiences together. Claudia stated: "It's interesting to do it all in one sitting. I don't usually talk about it sequentially like this."

Over the course of conducting the first few sets of interviews, I came to see that I needed to provide structure to the interviews that involved more than simply consulting my interview guide. I came to understand the first interview as akin to the beginning phase of clinical treatment, in which the patient joins the clinician and develops a sense of safety with her. I began asking first the questions "How did you decide to participate?" and "How comfortable are you talking about sex?" before asking anything substantive. The answers to these questions did provide me with data, but they also set the stage for the kinds of expectations and anxieties the respondent may have had going into the interviews. At the beginning of the first interview, I also offered to answer any questions that women had about me—an offer I had previously made at the end of the first interview, and which yielded few responses. The first interview often felt very intense, with women surprised at the amount of information and affect they revealed upon first meeting me.

I struggled with the second interview, as it often felt like a letdown after the intensity and revelations of the first interview. It often felt less intimate and less revelatory than the first. I came to understand this second interview as akin to the middle phase of a clinical treatment, in which the relationship is developed further and clinical work is engaged in, but the initial excitement of the first stage has abated. I considered doing only two interviews, as this middle interview seemed to fall so flat. But I came to understand that the second interview was crucial in building up to the third interview, which women experienced generally as consolidating. In the third interview, I asked women to make sense of their development, which we did together as we wrapped things up and provided some closure on the experience of the interviews. I began to frame the third interview as akin to the termination phase of clinical work, in which the patient and clinician take stock of what they have discovered and learned and attempt to consolidate the work they have done together.

CLINICAL LISTENING

I learned, through conducting interviews, that questions often were not the best way to get women to provide me with information that interested me. I found that when I asked women direct questions without context, they yielded few results. For example, initially I asked women to tell me when they felt sexual desire and how they knew what they were feeling. Women often responded with confusion to this question, and sometimes felt judged or criticized by it because they could not identify their sexual desire in this way. I began instead to ask, "Tell me about the last time you felt intense sexual desire. What was it like?" When given the direction to discuss a particular experience or memory, women had much less difficulty discussing their desires. Speaking to women in this way not only helped to locate information, but also to ease anxiety, because the way in which I phrased the question assumed that they *did* feel sexual desire, or that they *did* have sexual fantasies. For example, rather than asking respondents to tell me about a sexual fantasy, I asked them to tell me about the most recent sexual fantasy they had. Asking the question in the latter manner yielded far more information than it did in the prior.

At the beginning of the interviews, I let respondents know that it was up to them whether they answered particular questions, but that if they were uncomfortable discussing particular topics or answering particular questions, I wanted to know, and perhaps we could talk about their discomfort and not necessarily about the issue itself. This occurred multiple times during interviews, and this information was just as meaningful as literal content would have been. I learned, in this way, about my respondents' anxieties, fears, discomforts, and shame.

In listening to respondents, I worked to notice absences in the interview, and to point them out. For example, one woman was discussing her family and did not include her husband in her discussion. I asked her about this, and she commented that she was not sure if she yet considered her husband part of her family. She felt some ambivalence and conflict about her commitment to him. I also worked, between interviews, to notice topics or areas that I seemed to have left out or avoided discussing. For example, with one bisexual woman, we seemed to focus more on her relationships with men than with women. I pointed this out to her, and she commented that it seemed an important reflection of how she internally experienced those relationships—those with men were more troubled and dominated her psyche more than did those with women, which did not challenge her as much. I did not view these slippages or neglected topics as mistakes, but as important information for both the respondents and me about their experiences.

At the end of each interview, I asked if there was "anything I have not asked about this particular time in your life, anything that if I did not know, I would not have a complete picture of you." Responses to this question gave me important information about what was on the minds of the young women with whom I spoke, in addition to what I had anticipated. For example, in my original interview guide, I asked women about their vision of the future in terms of sexuality, but did not ask about their vision of the future generally. Several women, in response to this question, said, "You didn't ask me about the future," and proceeded to tell me how they imagined it. I subsequently added a general question about the future. This question also gave me additional insight into particular women, as they discussed topics I had not touched on. For example, for one woman, her parents' divorce was something we did not discuss enough; for another, her estranged relationship with her mother was not adequately addressed. While these topics may not all seem directly related to sexuality and relationships, they were crucial in these women's development generally, so their effects were felt throughout their lives.

SUBJECTIVITY OF THE RESEARCHER

In conducting interviews, I was attending not only to what respondents said and did not say, but also to how they responded to me and my subjectivity. With different women, different versions of my person felt highlighted: with some, I felt older, "settled," and potentially parental; with others, I felt like an older sister whose experience they valued; with some, I felt like a therapist whose counsel was being sought; and with others, I felt like a researcher whose expertise was valued. These varied experiences of myself had something to do with my actual presentation of self and the degree to which I made self-disclosures, but they also had to do with women's preexisting impressions of me based upon my recruiting materials and the topic of the research more generally.

In the interviews I expressed a willingness to answer some questions women may have had about me, but few asked. When women did ask me questions, the nature of the interview often changed, so that women's answers became richer and more intimate. This occurred regardless of the level of disclosure that I provided. Their merely asking a question of me seemed to shift their relationship to me and their ability to talk with me about the interview material. At the same time, sometimes I disclosed more about myself with certain women than with others, which I also understood to be data about the women's effect on people and about the nature of their relationships and relatedness to others.

Prior to meeting the women with whom I spoke, some assumed that I was an academic interested in this topic for purely intellectual reasons, and therefore took a more educational tone with me. Others assumed that I had a personal interest in the topic and so thought that I must have some personal insight into the dilemmas they were experiencing. Again, this was important information for me to understand the ways in which they were both locating me and positioning themselves in relation to me.

DIFFERENT TRANSFERENCES

Attention to transference—ways that women's past and present modes of relating inserted themselves into the current relationship with me— was crucial in my conduct and analysis of interviews.[8] These transferences were not static and consistent even with the same woman. I seemed to become, in some women's experience, a different person at different moments—sometimes a conservative, settled, straight, and bourgeois woman; sometimes a knowledgeable and wise woman; sometimes an understanding peer who may have been slightly ahead of them developmentally but who really understood their experience; and sometimes someone who seemed incapable of understanding their experience.

An example of a changing transferential experience occurred with Emma, a twenty-eight-year-old woman from an upper-middle-class background who seemed to feel guilty about how economically privileged she had been as a child. At first she framed participating in the study, and the study itself, as self-indulgent because it looked only at college-educated women and included such a small sample. I found myself feeling defensive of the project, but tolerated the attack and relatively quickly had the sense that Emma was attacking herself, finding her own experience to be less important and valuable than that of someone who had materially suffered more than she. I then felt empathy for her lack of entitlement to explore her own experiences. At the end of the first interview, Emma expressed surprise at how much she had gotten out of it. She seemed surprised by how seriously I took her experiences of her less-than-perfect body in relation to her sexuality, and consequently felt the project itself and her participation in it to be more worthwhile than she had at the start of the interview.

I was surprised by how many women said they did *not* feel comfortable talking about sex, given that they were willing to do three interviews about sex with me. Some of these women seemed likely to have a positive transference to me, experiencing me as safe and caring and the interviews as helping them. Others asked me challenging questions that seemed to be an effort to exert mastery over a situation in which they were quite vulnerable. Still others experienced me as alternately safe *and* dangerous.

The degree to which I appeared to understand them and their experiences seemed crucial in developing a positive or negative transference. With several women, if it felt as though I did not understand them, I began to feel that I was losing them. One woman who seemed to have experienced me as judging or distancing worried that she must not be very interesting because she did not have elaborate answers to my questions. She responded to my misattunement by not returning my calls and making it difficult to schedule subsequent interviews.

MULTIPLE INTERVIEWS

I began this project by theorizing that multiple interviews made sense in a project on twenty-something women, sexuality, and relationships, and I finished the project convinced of the utility of multiple interviews for conducting research on sexuality and relationships in particular.

I theorized that the complexity of sexuality and relationships, combined with feelings of shame, inadequacy, fear, competition, and exposure affiliated with these subjects, contributed to the case for conducting multiple interviews with respondents. And women did seem able to develop increasing levels of comfort with me and with the topic over the course of the three interviews. They and I could also notice ways in which they sometimes contradicted themselves, concluding one thing about a specific experience in one interview, and another thing about the same experience in a different interview. I would not have been able to capture the complexity of my respondents' experiences had I had only the data gathered from the first interview.

Conducting multiple interviews also afforded me and the women with whom I spoke the ability to see the impact of previous interviews—women would sometimes report that they had begun thinking or acting differently after our interview, and we could then think together about those changes. Multiple interviews also allowed the women with whom I spoke time and space to reflect on both the experience of the interview and their experiences of sexuality and relationships. Many women reported appreciation at knowing they could return to discuss their reactions to having talked about sexuality and relationships in great detail, and to share more thoughts and feelings about sexuality and relationships that were stimulated by the interviews. Emma began reconsidering nonmonogamy and, in a related vein, began breaking a pattern in which, as she said, "Any time a man expresses interest in me, suddenly I find him desirable." Taylor began wearing sexier clothes; Phoebe began feeling more ambivalence about her relationship with her partner; Carolina began thinking more about "experimentation" with women during and after college as important to her development; Mary concluded that she would "take a break" from sex for a while; and Claudia had a one-night stand the night before our first interview. It was fruitful for me and the women with whom I spoke to understand these feelings, thoughts, and actions not as coincidental or random, but as related to the interviews.

Multiple interviews allowed me to develop a relationship with a woman in which she could sometimes discuss increasingly vulnerable topics with me, and collaboration between us could develop over time. This provided me with richer data than I could have gathered otherwise, but it also offered a safer and more contained experience for the women with whom I spoke. With Alicia, the twenty-eight-year-old woman discussed in chapter 5, I found that the information I gathered in the first interview seemed somewhat rehearsed, as though they were stories she had told many times. But over the course of later interviews, the discussion felt more spontaneous and I gained more access to her. Alicia didn't discuss an experience of rape in the first interview, but she remembered it during the week when thinking about the interview: "I don't know why I forgot. I don't know. I realized after you had left.

Driving somewhere the next day, I was remembering meeting and talking to you and I thought, 'Oh, gosh.'" The rape fit Alicia's expectations of men, but did not fit with her self-image as a strong and resilient woman. This illustrates the utility of speaking with respondents multiple times. Had I met with her once, I would never have heard about this experience.

In previous research on sexuality that I carried out with teenage girls, I conducted only one interview with each respondent, and both the girls and I were often left feeling as though they had entrusted me with very intimate information and that the connection between us had been prematurely severed. In the interviews for this book, many women expressed gratitude at the end for the opportunity to reflect on their experiences, conveying that my attention and interest had provided a more digestible experience to the women than the girls had had. Many described feeling appreciative for being able to discuss aspects of previous interviews that felt disturbing, uncomfortable, stimulating, upsetting, or challenging in some way. Several talked about the comfort they felt in knowing they had more time than only one interview—several reported feeling more relaxed about being able to get to their material. They, and I, felt less anxious about taking detours and really exploring various topics and avenues that arose in the interviews than we would have felt had we had only one interview.

RECORDING DATA

In recording the data, I both wrote process notes immediately after the interviews and transcribed the interviews verbatim. In the process notes, I recorded what I recalled was said, in what order it was said, the affective tone of the exchanges, my observations of the respondents, my feelings and thoughts at particular moments during the interview, and connections that I was beginning to draw between this woman and others. I found that process notes best captured the experience of the interview, and the tape recorder served as a confirmation, but not as the source of most information. My most interesting findings and thoughts about those findings were generally the ones recorded immediately after interviews, when the experience was freshest in my mind and the surprise, curiosity, interest, disconnect, confusion, and discomfort were still clear and apparent.

From interview transcripts and process notes, I wrote a summary of each woman that read something like a case history. I organized the case histories according to themes that I found to be predominant among most or all respondents. These case histories provided me with a complex and rich depiction of each woman that attempted to capture her core conflicts with regard to relational desire and sexual desire. The case history also included information about the affective tone of the interview, my subjective experience of the respondent, and relational dynamics between the two of us.

By about the tenth interview I conducted, I began to see a pattern emerging in the themes, conflicts, and dilemmas in the data. And by about the fifteenth interview, I began to reach theoretical saturation. That is, while I was hearing new details about the lives of the women I was speaking with, the same broad themes were being repeated.

FROM DATA TO BOOK

In choosing how to present the data in this book, I debated between organizing the chapters thematically and using multiple examples of the theme in each chapter, and presenting one woman's story in each chapter to illustrate themes. After I'd identified the most predominant splits and dilemmas among the women with whom I spoke, I came to see that certain of the women most plainly exemplified these splits. I concluded that their stories would most clearly illustrate the causes and consequences of splits, and I chose to present one woman's story in each chapter. Many of the books that I remember most clearly from my undergraduate and graduate education—Lillian Rubin's *Worlds of Pain* and Arlie Hochschild's *The Second Shift* among them—present data in a similar fashion. I hoped to emulate their combination of astute analysis and humane presentation of multifaceted people in complex circumstances.

As I approached the end of writing the book, I contacted the women whose stories are featured here to ask for their feedback and reflection. I also wanted to make sure that their stories were disguised enough that they would be recognizable only to themselves or to others who knew the intimate details of their lives. This was a somewhat daunting prospect, as I had sat with this data for years, mulling it over and making sense of it. But it comprised a mere snapshot of these women's lives. I was also concerned about their reactions to my analyses, wondering if they might feel misunderstood, mischaracterized, or criticized. I have been heartened to find that most thought my characterizations of them were accurate. While they did not all agree with my analyses, they found them to be respectful, thoughtful, and thought-provoking. I could not have asked for more.

DEMOGRAPHIC INFORMATION ABOUT RESPONDENTS

Name	Age and Year of Birth	Race/ Ethnicity	Class Background[a]	Religious Background	Sexual Orientation
Lillian	24 1979	Chinese immigrant	Poor/ working class	Buddhist	Queer[b]
Katie	25 1978	White	Upper middle class	Nonreligious; half Jewish	Straight
Mary	25 1978	Eastern European immigrant	Working/ lower middle class	Nonreligious	Bisexual[c]

[a] To identify class, I used a combination of parents' educational attainment and occupation. Because Americans so often underestimate their class background, with families earning $100,000 per year claiming to be middle class, not upper middle class, despite being in the top 20 percent of income earners, I did not ask my respondents to identify their class background but instead determined it myself.

[b] The term *queer* identifies one's sexuality or gender as nonnormative. In addition to homosexual and bisexual sexual orientations, the term seeks to encompass diverse sexual and gender practices and identities such as sadomasochism, butch/femme relations, transsexuality, transgendered identity, polyamory, and even gender-normative heterosexuals whose sexual practices or gender identifications place them outside the mainstream.

[c] Mary identifies as bisensual, but for the purpose of clarity and because her sexual practices match those of someone who is bisexual, I have termed her bisexual.

Name	Age and Year of Birth	Race/ Ethnicity	Class Background[a]	Religious Background	Sexual Orientation
Sophia	25 1978	Half black, half white	Working/ lower middle class	Nonreligious	Queer[b]
Taylor	25 1978	White	Upper middle class	Catholic	Straight
Phoebe	26 1977	White	Middle/ upper middle class	Christian	Straight
Claudia	28 1976	Mexican	Poor/ working class	Catholic	Straight
Mildred	27 1976	White	Upper middle class	Nonreligious	Lesbian
Mona	27 1976	South Asian	Working/ lower middle class	Muslim	Straight
Alicia	28 1975	Hispanic	Poor/ working class	Catholic	Straight
Emma	28 1975	Latina	Upper middle class	Jewish	Bisexual
Jeanette	28 1975	White	Poor/ working class	Christian	Queer[b]
Maria	28 1975	Latina/ Filipina	Middle/ upper middle class	Catholic	Straight

Name	Age and Year of Birth	Race/ Ethnicity	Class Background[a]	Religious Background	Sexual Orientation
Susan	28 1975	White	Upper middle class	Nonreligious	Queer[b]
Vida	28 1975	White Canadian	Working/ lower middle class	Nonreligious; half Jewish	Straight
Angel	29 1974	White	Upper middle class	Nonreligious	Bisexual
Carolina	29 1974	White	Upper middle class	Nonreligious	Bisexual
Cecilia	29 1974	Half Latina, half white	Upper middle class	Christian	Straight
Jayanthi	29 1974	South Asian	Upper middle class	Hindu	Straight
Mia	29 1974	Hispanic	Working/ lower middle class	Nonreligious	Lesbian

[a] To identify class, I used a combination of parents' educational attainment and occupation. Because Americans so often underestimate their class background, with families earning $100,000 per year claiming to be middle class, not upper middle class, despite being in the top 20 percent of income earners, I did not ask my respondents to identify their class background but instead determined it myself.

[b] The term *queer* identifies one's sexuality or gender as nonnormative. In addition to homosexual and bisexual sexual orientations, the term seeks to encompass diverse sexual and gender practices and identities such as sadomasochism, butch/femme relations, transsexuality, transgendered identity, polyamory, and even gender-normative heterosexuals whose sexual practices or gender identifications place them outside the mainstream.

NOTES

CHAPTER ONE. THE PARADOX
OF SEXUAL FREEDOM

1. Throughout the book, I use the terms that the women themselves used to describe their own race, ethnicity, or sexual orientation. Claudia described herself as Mexican, while Alicia (another interviewee) described herself as Hispanic, and still other respondents described themselves as Latina.

2. S. Roberts, "For Young Earners in Big City, a Gap in Women's Favor," *New York Times,* August 3, 2007; A. Williams, "The New Math on Campus," *New York Times,* February 10, 2010.

3. For an illuminating analysis of why this new developmental period of the childless twenties does not predominate among poor women, see K. Edin and M. Kefalas, *Promises I Can Keep: Why Poor Women Put Motherhood before Marriage* (Berkeley: University of California Press, 2005). The authors argue that young women with few educational and professional opportunities make the logical choice to have children as teenagers because the care and nurturance of a child are the one promise they can keep in the absence of reliable earning potential from either themselves or their partners. They may not be able to promise financial security to their children, but they can promise love. Delaying

childbearing makes no logical sense for women whose late teens and early twenties would likely be spent in minimum-wage and dead-end jobs. Edin and Kefalas argue that, for poor women, motherhood, unlike education or marriage, is a "sure thing" at which they feel they can succeed. Investment in education and marriage may result in failure and disappointment, but motherhood's rewards are tangible and guaranteed.

4. Whether the twenties constitute a new developmental period is under rigorous debate both in the field of psychology, where a developmental period must have distinctive developmental tasks and challenges that set it apart from other periods, and in the culture at large. In 2010, the *New York Times* recently ran a cover story in its Sunday magazine on twenty-somethings and the particular struggles they face (R. M. Henig, "What Is It about 20-Somethings?" *New York Times Magazine*, August 18, 2010). J.J. Arnett, a psychologist, is the chief proponent of the notion that the twenties constitute a distinctive life stage— "emerging adulthood" is what he terms it (*Emerging Adulthood: The Winding Road from the Late Teens through the Twenties* [Oxford: Oxford University Press, 2006]). See also R. Settersten and B. Ray, *Not Quite Adults: Why 20-Somethings Are Choosing a Slower Path to Adulthood, and Why It's Good for Everyone* (New York: Bantam, 2010); and K. Hymowitz, *Manning Up: How the Rise of Women Has Turned Men into Boys* (New York: Basic Books, 2011). I am less concerned with whether the twenties now constitute an official developmental stage than I am with the unique struggles that twenty-something women contend with, given the particular opportunities, limitations, and messages they face.

5. See B. Schwartz, *The Paradox of Choice: Why More Is Less* (New York: HarperPerennial, 2003), for the psychological research on why increased choices do not necessarily result in greater happiness and in fact make us more miserable because they increase our perception that something better must be out there but not within our reach. See also S. Iyengar, *The Art of Choosing* (New York: Twelve, 2011).

6. Sociology has paid scant attention to adult development, perhaps because it seems such an individual and not a social phenomenon. And yet some sociological theorists have noted the importance of

generational experiences to development at both an individual and a group level. See, for example, K. Mannheim, "The Problem of Generations," in his *Essays on the Sociology of Knowledge* (London: Routledge, 1972 [1952]), 276–320; and N. Chodorow, "Born into a World at War: Listening for Affect and Personal Meaning," *American Imago* 59, no. 3 (2002): 297–315. Individual development, while seemingly a psychological matter, is also a sociological matter when it takes a new form among groups of people subject to similar social influences. And experiences of sexuality, which are both profoundly personal and inevitably socially influenced, cannot be understood without studying individuals in depth.

7. E. Fein and S. Schneider, *The Rules: Time-Tested Secrets for Capturing the Heart of Mr. Right* (New York: Grand Central Publishing, 1996); G. Behrendt and L. Tuccillo, *He's Just Not That into You: The No Excuses Truth to Understanding Guys* (New York: Gallery, 2009); L. Gottlieb, *Marry Him: The Case for Settling for Mr. Good Enough* (New York: Dutton Adult, 2010).

8. L. S. Stepp, *Unhooked: How Young Women Pursue Sex, Delay Love, and Lose at Both* (New York: Riverhead Books, 2007); W. Shalit, *A Return to Modesty: Discovering the Lost Virtue* (New York: Touchstone, 2000).

9. Despite all these efforts and advances, there is still a clear ceiling in many fields beyond which most women do not advance. In 2006, only 23 percent of U.S. college presidents were women (American Council on Education, *The American College President, 2007 Edition* [Washington, DC: American Council on Education, 2007]). In 2010, only 16.6 percent of representatives in the House of Representatives and 17 percent of U.S. senators were women. Also, in 2010, only fifteen heads of Fortune 500 companies were women. Additionally, women continue to earn less than men (R. Drago and C. Williams, *The Gender Wage Gap: 2009* [Washington, DC: Institute for Women's Policy Research, 2009]).

10. B. Friedan, *The Feminine Mystique* (New York: W. W. Norton, 1963).

11. Such efforts were aided by the leadership of activists such as Gloria Steinem, cofounder of the feminist *Ms.* magazine, and

organizations such as the National Organization for Women (NOW), founded in 1966 by Betty Friedan, Shirley Chisholm, and others.

12. S. Brownmiller, *Against Our Will: Men, Women, and Rape* (New York: Simon and Schuster, 1975).

13. See, for example, G. Greer, *The Female Eunuch* (New York: McGraw-Hill Books, 1971); N.J. Chodorow, *The Reproduction of Mothering: Psychoanalysis and the Sociology of Gender* (Berkeley: University of California Press, 1978); and A. Rich, *Of Woman Born: Motherhood as Experience and Institution* (New York: W.W. Norton, 1976).

14. P. Orenstein ably chronicles the rise of princess culture in *Cinderella Ate My Daughter: Dispatches from the Front Lines of the New Girlie-Girl Culture* (New York: HarperCollins, 2011).

15. See B. Thorne's excellent *Gender Play: Girls and Boys in School* (New Brunswick, NJ: Rutgers University Press, 1993).

16. M. Sadker and D. Sadker, *Failing at Fairness: How Our Schools Cheat Girls* (New York: Scribner, 1995); D. Sadker and K. Zittleman, *Still Failing at Fairness: How Gender Bias Cheats Girls and Boys in School and What We Can Do about It* (New York: Scribner, 2009).

17. See J. Irvine, *Talk about Sex: The Battles over Sex Education in the United States* (Berkeley: University of California Press, 2004); K. Luker, *When Sex Goes to School: Warring Views on Sex—and Sex Education—since the Sixties* (New York: W.W. Norton, 2007); and J. Fields, *Risky Lessons: Sex Education and Social Inequality* (New Brunswick, NJ: Rutgers University Press, 2008). Psychologist M. Fine's research on sexual education in schools in the 1980s also shows the ways in which girls were taught to be subject to boys' desires and not to recognize their own sexual desires ("Sexuality, Schooling, and Adolescent Females: The Missing Discourse of Desire," *Harvard Educational Review* 58 [1988]: 29–53).

18. The labor-force participation rate among adult women was 34 percent in 1950 and rose to 38 percent in 1960, 43 percent in 1970, 52 percent in 1980, and 58 percent in 1990 (U.S. Department of Commerce, *Statistical Abstract of the United States 2010* [Washington, DC: Census Bureau, 2010]). Average weekly hours of child care performed by married fathers living with children under the age of eighteen increased

from 2.6 in 1965 to 6.5 in 2000 (S. M. Bianchi, J. P. Robinson, and M. A. Milkie, *Changing Rhythms of American Family Life* [New York: Russell Sage Foundation, 2006]).

19. Divorce rates rose sharply in the 1970s, climbing from 10 divorces per 1,000 married couples in 1970 to 22.8 divorces per 1,000 married couples in 1979 (B. Stevenson and J. Wolfers, "Marriage and Divorce: Changes and Their Driving Forces," *Journal of Economic Perspectives* 21, no. 2 [Spring 2007]: 27–52).

20. In 1960, married-couple households composed more than 78 percent of American households. By 2005, according to the recently released *American Community Survey* (U.S. Department of Commerce [Washington, DC: Census Bureau, 2005]), households with a married couple at their core made up fewer than 50 percent of all households (S. Coontz, "Marriage as Social Contract: The Decline in Married-Couple Households," *Philadelphia Inquirer,* October 20, 2006). In 2011, more adult Americans (75 percent) were living outside the conventional nuclear family, composed of two married parents and their biological children, than in it. These figures are based on 2010 census data.

21. J. Stacey, *Brave New Families: Stories of Domestic Upheaval in Late Twentieth-Century America* (New York: Basic Books, 1990).

22. A. R. Hochschild, *The Second Shift: Working Parents and the Revolution at Home* (New York: Avon Books, 1989); A. R. Hochschild, *The Time Bind: When Work Becomes Home and Home Becomes Work* (New York: Henry Holt, 1997).

23. See also K. Gerson, *The Unfinished Revolution: How a New Generation Is Reshaping Family, Work, and Gender in America* (New York: Oxford University Press, 2009). For more on the effects of this "speed-up" in families, see also J. Schor, *The Overworked American: The Unexpected Decline of Leisure* (New York: Basic Books, 1991), and P. Stone, *Opting Out? Why Women Really Quit Careers and Head Home* (Berkeley: University of California Press, 2007).

24. In the 1980s, relational theorists critiqued the movement for overvaluing traditional "masculine" values of competition, aggression, and individualism. Instead they advocated that women (and men) behave in accordance with traditional "feminine" values of coopera-

tion, interdependence, and care. C. Gilligan, *In a Different Voice: Psychological Theory and Human Development* (Cambridge, MA: Harvard University Press, 1982); J. B. Miller, *Toward a New Psychology of Women* (Boston: Beacon Press, 1976); and S. Ruddick, *Maternal Thinking: Towards a Politics of Peace* (Boston: Beacon Press, 1989).

25. J. Butler, "Gender Trouble, Feminist Theory, and Psychoanalytic Discourse," in L. Nicholson, ed., *Feminism/Postmodernism* (New York: Routledge, 1990), 324–40; J. Butler, "Melancholy Gender / Refused Identification," in J. Butler, *The Psychic Life of Power: Theories in Subjection* (Stanford, CA: Stanford University Press, 1997 [1995]), 132–50; and J. Halberstam, *Female Masculinity* (Durham, NC: Duke University Press, 1998).

26. G. Anzaldúa, "*La Conciencia de la Mestiza:* Towards a New Consciousness," in G. Anzaldúa, ed., *Making Face, Making Soul: Haciendo Caras: Creative and Critical Perspectives by Feminists of Color* (San Francisco: Aunt Lute Books, 1995), 377–89; b. hooks, *Feminist Theory: From Margin to Center* (Boston: South End Press, 1984); b. hooks, *Ain't I a Woman: Black Women and Feminism* (Boston: South End Press, 1999); and T. M. H. Trinh, *Woman, Native, Other: Writing Postcoloniality and Feminism* (Bloomington: Indiana University Press, 1989).

27. Also in the 1980s, feminist scholars such as Catharine MacKinnon and Andrea Dworkin argued that pornography and rape are forms of sex discrimination and that they terrorize women—serving to control all women's behavior and sexuality, not just those of its direct victims (A. Dworkin, *Pornography: Men Possessing Women* [New York: Plume, 1981]; C. MacKinnon, *Toward a Feminist Theory of the State* [Cambridge, MA: Harvard University Press, 1989]). See also S. Bright, *The Sexual State of the Union* (New York: Simon & Schuster, 1997); G. Rubin, "Thinking Sex: Notes for a Radical Theory of the Politics of Sexuality," in C. Vance, ed., *Pleasure and Danger* (Boston: Routledge, 1984), 143–78; and P. Califia, *Public Sex: The Culture of Radical Sex* (Berkeley: Cleis Press, 2000).

28. In 1960, the median house price-to-income ratio was 1.86. In 2008, it was 3.34 (Joint Center for Housing Studies of Harvard University, *The State of the Nation's Housing* [2010], www.jchs.harvard.edu/

publications/markets/son2010/son2010.pdf). From 1995 to 2003, even before the housing bubble of 2006, the proportion of middle-class Americans who could be considered "house poor" because they spend more than 40 percent of their earnings on housing quadrupled (E. Warren and A.W. Tyagi, *The Two-Income Trap: Why Middle-Class Mothers and Fathers Are Going Broke* [New York: Basic Books, 2003], 133, 202).

29. According to a report by the Center for American Progress and the Center for WorkLife Law at UC Hastings College of the Law using data from the *Current Population Survey*, 37.9 percent of professional men in 2006–8 worked more than fifty hours a week, up from 34 percent in 1977–79 (J.C. Williams and H. Boushey, *The Three Faces of Work-Family Conflict: The Poor, the Professionals, and the Missing Middle* [Center for WorkLife Law, University of California, Hastings College of the Law, and Center for American Progress, 2010], www.americanprogress.org/issues/2010/01/pdf/threefaces.pdf). See S.A. Hewlett and C.B. Luce, "Extreme Jobs: The Dangerous Allure of a 70-Hour Workweek," *Harvard Business Review* 4 (2006): 49–59, for an account of extreme jobs requiring seventy-hour work weeks, which now predominate among the professional class. See M. Blair-Loy and A.S. Wharton, "Mothers in Finance: Surviving and Thriving," *Annals of the American Academy of Political and Social Science* 596 (2004): 151–71, for a description of a new norm of work devotion that has arisen in the field of finance that is often difficult to sustain for women seeking to combine work and family life. For further analyses of the gendered effects of the trend toward over forty-hour work weeks, see J. Jacobs and K. Gerson, *The Time Divide: Work, Family, and Gender Inequality* (Cambridge, MA: Harvard University Press, 2004); Schor, *The Overworked American;* and Stone, *Opting Out?*

30. U.S. Department of Commerce, *Statistical Abstract of the United States 2010*. According to a report from the Pew Research Center, based on data from the National Center for Health Statistics and the Census Bureau, the average age of U.S. mothers who had their first baby in 2006 was twenty-five, a year older than the average first-time mother in 1990 (G. Livingston and D. Cohn, *The New Demography of American Motherhood* [Pew Research Center, 2010], http://pewsocialtrends.org/

pubs/754/new-demography-of-american-motherhood). During the period between 2000 and 2006, only 31 percent of women ages twenty-five to twenty-nine with a college degree had borne a child (J.L. Dye, *Fertility of American Women: 2006: Current Population Reports* [Washington, DC: U.S. Census Bureau, 2008], www.census.gov/prod/2008pubs/p20–558.pdf). See also T.J. Mathews and B.E. Hamilton, *Delayed Childbearing: More Women Are Having Their First Child Later in Life,* National Center for Health Statistics Data Brief no. 21 (Washington, DC: Centers for Disease Control and Prevention, August 2009), www.cdc.gov/nchs/data/databriefs/db21.htm.

31. These figures are based on data from the census's 2009 *Survey of Income and Program Participation,* www.census.gov/sipp/index.html.

32. U.S. Department of Commerce, *Statistical Abstract of the United States 2011* (Washington, DC: Census Bureau, 2011b).

33. Freud's initial foray into psychoanalysis began with his trying to help women who suffered from hysteria. Through his work with them, he developed the notion of the unconscious to account for the manifestation of physical symptoms such as paralysis, shortness of breath, tics, and loss of sense of smell when there was nothing physically wrong with the women (J. Breuer and S. Freud, 1953 [1895], "Studies on Hysteria," in *The Standard Edition of the Complete Psychological Works of Sigmund Freud,* vol. 2 [London: Hogarth Press], 1–319). These women were previously assumed to be incurable, or, if curable, then only by medical science. Freud believed there to be meaning in the symptoms the young women manifested. Along with his colleague Breuer and one of Breuer's patients, Anna O., Freud came upon the "talking cure." After trying hypnosis and other techniques, Freud, Breuer, and their patients used talking to trace symptoms back to their origins, which sometimes led to the elimination of the symptoms when fully understood and accounted for. They found that, from the point of view of a person's unconscious fantasies or beliefs, there is meaning in symptoms that may appear to be crazy and irrational. An unconscious part of the mind reflects desires, wishes, and fantasies that are not conscious to us in our waking lives but which inform the ways that we think, act, and feel. Physical symptoms can be traced to meaningful experiences that

caused such profound inner conflict that women developed the symptoms to manage the conflict. For example, one patient could not tolerate the anger and resentment that she felt over having to tend her dying father. Another patient could not tolerate the shame and anger that she felt at having been sexually abused by her father's friend. They both developed physical symptoms rather than consciously experiencing personally and socially unacceptable feelings.

34. See A. Swidler, *Talk of Love: How Culture Matters* (Chicago: University of Chicago Press, 2001), in which she describes unsettled times as situations "when new strategies of action are being developed and tried out" (89). See also B. D. Whitehead, *Why There Are No Good Men Left: The Romantic Plight of the New Single Woman* (New York: Broadway, 2002), in which she chronicles this unsettled time. While she focuses chiefly on the absence of men for highly educated women, she also makes the point that while highly educated women are trained for professional success, they are not trained for dating and marriage in this new time.

35. For a discussion of the ways in which danger has always been a powerful disincentive for women to be sexually free, see C. Vance, ed., *Pleasure and Danger: Exploring Female Sexuality,* 1st ed. (Boston: Routledge, 1984). In it various authors argue that, throughout the ages, danger has been a reason for women to avoid sex, be wary of it, and be careful about it. And several authors in the volume argue that danger threatens not just physical safety, but emotional safety as well.

36. Hochschild introduces the notion of gender strategy in *The Second Shift* as a "plan of action through which a person tries to solve the problems at hand, given the cultural notions of gender at play" (15). Swidler also uses the concept of strategies in *Talk of Love* to discuss the ways that individuals mobilize the cultural resources available to them to solve life's difficulties. She argues that culture powerfully influences social action by shaping the selves, skills, and worldviews out of which people can build life strategies. A. C. Wilkins, in her *Wannabes, Goths, and Christians: The Boundaries of Sex, Style, and Status* (Chicago: University of Chicago Press, 2008), argues that the various groups of young people she studied mobilized various strategies depending upon the

cultural projects they were engaged in to develop, express, and live their identities.

37. While sociologists recognize the ways in which strategies are not entirely consciously formulated, sociologists do not generally use the concept of unconscious defenses to understand or elaborate individuals' use of strategies. For an exception to this, see *The Second Shift,* in which Hochschild points to something like a defense in describing the myths that families develop to cover the mismatch between what they believe and what they actually do regarding the second shift.

38. Thirty percent of my respondents (n = 6) used strategies of the Sexual Woman.

39. Settersten and Ray, in *Not Quite Adults,* found similar feelings among twenty-something women whom they researched: "Wary is probably the best word to describe her and most of her peers' feelings towards marriage—wary of compromise, wary of giving up one's individuality, wary of missing out on something better" (84).

40. Twenty-five percent of my respondents (n = 5) used strategies of the Relational Woman.

41. Forty-five percent of my respondents (n = 9) used strategies of the Desiring Woman.

42. I use the terms for sexual orientation used by the women with whom I spoke. In recent years, *queer* has become a term to identify one's sexuality or gender as nonnormative. Feeling confined by the labels *lesbian* and *bisexual,* as those connote only sexual orientation, the term *queer* seeks to encompass diverse sexual and gender practices and identities such as sadomasochism, butch/femme relations, transsexuals, transgendered individuals, polyamory, and even gender-normative heterosexuals whose sexual practices or gender identifications place them outside the mainstream.

43. These data are from the *Annual Social and Economic Supplement (ASEC) to the 2009 Current Population Survey (CPS),* www.census.gov/apsd/techdoc/cps/cpsmar09.pdf.

44. Gary Gates, a demographer at the Williams Institute at the University of California, Los Angeles, School of Law, looked at data from several population-based surveys and concluded that 3.5 percent of

adults in the United States identify as lesbian, gay, or bisexual and that 8.2 percent of adults in the United States report that they have engaged in same-sex sexual behavior. He did not break down these statistics by age (G. Gates, "How Many People Are Lesbian, Gay, Bisexual, and Transgender?" [Williams Institute, 2011], http://wiwp.law.ucla.edu/wp-content/uploads/Gates-How-Many-People-LGBT-Apr-2011.pdf). The National Survey of Sexual Health and Behavior found that 7 percent of adult women identified as lesbian or bisexual (these statistics were not broken down by age), and that 10 percent of women ages twenty-five to twenty-nine surveyed had engaged in same-sex sexual behavior (D. Herbenick et al., "Sexual Behavior in the United States: Results from a National Probability Sample of Men and Women Ages 14–94," *Journal of Sexual Medicine* 7, suppl. 5 [2010]: 255–65).

45. Clinical interviewing borrows some techniques and areas of emphasis from clinical work with patients: a focus on unspoken communication as well as what is said, attention to the nature of the relationship between researcher and interviewee and what it may say about the interviewee, an understanding of anxiety and the ways in which it may signal something important about the interviewee, and attention to the impact of previous interactions on subsequent interactions between the researcher and the interviewee. Clinical interviewing is decidedly different from clinical work, however, in that it is not an explicitly therapeutic process. While participating in the interviews may have felt illuminating, challenging, and interesting to interviewees, my role in relation to them was an investigative one, not a therapeutic one. Clinical interviewing is also different from clinical work in that it does generally involve the use of an interview guide to structure the interviews, while still allowing for the kind of open-ended discussion that characterizes clinical work.

CHAPTER TWO. THE NEW TABOO

1. Various theorists who argue for the centrality of relationships in women's development include L. M. Brown and C. Gilligan, *Meeting at the Crossroads: Women's Psychology and Girls' Development* (Cambridge, MA: Harvard University Press, 1992); C. Gilligan, *In a Different Voice:*

Psychological Theory and Human Development (Cambridge, MA: Harvard University Press, 1982); C. Gilligan, A. G. Rogers, and D. L. Tolman, eds., *Women, Girls, and Psychotherapy: Reframing Resistance* (New York: Harrington Park Press, 1991); J. Jordan, *Relational-Cultural Therapy* (Washington, DC: American Psychological Association, 2009); and J. B. Miller, *Toward a New Psychology of Women* (Boston: Beacon Press, 1976).

2. When discussing interview respondents, I sometimes changed the year of their birth by one or two years to disguise their identities. Please see appendix II for a more thorough discussion of the measures taken to protect their privacy and mask their identities.

3. N. Gerstel and N. Sarkisian, "Marriage: The Good, the Bad, and the Greedy," *Contexts* 5 (2006): 16–21; N. Glenn and E. Marquardt, *Hooking Up, Hanging Out, and Hoping for Mr. Right: College Women on Mating and Dating Today* (New York: Institute for American Values, 2001); L. Hamilton and E. Armstrong, "Double Binds and Flawed Options: Gendered Sexuality in Early Adulthood," *Gender & Sexuality* 23 (2009): 589–616; and A. Swidler, *Talk of Love: How Culture Matters* (Chicago: University of Chicago Press, 2001), argue that, like marriage, committed relationships can be greedy and can take time or motivation away from the pursuit of professional goals.

4. The ways in which increased choices may in fact lead to more constraints on pursuit of one's goals is documented by psychologist B. Schwartz, *The Paradox of Choice: Why More Is Less* (New York: Harper-Perennial, 2003); and by S. Iyengar, *The Art of Choosing* (New York: Twelve, 2011).

5. D. Tolman, *Dilemmas of Desire: Teenage Girls Talk about Sexuality* (Cambridge, MA: Harvard University Press, 2005). See also M. Pipher, *Reviving Ophelia: Saving the Selves of Adolescent Girls* (New York: Ballantine Books, 1994); and P. Orenstein, *School Girls: Young Women, Self-Esteem, and the Confidence Gap* (New York: Anchor Books, 1994).

6. This polarization of men and women into sexually desiring subjects and sexually desired objects is documented and theorized by many, including J. Benjamin, *The Bonds of Love: Psychoanalysis, Feminism, and the Problem of Domination* (New York: Pantheon, 1988); M. Fine, "Sexuality, Schooling, and Adolescent Females: The Missing Discourse of

Desire," *Harvard Educational Review* 58 (1988): 29–53; K. Martin, *Puberty, Sexuality, and the Self: Girls and Boys at Adolescence* (New York: Routledge, 1996); L. Phillips, *Flirting with Danger: Young Women's Reflections on Sexuality and Domination* (New York: New York University Press, 2000); and Tolman, *Dilemmas of Desire.*

7. Boston Women's Health Collective, *Our Bodies, Ourselves: A New Edition for a New Era* (Boston: Touchstone, 2005).

8. Lynne Layton, a psychologist, calls this stance that some women develop defensive autonomy. It is defensive because it is based upon a fear of closeness, vulnerability, and interdependence. Layton argues, and my research supports her conclusions, that many highly educated upper-middle-class women may adopt a version of defensive autonomy that is not based on a true appreciation of the virtues of independence, which include a capacity for intimacy (L. Layton, "Relational No More: Defensive Autonomy in Middle-Class Women," in J. Winer and J. W. Anderson, eds., *The Annual of Psychoanalysis: Psychoanalysis and Women,* vol. 32 [Hillsdale, NJ: Analytic Press, 2004], 29–42).

9. Some argue that women's focus on relationships is instrumental and positive in women's development. Chief among these are Gilligan, *In a Different Voice;* and Miller, *Toward a New Psychology of Women.* Others argue for women's equal investment in the work world as a solution to their inattention to themselves. Key examples of this point of view include N. J. Chodorow, *The Reproduction of Mothering: Psychoanalysis and the Sociology of Gender* (Berkeley: University of California Press, 1978); H. Hartmann, "Capitalism, Patriarchy, and Job Segregation by Sex," *Signs* 1, no. 3 (1976): 137–69; and S. B. Ortner, "Is Female to Male as Nature Is to Culture?," in M. Z. Rosaldo and L. Lamphere, eds., *Woman, Culture, and Society* (Stanford, CA: Stanford University Press, 1974), 67–88.

10. See D. de Marneffe's excellent *Maternal Desire: On Children, Love, and the Inner Life* (New York: Little, Brown, 2004) for a nuanced exploration of the ways that splitting deprives us of the opportunity to know our complicated feelings about our desires. De Marneffe focuses specifically on the societal and internal prohibitions on maternal desire (the desire to devote time and energy to mothering one's children) for high-achieving women.

11. For well-elaborated explorations of the causes and consequences of this split, see Benjamin, *The Bonds of Love;* Chodorow, *The Reproduction of Mothering;* Rosaldo and Lamphere, eds., *Woman, Culture, and Society;* and G. Rubin, "The Traffic in Women: Notes toward a Political Economy of Sex," in R. Reiter, ed., *Toward an Anthropology of Women* (New York: Monthly Review Press, 1975), 157–210.

12. These findings are based on data gathered by the National Science Foundation in the "Survey of Doctorate Recipients," a biennial, weighted, longitudinal study that follows more than 160,000 PhD recipients across all disciplines until they reach age 76. Among tenured faculty twelve years after achieving their PhDs, 26 percent of women and only 11 percent of men were single and without children, while 11 percent of women and only 4 percent of men were divorced with children. Cited in M. Mason and M. Goulden, "Do Babies Matter? Part II: Closing the Baby Gap," *Academe* 90, no. 6 (December 2004): 10–15.

13. As S.J. Correll et al. found, sending out résumés that reveal someone is a mother (e.g., through mentioning PTA as an extracurricular activity) does indeed lead to fewer callbacks from employers for high-level jobs, so my colleague wasn't being paranoid (S.J. Correll, S. Benard, and I. Paik, "Getting a Job: Is There a Motherhood Penalty?" *American Journal of Sociology* 112 [2007]: 1297–1338).

14. A. Williams, "Putting Money on the Table," *New York Times,* September 23, 2007.

CHAPTER THREE. THE BAD GIRL

1. While race and ethnicity shaped the ways in which my respondents' sexuality was received by others, they did not markedly influence my respondents' experiences of sexuality in any systematic way. That is, while race and ethnicity were factors in my respondents' sexual development, they did not cause my respondents to differ from one another according to race. This may be due to my relatively small sample size; or to self-selection, education, and class trumping race and ethnicity; or to my respondents' common experience of college. Throughout the book, then, I discuss the influence of race and ethnic-

ity on each particular woman and each woman's particular experience of sexualized or desexualized representations of women in the racial or ethnic group to which they belong.

2. A. Levy documents the rise of what she terms "raunch culture" in *Female Chauvinist Pigs: Women and the Rise of Raunch Culture* (New York: Free Press, 2006). She charts the rise in pressure on young women to adopt a stance of being a female chauvinist pig. But, she argues, in doing so they essentially open themselves up to being used by men. The rise of raunch culture, she argues, makes it acceptable and even required that young, liberated women make themselves into "liberated" objects of desire.

3. I argue here explicitly against the poststructuralist notion of a sturdy identity as merely a defensive formation to ward off anxieties about the inherently fractured and multiple nature of identity. Poststructuralists focus on the ultimately fragmented nature of identity, arguing that structuralism's assumptions of a unitary and constant identity that is consistent across space and time are merely defensive strategies with which we blindly comfort ourselves. See, for example, T. M. H. Trinh, *Woman, Native, Other: Writing Postcoloniality and Feminism* (Bloomington: Indiana University Press, 1989); and J. Butler, "Gender Trouble, Feminist Theory, and Psychoanalytic Discourse," in L. Nicholson, ed., *Feminism/Postmodernism* (New York: Routledge, 1990), 324–40. I argue instead, along with other feminist psychoanalytic theorists, for the importance of a sturdy yet flexible identity: see D. Bassin, "Beyond the He and the She: Toward the Reconciliation of Masculinity and Femininity in the Postoedipal Mind," *Journal of the American Psychoanalytical Association* 44, suppl. (1996): 157–90; M. Dimen, "Deconstructing Difference: Gender, Splitting, and Transitional Space," *Psychoanalytic Dialogues* 1, no. 3 (1991): 335–52; D. Elise, "Gender Repertoire: Body, Mind, and Bisexuality," *Psychoanalytic Dialogues* 8, no. 3 (1998): 353–71; V. Goldner, "Toward a Critical Relational Theory of Gender," *Psychoanalytic Dialogues* 1, no. 3 (1991): 249–72; A. Harris, "Gender as Contradiction," *Psychoanalytic Dialogues* 1, no. 2 (1991): 197–224; and A. Sweetnam, "The Changing Contexts of Gender: Between Fixed and Fluid Experience," *Psychoanalytic Dialogues* 6, no. 4 (1996): 437–59.

4. See N.J. Chodorow, *The Reproduction of Mothering: Psychoanalysis and the Sociology of Gender* (Berkeley: University of California Press, 1978); D. Dinnerstein, *The Mermaid and the Minotaur: Sexual Arrangements and Human Malaise* (New York: HarperCollins, 1976); and J. Benjamin, *The Bonds of Love: Psychoanalysis, Feminism, and the Problem of Domination* (New York: Pantheon, 1988), for original and influential accounts of the origins of various gendered versions of subjectivity in which men are generally experienced as subjects and women as objects. They each also speak to the dilemmas we confront when we persist in our cultural and individual insistence on being only a subject or only an object. See also my review of psychoanalytic theories of gender: L.C. Bell, "Psychoanalytic Theories of Gender," in A. Eagly et al., eds., *The Psychology of Gender,* 2nd ed. (New York: Guilford Press, 2005), 145–68.

5. Benjamin, *The Bonds of Love;* and psychoanalyst S. Mitchell, *Can Love Last? The Fate of Romance over Time* (New York: W.W. Norton, 1998), both provide accounts of the difficulties we have in maintaining closeness and individuality. Psychoanalyst and social theorist Benjamin argues that in a social structure characterized by sexual domination, closeness within heterosexual relationships comes to mean that one partner (generally the man) is granted subjectivity, and the other (generally the woman) is the object to the man's subjectivity. Thus, within heterosexual relationships, both partners maintaining their individuality and subjectivity is structurally difficult, if not impossible. Psychoanalyst Mitchell documents the ways in which couples may have difficulty retaining the knowledge of their separateness. Acknowledging that the person on whom you most depend is an independent actor capable not only of loving and supporting you, but also of betraying you and causing you pain, is a difficult challenge. And too often couples fall into the pattern of believing their partners to be extensions of themselves, rather than free agents. So Jayanthi was not alone in fearing the coexistence of closeness and separateness. But unlike the couples Mitchell describes, she chose to avoid closeness in relationships in order not to lose her separateness and strong identity.

6. See Benjamin, *The Bonds of Love;* and S. Contratto, "Father Presence in Women's Psychological Development," in J. Rabow and G.

Platt, eds., *Advances in Psychoanalytic Sociology* (Malabar, FL: Krieger, 1987), 138–57, for important accounts of the trouble that may ensue when fathers withdraw from their daughters.

7. J.B. Miller, *Toward a New Psychology of Women* (Boston: Beacon Press, 1976); and C. Gilligan, *In a Different Voice: Psychological Theory and Human Development* (Cambridge, MA: Harvard University Press, 1982), are the chief proponents of self-in-relation theory. Both argue that relationship and connection are instrumental in women's development and in women's identity. Miller argues for a new psychology of women that neither pathologizes nor ignores the particularities of women's experiences. Traditional psychoanalytic theorists maintained that development occurs through separation and individuation, but that this experience is often incomplete for women. Miller argues that women develop in the context of attachment and affiliation with others. This mode of development has been unrecognized and its outcome undervalued. Gilligan argues that boys and girls arrive at puberty with different interpersonal orientations and different ranges of social experiences. Since traditional psychoanalytic theorists have considered adolescence such a crucial time for separation, she does not find it surprising that female development has appeared most divergent from that of boys and most challenging at this point. She seeks to account for what adolescent girls are doing at adolescence, how they are distinct from boys, and why. According to Gilligan, relationships have been important in psychoanalytic theories of development only as they give way to the important goals of separation and individuation. For girls, however, relationships tend to continue to be important in their own right, making girls seem less than fully mature in the traditional models.

L. Kohlberg, *Essays on Moral Development,* vol. 1: *The Philosophy of Moral Development* (San Francisco: Harper & Row, 1981); D.J. Levinson, *The Seasons of a Man's Life* (New York: Ballantine, 1978); and G. Vaillant, *Adaptation to Life* (Boston: Little, Brown, 1977), are chief among the earlier male models.

8. Some second-wave psychoanalytic theorists—Chodorow, *The Reproduction of Mothering,* and Benjamin, *The Bonds of Love,* chief among

them—have a less essentializing, more socially constructed approach to understanding women's development. They argue that women are likely to be more relationship oriented than men as a result of culture, economy, and family structure.

9. On poststructural theories of gender identity and development, see, for example, J. Butler, "Melancholy Gender/Refused Identification," in J. Butler, *The Psychic Life of Power: Theories in Subjection* (Stanford, CA: Stanford University Press, 1997 [1995]), 132–50; and J. Halberstam, *Female Masculinity* (Durham, NC: Duke University Press, 1998). On feminist psychoanalytic theories of gender identity and development, see, for example, J. Benjamin, *Like Subjects, Love Objects: Essays on Recognition and Sexual Difference* (New Haven, CT: Yale University Press, 1995); J. Benjamin, *Shadow of the Other: Intersubjectivity and Gender in Psychoanalysis* (New York: Routledge, 1998); Bassin, "Beyond the He and the She"; Dimen, "Deconstructing Difference"; Elise, "Gender Repertoire"; Goldner, "Toward a Critical Relational Theory of Gender"; Harris, "Gender as Contradiction"; and Sweetnam, "The Changing Contexts of Gender."

But within popular culture, essentialism abounds when it comes to gender—I continue to be surprised when undergraduates wish to cite John Gray, *Men Are from Mars, Women Are from Venus* (New York: Harper, 1992), as a legitimate theory of gender.

CHAPTER FOUR. A PILL TO KILL DESIRE

1. Claudia's description of her experience of desire sounded remarkably similar to descriptions of adolescent male sexual desire—out of control, unbidden, powerful, and not always welcome. In some sense, Claudia sounded like a stereotypical adolescent American boy with "raging hormones" (A. Schalet, "Raging Hormones, Regulated Love: Adolescent Sexuality and the Constitution of the Modern Individual in the United States and the Netherlands," *Body & Society* 6, no. 1 [2000]: 75–105).

2. In L. Phillips, *Flirting with Danger: Young Women's Reflections on Sexuality and Domination* (New York: New York University Press, 2000), the

author interviewed a racially diverse group of college-age women and sought to understand how subjectivity and agency may be possible in the face of sexual aggression and domination in heterosexual sex and relationships. She found that girls often rewrite their experiences of aggression and domination in sex to feel themselves to have been more in control than they actually were. There was resistance to recognizing aggression and domination in their own lives, so new notions of empowerment, while positive in some sense, also served to make girls less likely to report rape or sexual assault. No one wants to be a "victim."

3. E. Fein and S. Schneider, *The Rules: Time-Tested Secrets for Capturing the Heart of Mr. Right* (New York: Grand Central Publishing, 1996); M. Titus and T. Fadal, *Why Hasn't He Called? New York's Top Date Doctors Reveal How Guys Really Think and How to Get the Right One Interested* (New York: McGraw-Hill, 2008).

4. The difference between the current specter of the ho and the old threat of the whore is that there is a brief reprieve from it during the decade of the twenties. This respite follows the period of adolescence, during which my respondents reported that being labeled a whore was still a fearsome thing. See L. Tanenbaum, *Slut: Growing Up Female with a Bad Reputation* (New York: Harper, 2000), for an account of how girls are held hostage by the threat of being labeled a slut. By contrast, in earlier eras, women were either a madonna or a whore throughout their lives. There was little fluidity, and little reprieve from the categories.

5. L. S. Stepp is chief among these handwringers in her *Unhooked: How Young Women Pursue Sex, Delay Love, and Lose at Both* (New York: Riverhead Books, 2007). For several well-researched pieces on the phenomenon of hooking up, see E. Armstrong, L. Hamilton, and P. England, "Is Hooking Up Bad for Young Women?" *Contexts* 9, no. 3 (August 2010): 22–27; K. Bogle, *Hooking Up: Sex, Dating, and Relationships on Campus* (New York: New York University Press, 2008); P. England, E. F. Shafer, and A. C. K. Fogarty, "Hooking Up and Forming Romantic Relationships on Today's College Campuses," in M. Kimmel and A. Aronson, eds., *The Gendered Society Reader,* 3rd ed. (New York: Oxford University Press, 2008), 531–46; N. Glenn and E. Marquardt, *Hooking Up,*

Hanging Out, and Hoping for Mr. Right: College Women on Mating and Dating Today (New York: Institute for American Values, 2001); and L. Hamilton and E. Armstrong, "Double Binds and Flawed Options: Gendered Sexuality in Early Adulthood," *Gender & Sexuality* 23 (2009): 589–616.

6. See C. Knapp, *Appetites: Why Women Want* (New York: Counterpoint Press, 2003), on female desire and wanting, and the ways in which women have been socialized not to want and to remain always in control. See also M. Fine's seminal article on adolescent female desire, "Sexuality, Schooling, and Adolescent Females: The Missing Discourse of Desire," *Harvard Educational Review* 58 (1988): 29–53; and D. Tolman's work on girls' experience of desire, *Dilemmas of Desire: Teenage Girls Talk about Sexuality* (Cambridge, MA: Harvard University Press, 2005). Fine argues that we lack a language of desire for girls, and that the antisex rhetoric surrounding sex education and school-based health clinics does little to enhance the development of sexual responsibility and subjectivity in adolescents. Tolman concludes that girls' experience of sexual desire and sexual subjectivity is complicated by our insistence on sexual objecthood for girls.

CHAPTER FIVE. THE GOOD GIRL

1. H. Brückner and P. Bearman ("After the Promise: The STD Consequences of Adolescent Virginity Pledges," *Journal of Adolescent Health* 36 [2005]: 271–78) find that communities with high rates of abstinence pledging among teens also have high rates of STDs. This could be because more teens pledge in communities where they perceive more danger from sex (in which case the pledge is doing some good), or it could be because fewer people in these communities use condoms when they break the pledge.

2. See chapter 1, note 3, on why many poor women put motherhood before marriage.

3. See J. Bettie, *Women without Class: Girls, Race, and Identity* (Berkeley: University of California Press, 2003), for an excellent account of how most working-class Latina girls grow into working-class lives, which is what Alicia was working so hard to avoid.

4. According to a 2007 report from the National Center for Education Statistics (*Status and Trends in the Education of Racial and Ethnic Minorities, NCES 2007–0039* [Washington, DC: U.S. Department of Education, 2007]), black women received twice as many associate's, bachelor's, and postsecondary degrees as their male counterparts between 2003 and 2004 (67 percent versus 33 percent)—a larger disparity between genders than in any other racial group. In 2001, Hispanic women were awarded 60 percent of associate's and bachelor's degrees conferred to Hispanic undergraduates, and Hispanic men only 40 percent. Similarly, and only slightly less dramatically, in 2001, white women were awarded 57 percent of associate's and bachelor's degrees conferred on white undergraduates, and white men only 43 percent (National Center for Education Statistics, *Gender Differences in Participation and Completion of Undergraduate Education and How They Have Changed over Time* [Washington, DC: U.S. Department of Education, 2005]).

5. Legal scholars N. Cahn and J. Carbone ("Red Families v. Blue Families," *GWU Legal Studies Research Paper* 343 [August 16, 2007]) identify what they term "the new middle-class morality," which involves delaying family formation until the late twenties or early thirties. This new morality correlates more closely to blue-state demographic patterns, and presumably Alicia's childhood, spent in Northern California, a model of blue-state demographic patterns, influenced her determination to delay family formation.

6. Alicia's experience with a man who was selfish while she catered to his needs is all too common among women, although more frequent in casual sexual encounters than in committed relationships. Recent evidence from a study by E. A. Armstrong, P. England, and A. Fogarty ("Orgasm in College Hookups and Relationships," in B. Risman, ed., *Families as They Really Are* [New York: W. W. Norton, 2010], 362–77), in which they surveyed twelve thousand college students across the country, shows that as the degree of the relationship progressed (e.g., from first hook-up to repeat hook-up to committed relationship), the more likely both sex partners were to orgasm. However, this was not equally true for men and women: women orgasm close to 80 percent as often as men do in close relationships, but only 32 percent as often in first

hook-ups. Armstrong et al.'s evidence suggests that men engaged in hook-ups are less invested in their partners' pleasure than they are when in relationships, performing cunnilingus more frequently and regularly as the relationship progresses.

7. Guttmacher Institute, *Facts on Sexually Transmitted Infections in the United States* (New York: Guttmacher Institute, 2009); C. Willard, "Estimates of the Incidence and Prevalence of Sexually Transmitted Diseases in the United States," *Sexually Transmitted Diseases* 26, no. 4 (1999): S2–S7.

8. E. Fein and S. Schneider, *The Rules: Time-Tested Secrets for Capturing the Heart of Mr. Right* (New York: Grand Central Publishing, 1996).

CHAPTER SIX. ON NOT HAVING IT ALL

1. See A. Hochschild, *The Time Bind: When Work Becomes Home and Home Becomes Work* (New York: Henry Holt, 1997); and J. Schor, *The Overworked American: The Unexpected Decline of Leisure* (New York: Basic Books, 1991). For statistics on sexual satisfaction among women, see the National Survey of Sexual Health and Behavior, "Findings from the National Survey of Sexual Health and Behavior (NSSHB), Center for Sexual Health Promotion, Indiana University," *Journal of Sexual Medicine* 7, suppl. 5 (2010): 243–373. In this survey, researchers found that 64 percent of women reported having had an orgasm at their most recent sexual event, compared to 85 percent of men. See also E. Laumann, J.H. Gagnon, R.T. Michael, and S. Michaels, *The Social Organization of Sexuality: Sexual Practices in the United States* (Chicago: University of Chicago Press, 1994). In this survey, researchers found that 29 percent of women reported always having an orgasm with their partner, compared to 75 percent of men.

2. For evidence of the positive relationship among athletics, self-esteem, and positive body image, see M. Colton and S. Gore, *Risk, Resiliency, and Resistance: Current Research on Adolescent Girls* (New York: Ms. Foundation, 1991); S. Gadbois and A. Bowker, "Gender Differences in the Relationships between Extracurricular Activities Participation, Self-Description, and Domain-Specific and General Self-Esteem," *Sex*

Roles: A Journal of Research 56, nos. 9–10 (2007): 675–89; C. Greenleaf, E. M. Boyer, and T. A. Petrie, "High School Sport Participation and Subsequent Psychological Well-Being and Physical Activity: The Mediating Influences of Body Image, Physical Competence, and Instrumentality," *Sex Roles: A Journal of Research* 61, nos. 9–10 (2009): 714–26.

3. Her mother doled out advice similar to that dispensed in the recent self-help book by L. Gottlieb, *Marry Him: The Case for Settling for Mr. Good Enough* (New York: Dutton Adult, 2010).

4. See, for example, the now notorious article by Lisa Belkin, "The Opt-Out Revolution," *New York Times Magazine,* October 26, 2003, profiling high-achieving women whom the author characterizes as opting out of high-powered careers in order to stay home with their children. Since that article's publication, researchers have focused on understanding whether opting out is indeed as widespread a phenomenon as it's perceived to be, and on understanding why some women might opt out. See, for example, P. Stone, *Opting Out? Why Women Really Quit Careers and Head Home* (Berkeley: University of California Press, 2007); and J. C. Williams and H. Boushey, *The Three Faces of Work-Family Conflict: The Poor, the Professionals, and the Missing Middle* (Berkeley: Center for WorkLife Law, University of California, Hastings College of the Law, and Center for American Progress, 2010), 56, www.americanprogress .org/issues/2010/01/pdf/threefaces.pdf, in which the authors find that having a husband who works more than fifty hours a week increases the odds of a woman quitting her job by 44 percent. Having a husband who works more than sixty hours a week increases her odds of quitting by 112 percent. Both publications argue that rather than opting out of work, women in high-powered careers are being forced out by the expectations for "extreme work" that now predominate.

5. See, for example, K. Gerson, *Unfinished Revolution: How a New Generation Is Reshaping Family, Work, and Gender in America* (Oxford: Oxford University Press, 2009); and P. Orenstein, *Flux: Women on Sex, Work, Love, Kids, and Life in a Half-Changed World* (New York: Anchor, 2001).

6. Gerson, in *Unfinished Revolution,* also finds evidence of twenty-somethings scaling down their expectations about the degree to which

they'll be able to have it all; and Stone, in *Opting Out?* finds that women who appear to be opting out by leaving their careers are in fact often feeling pushed out by workplace demands for well over fifty-hour work weeks.

7. See, for example, A. Lareau, *Unequal Childhoods: Class, Race, and Family Life* (Berkeley: University of California Press, 2003).

8. See Orenstein, *Flux*, in which she coins the term "half-changed world."

CHAPTER SEVEN. HOW DOES SHE DO IT?

1. See L. Tanenbaum, *Slut: Growing Up Female with a Bad Reputation* (New York: Harper, 2000), for an account of how not just sexual activity, but the slightest deviation from social norms, can earn girls the reputation of a "slut." This is similar to the dynamic at work in C.J. Pascoe's excellent *Dude, You're a Fag: Masculinity and Sexuality in High School* (Berkeley: University of California Press, 2007), in which boys are subject to the specter of the "fag" in order to police and control their masculinity.

2. Sexual orientation certainly played a role in my respondents' sexual development, and it did so in a systematic way. I found more acknowledgment of multiple desires (for sex, intimacy, and independence) among my queer respondents than I did among my straight respondents. I discuss this finding further in chapter 9.

3. L. Diamond, *Sexual Fluidity: Understanding Women's Love and Desire* (Cambridge, MA: Harvard University Press, 2009).

CHAPTER EIGHT. MAYBE SHE'S BORN WITH IT

1. Some researchers have found that a factor more important than strength of religiosity is the nature of the religion, with Catholicism engendering more guilt and shame about sex, and conservative evangelical churches being relatively unsuccessful in promoting abstinence, guilt, and shame. See, for example, A.M. Burdette and T.D. Hill, "Religious Involvement and Transitions into Adolescent Sexual Activities,"

Sociology of Religion 70, no. 1 (2009): 28–48; and A. Ovadia and L. M. Moore, "Decomposing the Moral Community: Religious Contexts and Teen Childbearing," *City & Community* 9, no. 3 (2010): 320–34.

2. We have ample documentation that what we've historically considered a "traditional family structure" is not necessarily as predominant as it once was. Census Bureau statistics from 2004 indicate that 60 percent of children were living with both biological parents, while 40 percent were living in a variety of other family forms (S. Roberts, "Most Children Still Live in Two-Parent Homes, Census Bureau Reports," *New York Times,* February 21, 2008). See also J. Stacey, *Brave New Families: Stories of Domestic Upheaval in Late Twentieth-Century America* (New York: Basic Books, 1990).

CHAPTER NINE. CONCLUSION

1. E. Fein and S. Schneider, *The Rules: Time-Tested Secrets for Capturing the Heart of Mr. Right* (New York: Grand Central Publishing, 1996).

2. Many women's experiences of sexual coercion, assault, and exploitation are the absolute opposite of this developmental model. They are treated as a body and not a person and their own desires are made irrelevant. In a nation in which one out of every six American women has been or will be the victim of an attempted or completed rape in her lifetime (National Institute of Justice, *Prevalence, Incidence, and Consequences of Violence against Women: Findings from the National Violence against Women Survey* [Washington, DC: National Institute of Justice, U.S. Department of Justice; Centers for Disease Control and Prevention, 1998]), we need to change the sexual landscape so that these experiences will be anomalous and uncommon. In our families, schools, churches, and communities, boys and girls both must be raised and educated to be sexual subjects, not sexual objects or sexual aggressors. The judicial system must be reformed so that more victims of sexual assault can press charges and win their cases. For example, a 2004 study of sex crimes in Philadelphia and Kansas City, Missouri, found that only half of the cases that resulted in an arrest were prosecuted (C. Bushey, "Why Don't More Women Sue Their Rapists?

Because the Supreme Court Took Away Part of the Violence against Women Act," *Slate,* May 26, 2010).

3. J. Benjamin (*The Bonds of Love: Psychoanalysis, Feminism, and the Problem of Domination* [New York: Pantheon Books, 1988]) argues that early experiences with assertive parents are crucial to girls for purposes of both identification and practice. With an assertive mother, a girl may develop the sense that she too can be strong and have desires of her own. And with an assertive father who values and nurtures her, a girl may develop the sense that she can expect a similar reception from boys and other men in her life.

4. Such a father receives his daughter not as a nascent sex object, which Benjamin, in *The Bonds of Love,* identifies as a problematic experience for many women, but as a smart, competent, and agentic person with ideas, thoughts, and feelings of her own. Feminist psychoanalytic theorists have identified these experiences with parents as important to development: M. Jay ("Melancholy Femininity and Obsessive-Compulsive Masculinity: Sex Differences in Melancholy Gender," *Studies in Gender and Sexuality* 8 [2007]: 115–35) emphasizes the importance of a strong attachment to a mother who is not a caricature of gender in developing inclusive and nonmelancholic gender identifications, and K. Martin (*Puberty, Sexuality, and the Self: Girls and Boys at Adolescence* [New York: Routledge, 1996]) highlight the importance of a recognizing father in girls' development of subjectivity.

5. While many of the women with whom I spoke had difficulty asserting themselves in relationships, women (Alicia, Taylor, Mia, Vida) who had particularly limited or troubled relationships with their fathers found the struggle to be especially challenging. In Martin's study of teenage sexuality, *Puberty, Sexuality, and the Self,* she also found this to be the case among teenage girls. She found that these relationships varied by class, so that girls from poor and working-class backgrounds were more likely to have limited or troubled relationships with their fathers. She found that upper-middle-class girls were more likely to have fathers who were involved in their daughters' lives in positive ways—coaching sports teams, encouraging their daughters' achievements—and that this provided

some protection from later sexual exploitation among these girls. My findings support Martin's to a certain degree, but I would also argue that a critical ingredient in girls' developing comfort with assertion involves having parents (both mothers and fathers) who assert themselves productively and allow their daughters to practice doing the same.

6. Of those nine women I spoke with who managed to get what they wanted, seven were queer and two were straight (seven-ninths = 78 percent).

7. Straight women made up about two-thirds (67 percent) of women using strategies of the Sexual Woman, and four-fifths (80 percent) of women using strategies of the Relational Woman.

8. See, for example, J. M. Irvine, *Talk about Sex: The Battles over Sex Education in the United States* (Berkeley: University of California Press, 2004); and K. Luker, *When Sex Goes to School: Warring Views on Sex—and Sex Education—since the Sixties* (New York: W. W. Norton, 2007).

9. M. Fine, "Sexuality, Schooling, and Adolescent Females: The Missing Discourse of Desire," *Harvard Educational Review* 58 (1988): 29–53. See also J. Fields, *Risky Lessons: Sex Education and Social Inequality* (New Brunswick, NJ: Rutgers University Press, 2008).

10. P. Tjaden and N. Thoennes, *Full Report of the Prevalence, Incidence, and Consequences of Violence against Women: Findings from the National Violence against Women Survey* (Washington, DC: U.S. Department of Justice, 2000).

11. See P. Stone, *Opting Out? Why Women Really Quit Careers and Head Home* (Berkeley: University of California Press, 2007); and E. Leonhardt, "A Labor Market Punishing to Mothers," *New York Times,* Business section, August 3, 2010.

12. K. Gerson (*The Unfinished Revolution: How a New Generation Is Reshaping Family, Work, and Gender in America* [New York: Oxford University Press, 2009]) finds, in her study of young adults, that a majority of young men (68 percent of her sample) and young women (80 percent of her sample) may hold what she describes as an egalitarian ideal, expressing the belief that men and women *ought* to share equally the responsibilities for work and family life in their marriages. However,

when asked to imagine what will *actually* happen in their work and family lives, given the exigencies of the workplace (where work often exceeds sixty hours per week), family life, and a demand for intensive parenting, or what A. Lareau (*Unequal Childhoods: Class, Race, and Family Life* [Berkeley: University of California Press, 2003]) calls "concerted cultivation," which requires an intense investment of time and energy in one's children and their development, a majority of men in her sample (70 percent) fall back to a neotraditional strategy. Gerson writes, "Worried about time-greedy workplaces and convinced that work remains at the core of manly success, they hope to avoid the sacrifices of equal sharing through a neotraditional arrangement in which they can continue to place a high priority on work while their partner provides more of the caregiving" (123). Meanwhile, a majority of women in Gerson's sample (73 percent) fall back on a self-reliant strategy. "Hoping to avoid being stuck in an unhappy marriage or deserted by an unfaithful spouse, these women see paid work as essential to their survival and to the well-being of any children they might bear. Women look to self-reliance and personal autonomy, within and outside the boundaries of marriage, to protect against economic dependence on a partner or personal malaise in domesticity" (122–23).

13. Stone, in *Opting Out?*—her study of high-achieving women who seemingly opt out of their careers to stay home with their children—notes that "there exists among these high-achieving stay-at-home mothers a large unmet demand to work, specifically an unmet demand to work flexibly in their high-status, high-knowledge professional and executive fields without incurring huge penalties" (220). She suggests that instead of describing these women as opting out, we should more accurately describe them as being shut out of their high-status, high-knowledge careers.

14. M. Cooper (*Doing Security in Insecure Times: Class and Family Life in Silicon Valley*, PhD diss., University of California, Berkeley, 2008) describes the "upscaling" of security at the top of the income ladder, such that the amount of money upper-income people consider necessary to feel "secure" requires incomes that are achievable only by extremely time-intensive jobs.

APPENDIX I. SPLITTING

1. M. Klein, "Notes on Some Schizoid Mechanisms," in J. Mitchell, ed., *The Selected Melanie Klein* (New York: Free Press, [1946] 1986), 175–200.

2. J. Benjamin, *The Bonds of Love: Psychoanalysis, Feminism, and the Problem of Domination* (New York: Pantheon Books, 1988); N. J. Chodorow, *The Reproduction of Mothering: Psychoanalysis and the Sociology of Gender* (Berkeley: University of California Press, 1978); J. Chasseguet-Smirgel, *Sexuality and Mind: The Role of the Father and the Mother in the Psyche* (New York: New York University Press, 1986); D. Dinnerstein, *The Mermaid and the Minotaur: Sexual Arrangements and Human Malaise* (New York: HarperCollins, 1976).

3. J. Butler, "Gender Trouble, Feminist Theory, and Psychoanalytic Discourse," in L. Nicholson, ed., *Feminism/Postmodernism* (New York: Routledge, 1990), 324–40; J. Halberstam, *Female Masculinity* (Durham, NC: Duke University Press, 1998); T. de Lauretis, "Queer Theory: Lesbian and Gay Sexualities," *Differences: A Journal of Feminist Cultural Studies* 3, no. 2 (1991): iii–xviii; F. Fanon, *Black Skin, White Masks* (New York: Grove Press, [1952] 1967); E. Sedgwick, *Epistemology of the Closet* (Berkeley: University of California Press, 1990); and T. T. Minh-ha, *Woman, Native, Other: Writing Postcoloniality and Feminism* (Bloomington: Indiana University Press, 1989).

4. Butler, "Gender Trouble"; de Lauretis, "Queer Theory"; F. Fanon, *Black Skin, White Masks;* M. Foucault, *The History of Sexuality* (New York: Vintage Books, [1978] 1990); and Sedgwick, *Epistemology of the Closet.*

5. Benjamin, *The Bonds of Love.*

APPENDIX II. CLINICAL INTERVIEWING

1. See, for example, L. Irigaray, *This Sex Which Is Not One* (Ithaca, NY: Cornell University Press, 1985); and J. Kristeva, *In the Beginning Was Love: Psychoanalysis and Faith* (New York: Columbia University Press, 1987).

2. M. Fine, "Sexuality, Schooling, and Adolescent Females: The Missing Discourse of Desire," *Harvard Educational Review* 58 (1988): 29–53.

3. E. S. Person, "From Sexual Desire to Excitement: The Role of Sexual Fantasy," in E. Person, *The Sexual Century* (New Haven, CT: Yale University Press, 1999), 211–29.

4. N. J. Chodorow, *The Power of Feelings: Personal Meaning in Psychoanalysis, Gender, and Culture* (New Haven, CT: Yale University Press, 1999).

5. I was concerned about the problem of self-selection were I to advertise the study; I imagined that the people who would agree to speak with a stranger about their sexuality for four and a half to six hours would likely be sex-positive activists or people for whom sexuality was an organizing feature of their public lives. I still confronted the problem of self-selection in that respondents needed to be willing and interested enough to speak with a relative stranger, albeit one whose credibility was vouched for by a friend, for several hours about their sexuality.

6. U.S. Department of Commerce, *State and County QuickFacts* (Washington, DC: Census Bureau, 2011a).

7. See, for example, K. Anderson and D. C. Clark, "Learning to Listen," in S. Gluck and D. Patai, eds., *Women's Words: The Feminist Practice of Oral History* (New York: Routledge, 1990), 11–26; K. Borland, "That's Not What I Said," in Gluck and Patai, eds., *Women's Words,* 63–76; S. Harding, "Introduction: Is There a Feminist Method?" in S. Harding, ed., *Feminism and Methodology* (Bloomington: Indiana University Press, 1987), 1–14; A. Oakley, "Interviewing Women: A Contradiction in Terms?" in H. Roberts, ed., *Doing Feminist Research* (London: Routledge, 1981), 30–61; and J. Stacey, "Can There Be a Feminist Ethnography?" in Gluck and Patai, eds., *Women's Words,* 111–20.

8. See, for example, Chodorow, *The Power of Feelings;* and W. Kracke, "Reflections on the Savage Self," in M. M. Suarez-Orozco, ed., *Making of Psychological Anthropology II* (New York: Harcourt Brace, 1991), 195–222.

REFERENCES

American Council on Education. 2007. *The American College President, 2007 Edition.* Washington, DC: American Council on Education.

Anderson, K., and D.C. Clark. 1990. "Learning to Listen." In S. Gluck and D. Patai, eds., *Women's Words: The Feminist Practice of Oral History.* New York: Routledge, 11–26.

Annual Social and Economic Supplement (ASEC) to the 2009 Current Population Survey (CPS). 2009. www.census.gov/apsd/techdoc/cps/cpsmar09 .pdf.

Anzaldúa, G. 1995. "*La Conciencia de la Mestiza:* Towards a New Consciousness." In G. Anzaldúa, ed., *Making Face, Making Soul: Haciendo Caras: Creative and Critical Perspectives by Feminists of Color.* San Francisco: Aunt Lute Books, 377–89.

Armstrong, E., L. Hamilton, and P. England. 2010. "Is Hooking Up Bad for Young Women?" *Contexts* 9, no. 3: 22–27.

Armstrong, E.A., P. England, and A. Fogarty. 2010. "Orgasm in College Hookups and Relationships." In B. Risman, ed., *Families as They Really Are.* New York: W.W. Norton, 362–77.

Arnett, J.J. 2006. *Emerging Adulthood: The Winding Road from the Late Teens through the Twenties.* Oxford: Oxford University Press.

Bassin, D. 1996. "Beyond the He and the She: Toward the Reconciliation of Masculinity and Femininity in the Postoedipal Mind." *Journal of the American Psychoanalytic Assocation* 44, suppl.: 157–90.

Behrendt, G., and L. Tuccillo. 2009. *He's Just Not That into You: The No Excuses Truth to Understanding Guys.* New York: Gallery.

Belkin, L. 2003. "The Opt-Out Revolution." *New York Times Magazine,* October 26.

Bell, L. C. 2005. "Psychoanalytic Theories of Gender." In A. Eagly et al., eds., *The Psychology of Gender,* 2nd ed. New York: Guilford Press, 145–68.

Benjamin, J. 1988. *The Bonds of Love: Psychoanalysis, Feminism, and the Problem of Domination.* New York: Pantheon.

———. 1995. *Like Subjects, Love Objects: Essays on Recognition and Sexual Difference.* New Haven, CT: Yale University Press.

———. 1998. *Shadow of the Other: Intersubjectivity and Gender in Psychoanalysis.* New York: Routledge.

Bettie, J. 2003. *Women without Class: Girls, Race, and Identity.* Berkeley: University of California Press.

Bianchi, S. M., J. P. Robinson, and M. A. Milkie. 2006. *Changing Rhythms of American Family Life.* New York: Russell Sage Foundation.

Blair-Loy, M., and A. S. Wharton. 2004. "Mothers in Finance: Surviving and Thriving." *Annals of the American Academy of Political and Social Science* 596: 151–71.

Bogle, K. 2008. *Hooking Up: Sex, Dating, and Relationships on Campus.* New York: New York University Press.

Borland, K. 1990. "That's Not What I Said." In S. Gluck and D. Patai, eds., *Women's Words: The Feminist Practice of Oral History.* New York: Routledge, 63–76.

Boston Women's Health Collective. 2005. *Our Bodies, Ourselves: A New Edition for a New Era.* Boston: Touchstone.

Breuer, J., and S. Freud. 1953 [1895]. "Studies on Hysteria." In *The Standard Edition of The Complete Psychological Works of Sigmund Freud,* vol. 2. London: Hogarth Press, 1–319.

Bright, S. 1997. *The Sexual State of the Union.* New York: Simon & Schuster.

Brown, L.M., and C. Gilligan. 1992. *Meeting at the Crossroads: Women's Psychology and Girls' Development.* Cambridge, MA: Harvard University Press.

Brownmiller, S. 1975. *Against Our Will: Men, Women, and Rape.* New York: Simon & Schuster.

Brückner, H., and P. Bearman. 2005. "After the Promise: The STD Consequences of Adolescent Virginity Pledges." *Journal of Adolescent Health* 36: 271–78.

Burdette, A.M., and T.D. Hill. 2009. "Religious Involvement and Transitions into Adolescent Sexual Activities." *Sociology of Religion* 70, no. 1: 28–48.

Bushey, C. 2010. "Why Don't More Women Sue Their Rapists? Because the Supreme Court Took Away Part of the Violence against Women Act." *Slate,* May 26.

Butler, J. 1990. "Gender Trouble, Feminist Theory, and Psychoanalytic Discourse." In L. Nicholson, ed., *Feminism/Postmodernism.* New York: Routledge, 324–40.

———. 1997 [1995]. "Melancholy Gender/Refused Identification." In J. Butler, *The Psychic Life of Power: Theories in Subjection.* Stanford, CA: Stanford University Press, 132–50.

Cahn, N.R., and J. Carbone. 2007. "Red Families v. Blue Families." *GWU Legal Studies Research Paper* 343, August 16.

Califia, P. 2000. *Public Sex: The Culture of Radical Sex.* Berkeley: Cleis Press.

Chasseguet-Smirgel, J. 1986. *Sexuality and Mind: The Role of the Father and the Mother in the Psyche.* New York: New York University Press.

Chodorow, N.J. 1978. *The Reproduction of Mothering: Psychoanalysis and the Sociology of Gender.* Berkeley: University of California Press.

———. 1999. *The Power of Feelings: Personal Meaning in Psychoanalysis, Gender, and Culture.* New Haven, CT: Yale University Press.

———. 2002. "Born into a World at War: Listening for Affect and Personal Meaning." *American Imago* 59, no. 3: 297–315.

Colton, M., and S. Gore. 1991. *Risk, Resiliency, and Resistance: Current Research on Adolescent Girls.* New York: Ms. Foundation.

Contratto, S. 1987. "Father Presence in Women's Psychological Development." In J. Rabow and G. Platt, eds., *Advances in Psychoanalytic Sociology*. Malabar, FL: Krieger.

Coontz, S. 2006. "Marriage as Social Contract / The Decline in Married-Couple Households." *Philadelphia Inquirer*, October 20.

Cooper, M. 2008. *Doing Security in Insecure Times: Class and Family Life in Silicon Valley*. PhD diss., University of California, Berkeley.

Correll, S. J., S. Benard, and I. Paik. 2007. "Getting a Job: Is There a Motherhood Penalty?" *American Journal of Sociology* 112: 1297–1338.

de Marneffe, D. 2004. *Maternal Desire: On Children, Love, and the Inner Life*. New York: Little, Brown.

Diamond, L. 2009. *Sexual Fluidity: Understanding Women's Love and Desire*. Cambridge, MA: Harvard University Press.

Dimen, M. 1991. "Deconstructing Difference: Gender, Splitting, and Transitional Space." *Psychoanalytic Dialogues* 1, no. 3: 335–52.

Dinnerstein, D. 1976. *The Mermaid and the Minotaur: Sexual Arrangements and Human Malaise*. New York: HarperCollins.

Drago, R., and C. Williams. 2009. *The Gender Wage Gap: 2009*. Washington, DC: Institute for Women's Policy Research.

Dworkin, A. 1981. *Pornography: Men Possessing Women*. New York: Plume.

Dye, J. L. 2008. *Fertility of American Women: 2006: Current Population Reports*. Washington, DC: U.S. Census Bureau. www.census.gov/prod/2008pubs/p20-558.pdf.

Edin, K., and M. Kefalas. 2005. *Promises I Can Keep: Why Poor Women Put Motherhood before Marriage*. Berkeley: University of California Press.

Elise, D. 1998. "Gender Repertoire: Body, Mind, and Bisexuality." *Psychoanalytic Dialogues* 8, no. 3: 353–71.

England, P., E. F. Shafer, and A. C. K. Fogarty. 2008. "Hooking Up and Forming Romantic Relationships on Today's College Campuses." In M. Kimmel and A. Aronson, eds., *The Gendered Society Reader*, 3rd ed. Oxford: Oxford University Press, 531–49.

Erikson, E. 1959. *Identity and the Life Cycle*. New York: W. W. Norton.

Fanon, F. 1967 [1952]. *Black Skin, White Masks*. New York: Grove Press.

Fein, E., and S. Schneider. 1996. *The Rules: Time-Tested Secrets for Capturing the Heart of Mr. Right*. New York: Grand Central Publishing.

Fields, J. 2008. *Risky Lessons: Sex Education and Social Inequality.* New Brunswick, NJ: Rutgers University Press.

Fine, M. 1988. "Sexuality, Schooling, and Adolescent Females: The Missing Discourse of Desire." *Harvard Educational Review* 58: 29–53.

Foucault, M. 1990 [1978]. *The History of Sexuality.* New York: Vintage Books.

Freud, S. 1959 [1908]. "'Civilized' Sexual Morality and Modern Nervous Illness." In J. Strachey, ed., *The Standard Edition of the Complete Psychological Works of Sigmund Freud,* vol. 8. London: Hogarth Press, 181–204.

———. 1959 [1930]. "Civilization and Its Discontents." In J. Strachey, ed., *The Standard Edition of the Complete Psychological Works of Sigmund Freud,* vol. 21. London: Hogarth Press, 64–148.

Friedan, B. 1963. *The Feminine Mystique.* New York: W. W. Norton.

Gadbois, S., and A. Bowker. 2007. "Gender Differences in the Relationships between Extracurricular Activities Participation, Self-Description, and Domain-Specific and General Self-Esteem." *Sex Roles: A Journal of Research* 56, nos. 9–10: 675–89.

Gates, G. 2011. "How Many People Are Lesbian, Gay, Bisexual, and Transgender?" Williams Institute. http://wiwp.law.ucla.edu/wp-content/uploads/Gates-How-Many-People-LGBT-Apr-2011.pdf.

Gerson, K. 2009. *The Unfinished Revolution: How a New Generation Is Reshaping Family, Work, and Gender in America.* New York: Oxford University Press.

Gerstel, N., and N. Sarkisian. 2006. "Marriage: The Good, the Bad, and the Greedy." *Contexts* 5: 16–21.

Gilligan, C. 1982. *In a Different Voice: Psychological Theory and Human Development.* Cambridge, MA: Harvard University Press.

Gilligan, C., A. G. Rogers, and D. L. Tolman, eds. 1991. *Women, Girls, and Psychotherapy: Reframing Resistance.* New York: Harrington Park Press.

Glenn, N., and E. Marquardt. 2001. *Hooking Up, Hanging Out, and Hoping for Mr. Right: College Women on Mating and Dating Today.* New York: Institute for American Values.

Goldner, V. 1991. "Toward a Critical Relational Theory of Gender." *Psychoanalytic Dialogues* 1, no. 3: 249–72.

Gottlieb, L. 2010. *Marry Him: The Case for Settling for Mr. Good Enough.* New York: Dutton Adult.

Gray, J. 1992. *Men Are from Mars, Women Are from Venus.* New York: Harper.

Greenleaf, C., E. M. Boyer, and T. A. Petrie. 2009. "High School Sport Participation and Subsequent Psychological Well-Being and Physical Activity: The Mediating Influences of Body Image, Physical Competence, and Instrumentality." *Sex Roles: A Journal of Research* 61, nos. 9–10: 714–26.

Greer, G. 1971. *The Female Eunuch.* New York: McGraw-Hill Books.

Guttmacher Institute. 2009. *Facts on Sexually Transmitted Infections in the United States.* New York: Guttmacher Institute.

Halberstam, J. 1998. *Female Masculinity.* Durham, NC: Duke University Press.

Hamilton, L., and E. Armstrong. 2009. "Double Binds and Flawed Options: Gendered Sexuality in Early Adulthood." *Gender & Sexuality* 23: 589–616.

Harding, S. 1987. "Introduction: Is There a Feminist Method?" In S. Harding, ed., *Feminism and Methodology.* Bloomington: Indiana University Press, 1–14.

Harris, A. 1991. "Gender as Contradiction." *Psychoanalytic Dialogues* 1, no. 2: 197–224.

Hartmann, H. 1976. "Capitalism, Patriarchy, and Job Segregation by Sex." *Signs* 1, no. 3: 137–69.

Henig, R. M. 2010. "What Is It about 20-Somethings?" *New York Times Magazine,* August 18.

Herbenick, D., et al. 2010. "Sexual Behavior in the United States: Results from a National Probability Sample of Men and Women Ages 14–94." *Journal of Sexual Medicine* 7, suppl. 5: 255–65.

Hewlett, S. A., and C. B. Luce. 2006. "Extreme Jobs: The Dangerous Allure of a 70-Hour Workweek." *Harvard Business Review* 4: 49–59.

Hochschild, A. 1989. *The Second Shift: Working Parents and the Revolution at Home.* New York: Avon Books.

———. 1997. *The Time Bind: When Work Becomes Home and Home Becomes Work.* New York: Henry Holt.

Hooks, B. 1984. *Feminist Theory: From Margin to Center.* Boston: South End Press.

——. 1999. *Ain't I a Woman: Black Women and Feminism.* Boston: South End Press.

Hymowitz, K. 2011. *Manning Up: How the Rise of Women Has Turned Men into Boys.* New York: Basic Books.

Irigaray, L. 1985. *This Sex Which Is Not One.* Ithaca, NY: Cornell University Press.

Irvine, J. M. 2004. *Talk about Sex: The Battles over Sex Education in the United States.* Berkeley: University of California Press.

Iyengar, S. 2011. *The Art of Choosing.* New York: Twelve.

Jacobs, J., and K. Gerson. 2004. *The Time Divide: Work, Family, and Gender Inequality.* Cambridge, MA: Harvard University Press.

Jay, M. 2007. "Melancholy Femininity and Obsessive-Compulsive Masculinity: Sex Differences in Melancholy Gender." *Studies in Gender and Sexuality* 8: 115–35.

Joint Center for Housing Studies of Harvard University. 2010. *The State of the Nation's Housing.* www.jchs.harvard.edu/publications/markets/son2010/son2010.pdf.

Jordan, J. 2009. *Relational-Cultural Therapy.* Washington, DC: American Psychological Association.

Klein, M. 1986 [1940]. "Mourning and Its Relation to Manic-Depressive States." In J. Mitchell, ed., *The Selected Melanie Klein.* New York: Free Press, 146–74.

——. 1986 [1946]. "Notes on Some Schizoid Mechanisms." In J. Mitchell, ed., *The Selected Melanie Klein.* New York: Free Press, 175–200.

Knapp, C. 2003. *Appetites: Why Women Want.* New York: Counterpoint Press.

Kohlberg, L. 1981. *Essays on Moral Development.* Vol. I: *The Philosophy of Moral Development.* San Francisco: Harper & Row.

Kracke, W. 1991. "Reflections on the Savage Self." In M. M. Suarez-Orozco, ed., *Making of Psychological Anthropology II.* New York: Harcourt Brace, 195–222.

Kristeva, J. 1987. *In the Beginning Was Love: Psychoanalysis and Faith.* New York: Columbia University Press.

Lareau, A. 2003. *Unequal Childhoods: Class, Race, and Family Life.* Berkeley: University of California Press.

Laumann, E., J.H. Gagnon, R.T. Michael, and S. Michaels. 1994. *The Social Organization of Sexuality: Sexual Practices in the United States.* Chicago: University of Chicago Press.

Lauretis, T. de. 1991. "Queer Theory: Lesbian and Gay Sexualities." *differences: A Journal of Feminist Cultural Studies* 3, no. 2: iii–xviii.

Layton, L. 2004. "Relational No More: Defensive Autonomy in Middle-Class Women." In J. Winer and J.W. Anderson, eds., *The Annual of Psychoanalysis: Psychoanalysis and Women,* vol. 32. Hillsdale, NJ: Analytic Press, 29–42.

Leonhardt, D. 2010. "A Labor Market Punishing to Mothers." *New York Times,* Business section, August 3.

Levinson, D.J. 1978. *The Seasons of a Man's Life.* New York: Ballantine.

Levy, A. 2006. *Female Chauvinist Pigs: Women and the Rise of Raunch Culture.* New York: Free Press.

Livingston, G., and D. Cohn. 2010. *The New Demography of American Motherhood.* Pew Research Center. http://pewsocialtrends.org/pubs/754/new-demography-of-american-motherhood.

Luker, K. 2007. *When Sex Goes to School: Warring Views on Sex—and Sex Education—since the Sixties.* New York: W.W. Norton.

MacKinnon, C. 1989. *Toward a Feminist Theory of the State.* Cambridge, MA: Harvard University Press.

Mannheim, K. 1972 [1952]. "The Problem of Generations." In K. Mannheim, *Essays on the Sociology of Knowledge.* London: Routledge, 276–320.

Martin, K. 1996. *Puberty, Sexuality, and the Self: Girls and Boys at Adolescence.* New York: Routledge.

Mason, M., and M. Goulden. 2004. "Do Babies Matter? Part II: Closing the Baby Gap." *Academe* 90, no. 6 (December): 10–15.

Mathews, T.J., and B.E. Hamilton. 2009. *Delayed Childbearing: More Women Are Having Their First Child Later in Life.* National Center for Health Statistics Data Brief no. 21. Washington, DC: Centers for Disease Control and Prevention, August. www.cdc.gov/nchs/data/databriefs/db21.htm.

Miller, J. B. 1976. *Toward a New Psychology of Women.* Boston: Beacon Press.

Minh-ha, T. T. 1989. *Woman, Native, Other: Writing Postcoloniality and Feminism.* Bloomington: Indiana University Press.

Mitchell, S. 1998. *Can Love Last? The Fate of Romance over Time.* New York: W. W. Norton.

National Center for Education Statistics. 2005. *Gender Differences in Participation and Completion of Undergraduate Education and How They Have Changed over Time.* Washington, DC: U.S. Department of Education.

———. 2007. *Status and Trends in the Education of Racial and Ethnic Minorities,* NCES 2007–0039. Washington, DC: U.S. Department of Education.

National Institute of Justice. 1998. *Prevalence, Incidence, and Consequences of Violence against Women: Findings from the National Violence against Women Survey.* Washington, DC: National Institute of Justice, U.S. Department of Justice; Centers for Disease Control and Prevention.

National Survey of Sexual Health and Behavior. 2010. "Findings from the National Survey of Sexual Health and Behavior (NSSHB), Center for Sexual Health Promotion, Indiana University." *Journal of Sexual Medicine* 7, suppl. 5: 243–373.

Oakley, A. 1981. "Interviewing Women: A Contradiction in Terms?" In H. Roberts, ed., *Doing Feminist Research.* London: Routledge, 30–61.

Orenstein, P. 1994. *School Girls: Young Women, Self-Esteem, and the Confidence Gap.* New York: Anchor Books.

———. 2001. *Flux: Women on Sex, Work, Love, Kids, and Life in a Half-Changed World.* New York: Anchor.

———. 2011. *Cinderella Ate My Daughter: Dispatches from the Front Lines of the New Girlie-Girl Culture.* New York: HarperCollins.

Ortner, S. B. 1974. "Is Female to Male as Nature Is to Culture?" In M. Z. Rosaldo and L. Lamphere, eds., *Woman, Culture, and Society.* Stanford, CA: Stanford University Press, 68–87.

Ovadia, S., and L. M. Moore. 2010. "Decomposing the Moral Community: Religious Contexts and Teen Childbearing." *City & Community* 9, no. 3: 320–34.

Pascoe, C.J. 2007. *Dude, You're a Fag: Masculinity and Sexuality in High School.* Berkeley: University of California Press.

Person, E.S. 1999. "From Sexual Desire to Excitement: The Role of Sexual Fantasy." In E. Person, *The Sexual Century.* New Haven, CT: Yale University Press, 211–29.

Phillips, L. 2000. *Flirting with Danger: Young Women's Reflections on Sexuality and Domination.* New York: New York University Press.

Pipher, M. 1994. *Reviving Ophelia: Saving the Selves of Adolescent Girls.* New York: Ballantine Books.

Rich, A. 1976. *Of Woman Born: Motherhood as Experience and Institution.* New York: W.W. Norton.

Roberts, S. 2007. "For Young Earners in Big City, a Gap in Women's Favor." *New York Times,* August 3.

———. 2008. "Most Children Still Live in Two-Parent Homes, Census Bureau Reports." *New York Times,* February 21.

Rosaldo, M.Z., and L. Lamphere, eds. 1974. *Woman, Culture, and Society.* Stanford, CA: Stanford University Press.

Rubin, G. 1975. "The Traffic in Women: Notes toward a Political Economy of Sex." In R. Reiter, ed., *Toward an Anthropology of Women.* New York: Monthly Review Press, 157–210.

———. 1984. "Thinking Sex: Notes for a Radical Theory of the Politics of Sexuality." In C. Vance, ed., *Pleasure and Danger.* Boston: Routledge, 143–78.

Ruddick, S. 1989. *Maternal Thinking: Towards a Politics of Peace.* Boston: Beacon Press.

Sadker, D., and K. Zittleman. 2009. *Still Failing at Fairness: How Gender Bias Cheats Girls and Boys in School and What We Can Do about It.* New York: Scribner.

Sadker, M., and D. Sadker. 1995. *Failing at Fairness: How Our Schools Cheat Girls.* New York: Scribner.

Schalet, A. 2000. "Raging Hormones, Regulated Love: Adolescent Sexuality and the Constitution of the Modern Individual in the United States and the Netherlands." *Body & Society* 6, no. 1: 75–105.

Schor, J. 1991. *The Overworked American: The Unexpected Decline of Leisure.* New York: Basic Books.

Schwartz, B. 2003. *The Paradox of Choice: Why More Is Less.* New York: HarperPerennial.

Sedgwick, E. 1990. *Epistemology of the Closet.* Berkeley: University of California Press.

Settersten, R., and B. Ray. 2010. *Not Quite Adults: Why 20-Somethings Are Choosing a Slower Path to Adulthood, and Why It's Good for Everyone.* New York: Bantam.

Shalit, W. 2000. *A Return to Modesty: Discovering the Lost Virtue.* New York: Touchstone.

Shapira, I. 2008. "Bringing Up Babies, and Defying the Norms: Some Young College Grads Embrace Parenthood as Their Peers Postpone It." *Washington Post,* January 15.

Stacey, J. 1990a. *Brave New Families: Stories of Domestic Upheaval in Late Twentieth-Century America.* New York: Basic Books.

———. 1990b. "Can There Be a Feminist Ethnography?" In S. Gluck and D. Patai, eds., *Women's Words: The Feminist Practice of Oral History.* New York: Routledge, 111–20.

Stepp, L. S. 2007. *Unhooked: How Young Women Pursue Sex, Delay Love, and Lose at Both.* New York: Riverhead Books.

Stern, L. 1991. "Disavowing the Self in Female Adolescence." In C. Gilligan, A. G. Rogers, and D. L. Tolman, eds., *Women, Girls, and Psychotherapy: Reframing Resistance.* New York: Harrington Park Press, 105–17.

Stevenson, B., and J. Wolfers. 2007. "Marriage and Divorce: Changes and Their Driving Forces." *Journal of Economic Perspectives* 21, no. 2 (Spring): 27–52.

Stone, P. 2007. *Opting Out? Why Women Really Quit Careers and Head Home.* Berkeley: University of California Press.

Sweetnam, A. 1996. "The Changing Contexts of Gender: Between Fixed and Fluid Experience." *Psychoanalytic Dialogues* 6, no. 4: 437–59.

Swidler, A. 2001. *Talk of Love: How Culture Matters.* Chicago: University of Chicago Press.

Tanenbaum, L. 2000. *Slut: Growing Up Female with a Bad Reputation.* New York: Harper.

Thompson, S. 1995. *Going All the Way: Teenage Girls' Tales of Sex, Romance, and Pregnancy.* New York: Hill and Wang.

Thorne, B. 1993. *Gender Play: Girls and Boys in School.* New Brunswick, NJ: Rutgers University Press.

Titus, M., and T. Fadal. 2008. *Why Hasn't He Called? New York's Top Date Doctors Reveal How Guys Really Think and How to Get the Right One Interested.* New York: McGraw-Hill.

Tjaden, P., and N. Thoennes. 2000. *Full Report of the Prevalence, Incidence, and Consequences of Violence against Women: Findings from the National Violence against Women Survey.* Washington, DC: U.S. Department of Justice.

Tolman, D. 2005. *Dilemmas of Desire: Teenage Girls Talk about Sexuality.* Cambridge, MA: Harvard University Press.

U.S. Department of Commerce. 2005. *American Community Survey.* Washington, DC: Census Bureau.

———. 2009. *Survey of Income Program Participation.* Washington, DC: Census Bureau.

———. 2010. *Statistical Abstract of the United States 2010.* Washington, DC: Census Bureau.

———. 2011a. *State and County QuickFacts.* Washington, DC: Census Bureau.

———. 2011b. *Statistical Abstract of the United States 2011.* Washington, DC: Census Bureau.

Vaillant, G. 1977. *Adaptation to Life.* Boston: Little, Brown.

Valenti, J. 2009. *The Purity Myth.* New York: Seal Press.

Vance, C., ed. 1984. *Pleasure and Danger: Exploring Female Sexuality,* 1st ed. Boston: Routledge.

Warren, E., and A. W. Tyagi. 2003. *The Two-Income Trap: Why Middle-Class Mothers and Fathers Are Going Broke.* New York: Basic Books.

Whitehead, B. D. 2002. *Why There Are No Good Men Left: The Romantic Plight of the New Single Woman.* New York: Broadway.

Wilkins, A. C. 2008. *Wannabes, Goths, and Christians: The Boundaries of Sex, Style, and Status.* Chicago: University of Chicago Press.

Willard, C. 1999. "Estimates of the Incidence and Prevalence of Sexually Transmitted Diseases in the United States." *Sexually Transmitted Diseases,* 26, no. 4: S2–S7.

Williams, A. 2007. "Putting Money on the Table." *New York Times,* September 23.

———. 2010. "The New Math on Campus." *New York Times,* February 10.

Williams, J.C., and H. Boushey. 2010. *The Three Faces of Work-Family Conflict: The Poor, the Professionals, and the Missing Middle.* San Francisco: Center for WorkLife Law, University of California, Hastings College of the Law, and Center for American Progress. www.americanprogress.org/issues/2010/01/pdf/threefaces.pdf.

INDEX

Text:	10.75/15 Janson
Display:	Janson MT Pro
Compositor:	Toppan Best-set Premedia Limited
Printer and binder:	Maple Press